YOUR LAST CHANCE TO GET IT RIGHT!

(A Journey from Darkness into Light)

ALAN W. HAYDEN

WESTBOW
PRESS®
A DIVISION OF THOMAS NELSON
& ZONDERVAN

Copyright © 2016 Alan W. Hayden.

All rights reserved. No part of this book may be used or reproduced by any means, graphic, electronic, or mechanical, including photocopying, recording, taping or by any information storage retrieval system without the written permission of the author except in the case of brief quotations embodied in critical articles and reviews.

Scripture taken from the Holy Bible, NEW INTERNATIONAL VERSION®. Copyright © 1973, 1978, 1984 by Biblica, Inc. All rights reserved worldwide. Used by permission. NEW INTERNATIONAL VERSION® and NIV® are registered trademarks of Biblica, Inc. Use of either trademark for the offering of goods or services requires the prior written consent of Biblica US, Inc.

Please note that all Bible references are from the New Testament Version (NIV) unless stated otherwise

WestBow Press books may be ordered through booksellers or by contacting:

WestBow Press
A Division of Thomas Nelson & Zondervan
1663 Liberty Drive
Bloomington, IN 47403
www.westbowpress.com
1 (866) 928-1240

Because of the dynamic nature of the Internet, any web addresses or links contained in this book may have changed since publication and may no longer be valid. The views expressed in this work are solely those of the author and do not necessarily reflect the views of the publisher, and the publisher hereby disclaims any responsibility for them.

Any people depicted in stock imagery provided by Thinkstock are models, and such images are being used for illustrative purposes only. Certain stock imagery © Thinkstock.

ISBN: 978-1-5127-3157-6 (sc)
ISBN: 978-1-5127-3159-0 (hc)
ISBN: 978-1-5127-3158-3 (e)

Library of Congress Control Number: 2016902699

Printed in the USA.

WestBow Press rev. date: 05/12/2016

CONTENTS

Dedication vii
Acknowledgements ix
Introduction xi
Chapter 1   A Little Perspective 1
Chapter 2   Discovering and Understanding Christianity 27
Chapter 3   God's Written Manual for Mankind 56
Chapter 4   A Search for the Meaning of Life 79
Chapter 5   Eastern Based Religions (Oriential) 105
Chapter 6   World-Wide Western Religions (Occidental) 141
Chapter 7   Insights into Islam and World-Wide Animism 163
Chapter 8   Man's War Against God 194
Chapter 9   Excelling in Evil 222
Chapter 10   Is America going the Way of Europe? 248
Chapter 11   Imagine a World without Jesus 277
Chapter 12   A Glimpse into the Future 311
Chapter 13   The Tribulation and Beyond 332
Chapter 14   Is the Bible True and Authentic? 359
Chapter 15   The Case for Christ 377
Bibliography – End Notes 397

DEDICATION

I dedicate this book to my deceased wife, Karen Carlson Hayden, who, through her daily example, taught me the true Christian way to live my life. She alone, with the help of the Holy Spirit, led me from darkness and ignorance into the light of Jesus Christ, as my Lord and Savior. John Newton could not have said it better when he wrote: "Amazing Grace – how sweet the sound – that saved a wretch like me! I once was lost but now am found, was blind but now I see." Thank you Karen for 25 glorious years!

ACKNOWLEDGEMENTS

Many thanks to my librarian friend, Vickie Hoff, and my two pastor friends, Joel Tetrau and Steven Speichinger, who have taught me many important Christian concepts over the years. Finally a great thank you to my dear friend, Irene Williams, who continued to encourage me when I thought this book would never get finished. This book is now being read thanks to Irene's consistent reminders to me that God wanted the book finished too!

INTRODUCTION

It would be ever so noble of me if I told you I decided to write this book when I became seventy years of age as a way of giving back to younger people the benefits of the many mistakes I have made, and the lessons learned along the way. Although this motivation is somewhat true, I must admit I began to sketch out my ideas for writing this book after my dear wife passed away, more than twelve-years ago, but life continually kept getting in the way until now. In the back of my mind I knew that time was running out, and if I did not finish and publish this book now, then it may never happen. So I began this project simply because the book had been pent up inside me to a point it just had to find an outlet. Like a pregnant woman, I had to give birth to this idea as it's time had come.

In scouring through many bookstores over the years, I noticed that most books promoting Christianity are written for Christian audiences because that is where the book sales are! This book is somewhat counter-intuitive to that trend as you will soon discover. Although Christians will receive substantial benefit from a reading of this book, I must say at the outset that it is primarily addressed to the audience of non-believers who do not believe in, or have serious doubts about, a loving, monotheistic, Christian God who created our world, our solar system, our universe, and everything in it.

MY FOCUS THEN IS ON NON-BELIEVERS, people who do not believe in the God of the Bible, or his Son, Jesus Christ, who is God incarnate, who spent a short time fellowshipping with man in the flesh so many years ago, showing man the gold standard of how he should live his life while temporarily trapped on earth in a mortal body. So I am addressing most of my thoughts to atheists (people who do not believe in God), agnostics (people who are not sure there is a God), Muslims (who do not believe Jesus Christ is God), Buddhists (who are atheistic and are not sure of the concept of an Almighty God), Jews (who do not believe that Jesus Christ is God, and therefore reject most of the New Testament teachings), Hindus (who serve millions of deities, or gods), animists (who look to animals, rivers, trees, and all of the natural world for answers), Europeans and North Americans, and much of the affluent world (who are like starving men at a banquet – educated and prospering with access to freedom of religion, but living in a spiritual dead zone in the way they live their lives), cultists (people who have created their own spiritual way that is contrary to God's plan for their lives, and is often non-biblically based), and all those other frustrated souls who are either confused, or just have not spent much time worrying about their future lives after they leave this earthly existence, which they know they one day will.

It should also be pointed out that this book is not meant to be another Christian theological treatise, although Christian doctrine is laced throughout it, but rather it is a book in many ways about my own personal journey from darkness into light, which parallels the story of millions of men and women almost from the very beginning. Upfront, however, I must offer a disclaimer that I am not a theologian, but just an ordinary man who has been truly blessed by God to live an incredibly rich life. It is a life full of unique experiences and challenges along a journey of many mistakes, and many blessings. I am appreciative to many pastors and theologians who have inspired me throughout the last forty years; a group of men and women who have swum in the much deeper end of God's water, while I stayed much closer to the shoreline. However, I have been encouraged by the simplicity of God's truth, a truth that a young child can understand, while also being deep enough to inspire the most brilliant minds throughout the last two thousand years.

As this book will point out, man has searched down many "rabbit holes" looking for the meaning of life, and huge and extravagant efforts have gone into creating alternative spiritual faith based systems to solve this issue, that live on in our world today. This book makes a valiant attempt to eliminate some of the confusion, and inject clarity into our thinking by "connecting the dots" in explaining man's journey from his beginning up to the present day. We will be exploring man's many mistakes in rebelling against God, the lessons he has learned, and then I will be offering a number of ways to assist the reader in getting back on the right course with God, especially for those who are struggling with feelings of emptiness and other life based issues. I have traveled the road you are now on, and I know the importance of making a detour with your life,

At this point in your life you may be suffering with a serious illness, a major life change, old age issues, depression, or any one of a number of issues that are creating in you disillusionment in your life, especially as it concerns your future. Or you may be like me when I was young, feeling frustrated that life did not have the meaning that I yearned for, or it may be that your goals and ambitions, and your general life direction, are going nowhere. Any one of these issues should cause you to think hard and deep about your limited mortality, causing you to wonder about your present condition, your future, and perhaps what happens when you die.

Further perspective tells us that two great forces have dogged mankind right from the beginning of his existence on this planet. The forces of good and evil, of light and dark, and they have had, and continue to have, an impact on just about everything we do. Unlike many Christians, I have experienced what it is like to live a life in ignorance of God's Word; to experience unbridled ambition while racing selfishly to accumulate as many assets as possible. Although I considered myself a reasonably intelligent fellow, I made lots of mistakes that could have been avoided if I had known God more intimately. This race to get rich was motivated strictly by selfish ego, my poor background and my need at that time to be esteemed by men. All it brought me was anguish and an empty feeling inside, which I will explain later. I knew there had to be a better way, but I didn't know where to turn. My heart was empty, and I was out of ideas. My prayers, however, were answered when God introduced a Christian lady into my life who later became my wife. From that point forward there was no turning back for me. It took me very little time to then realize that man was created by a loving God, and that man has spent most of his time on earth rebelling against Him.

So, with the aid of the Holy Spirit, if I can in some way make a small contribution that causes just one reader to take a serious look at his or her life, and then realize that accepting the Christian God will save that person's soul for all eternity, then my mission will have been accomplished.

Light and darkness cannot co-exist. Light can be described in two ways: pure light is transparent, open, and promotes growth; translucent light creates confusion and an inability to see clearly. Darkness, however, is opaque and promotes death. Nothing, however, is hidden from God. I spent more than thirty years living in darkness before finding the light of Christ, and hence my motivation for writing this book, to help bring someone into the light – perhaps you. We are all grappling with an unfinished education, and with so little time to get it all right so that we can end this mortal existence with an "A" stamped on our life experience. This life is only a prelude to our next life, which is eternal. This is a solemn promise from God, but the offer only extends to people who believe in Him, and have faith in His Word.

We have all sinned, and made bad choices in the way we have conducted our lives. Many lose hope in their future because they feel they have no one to turn to in order to confess their sins and release the burdens on their hearts. Most people are genuinely seeking something that provides a grounding and explanation for the deep questions of life that they have thought about for years. They feel a need for a higher sense of purpose for their lives, but are unsure where to find the answers. They are aware of the conflicts between science and God, and are sometimes unable to resolve this conflict for themselves because they believe science is proven, while faith seems unreasonable and untenable. They are also affected by newspaper headlines where religious fanatics claim responsibility for ghastly atrocities committed against innocent people. These religious fanatics, however, are grossly misinformed, and are not true followers of the Christian God who promotes love and peace for all mankind.

People live very busy lives, and often complain there is not enough time to do all the learning they would like to do in order to develop their own true convictions about what they really believe in. Consequently, they listen to sound bites on television or the opinions of others in social gatherings, and they read articles in newspapers or Internet blogs, all of which generates a jumble of information that is never properly tied together. This experience creates frustration, a feeling of uncertainty, and is a result of having no solid core convictions they can wrap their heads around and consistently believe in, regardless of circumstances.

In designing the flow of this book, I wanted to provide a panoramic overview of a multiple number of Christian theological issues all under one cover to make it easier for the reader to grasp a greater understanding of the "big picture," so that a clear perspective can be explained in why the world is in the mess that it is in, why men do what they do, and why man needs God more than ever before. Many of these concerns are addressed in this book, and perhaps other issues that you may not have considered. I will demonstrate to the reader the following:

- That man really does need God whether he realizes it or not
- That Christianity is the only true way to have a loving relationship with the creator

- That following the ways of Jesus can give you a fulfilling life
- That there is life beyond this mortal existence
- That you can be saved no matter how bad your life has been to date
- That it is the work of Jesus Christ that founded the principles of Europe and America
- That science and faith can work together
- That it was atheism and not religion that created the godless societies in the East
- That it is normal and rational to have faith in God without actually seeing Him
- That God truly has a plan for you, and the ending of this world as we know it
- That you can have the opportunity to live forever with God, if you accept His call.

This book puts God in the dock, (i.e. on trial), and you will find that when you have read it completely, God is proven innocent.

It should be stated right at the beginning that God clearly states in the Bible that everyone has the opportunity to become a child of God irrespective of how badly their life has turned out so far, or how many sins or crimes they have committed. As the popular saying goes, "God don't make no junk!" There is nothing you can do on this side of death that cannot be forgiven by God, and your soul can be saved for all eternity. It is never too late to ask God for forgiveness and enter into His light. God's love for you is a pure, unconditional love that is far greater than your love for Him. It is the greatest, most liberating feeling you will ever experience when you enter into a two-way loving relationship with God. Don't allow yourself to miss out on this glorious opportunity. After all, He is in the redemption business. He is the creator, we are the created. He is the potter, we are the clay, and we are all made in His image.

My own personal life attests to the power of Jesus Christ, and how He can turn any man or woman away from darkness and into the light. Just like you, I did not choose my parents, or the place or time that I was going to be born. In my case I was born in England during WWII, when the Germans were doing considerable damage to the British Isles. The tremendous loss of life, and destruction of so many homes and businesses, was too immeasurable to count. The British may have come out winners in that war, but did they really? The great casualty of the war was the loss of faith in God that developed in much of the population. Wives lost their husbands, and husbands came home to find their wives had left them. Soldiers arriving home with severe disabilities, such as amputations, blindness, deafness, and mental disorders were numerous. Many left home never to return, thus creating incalculable heart-ache for their loved ones. There was a feeling of hopelessness and people were demoralized. I fully remember growing up without a feeling of God in my life. There was no Bible in our home, and we never went to church. In fact none of my friends, neighbors or extended family went to church either. Looking back it is almost like everyone I knew was caught up in a vortex of thinking that they didn't need God in their lives, although it was never openly admitted.

My parents were good, loving, hard working people who held low paying jobs due to their limited education. But they did their very best to provide for my sister and me by instilling in us a good, strong work ethic, and a sense of independence that I personally cherish to this day. In many ways my parents represented a microcosm of a larger portrait of British families who had been eye-witnesses to the ravages of war, and the horror, pain, and suffering inflicted by the madness of men. This small island off the coast of Europe had suffered terribly, and God seemed to be far, far away. So during my formative years I grew up without God, and lived a life in darkness.

In the public school system I was taught all the great achievements the British had accomplished, and I often looked at a world map colored coated to represent all the places where either we had control or had established a heavy foot print before giving independence back to the natives (I had no idea at the time that one day I would enjoy the privilege of visiting every one of those former British Colonies). We were taught the sun never set on the British Empire, and mad dogs of Englishmen sat out in the noon day sun. We were filled with patriotic pride, and our love for the royal family was strong. But deep down inside we all instinctively knew the empire was fading, and there was a huge hole in our hearts. Something was clearly missing, but I was too young to understand it at the time.

When we look back to the late 19th and early 20th centuries, we find that European men came to believe they had all the answers, and God was no longer needed. Science had made huge strides in solving all kinds of problems that had plagued society for centuries. The ego and arrogance of the scientific community, was unbounded. Religion had, according to many people, already been discredited by Charles Darwin's book,

The Origin of Species, that intimated man was an evolutionary creation formed from some ancient primordial cesspool millions of years ago without any help from God. Meanwhile, Karl Marx was busy promoting his *Communist Manifesto,* which encouraged a system for man that had no use for religion or God. Friedrich Nietzsche, the great German philosopher, claimed God was dead, and a new approach for the governing of mankind was needed. Scientists were making the claim that the earth was much older than the Bible's Genesis account, which was disconcerting to many Christian leaders. Yes, man was on a roll, and God was being pushed further and further from the affairs of men. This was man's big mistake, and it later led to a major catastrophe.

A few years later World War I broke out, and within 20 years from the end of that war, another major war started, all on the smallest continent on earth. These two great wars resulted in more than 125 million casualties, to say nothing of the millions who lost their personal freedoms. [1] Many survivors blamed God, while others wondered if God was teaching man a lesson.

I have visited the German death camps in Poland, such as Auschwitz and Birkenau, and I have seen where human beings by the millions were slaughtered like cattle. The Germans systematically, and tortuously, poisoned millions of Jewish men, women and their children, along with Slavs, gypsies and homosexuals in the infamous German gas chambers. The Nazi officers who perpetrated the torture and murder of their fellow human beings were well educated, some even with a PhD after their names. By all outward appearances they looked very normal, but they were not educated in the ways of God. The camp's commander, Rudolph Hoss, lived with his wife and five children just down the road from Auschwitz, and every day he would have a normal breakfast with his family, then head to the camp in his chauffeur driven vehicle to make thousands of life and death decisions. He would go home at the end of the day to spend a quiet evening with his family. This routine went on for years without any conscience for what he was doing.

By Hoss' own admission, he was responsible for the extermination of about three million human beings, but just before sentencing he stated: "My conscience compels me to make the following declaration. In the solitude of my prison cell I have come to the bitter recognition that I have sinned gravely against humanity. As commandant of Auschwitz I was responsible for carrying out part of the cruel plans of the Third Reich for human destruction. In so doing I have inflicted a terrible wound on humanity. I caused unspeakable suffering, and I am to pay for this with my life. May the Lord God forgive one day what I have done." [2]

When I stood at the very spot where Hoss was hanged from a tree in 1946, after his wife had told the British where he was hiding, I could not help but think that Nazi officers were nothing more than intellectual barbarians who had lived for the moment, which was to do everything to please one man – Adolf Hitler, their leader, their god if you will. Almighty God, the creator of all things, was completely ignored, again.

Evil is still rampant in this world, and it continues with men attempting to enslave other men. Dietrich Bonheoffer, the German priest who resisted Hitler and was executed for his beliefs, once said: "Silence in the face of evil is itself evil. God will not hold us guiltless. Not to speak is to speak. Not to act is to act." Someone, somewhere is always trying to take away freedom from someone else, and someone somewhere is always paying the price for freedom. That someone, incidentally, is often someone we only know in the abstract, and somehow we are just never grateful enough for the sacrifices they have made on our behalf. President Ronald Reagan once said, "Freedom is just one generation away from extinction. We do not pass freedom on to our children through our blood-line."

In a world where there are more people subjugated under tyrannical rulers than are actually free, we must all turn our attention to the one person who can free us from the tyrannies of this world. We must accept Jesus Christ as Lord and Savior. Only when we put on the armor plate of Jesus do we have any hope of pleasing a loving, gracious God who will protect us from evil, and provide us with an eternal life beyond this cruel world where children die so young, and evil men live to an old age; a world where some people experience sickness all their life, and others sail through it all in good health; where some people possess fortunes, and others struggle to put the next meal on the table for their family. It is also a world where men are continually enslaving other men, and a world where justice is hard to understand.

Evil will only get worse in the future according to the Bible. So the choice lying before us is quite simple. We must either choose God or reject Him, because in this matter there are no abstentions. My fervent wish for you, therefore, is that this book will assist you in reaching a level of knowledge to help you make the right decision for your life, so your cup will be filled with love for God. If you think that this is an invitation to accept Jesus Christ into your life, it is. So I implore you to read every chapter of this book as though your future life depends on the knowledge contained within its pages, because in many ways it just might.

In Chapter One I ask the reader to step back for a moment and appreciate the big picture of man's existence here on earth, by applying some perspectives to separate the really important issues from the not so important ones as we explore our relationship with God. For the benefit of non- believers I devote Chapter Two to an understanding of Christian fundamentals to make it easier to understand when I discuss Christian issues in later chapters. Then in Chapter Three I follow the previous chapter with a better understanding of the core, central document of Christianity, the Bible, which is God's written manual for all mankind. Chapter Four takes us back in time to discuss man's evolutionary journey in his search for meaning, and to make sense of the world around him leading up to a better understanding of our contemporary condition. Chapter Five provides a discussion of how the world-wide faith based religious systems began, and the impact on our lives today starting with a look at Eastern religions, followed in Chapter Six where we take a careful look at the Western religions of Judaism and Christianity. In Chapter Seven we round out our discussion of world religions with a look at Islam and Animism.

There has been a long war against God, and in Chapter Eight I discuss the horrors that have come about as a result. Some of these horrors are discussed in Chapter Nine when we discuss how evil is being promoted in contemporary society, and the effect it is having on our young. Chapter Ten discusses how America is given a wonderful opportunity to learn some valuable lessons from the more advanced secular Europe before it is too late. One cannot help but wonder what life on our planet would have been like without Jesus coming here to minister to mankind, and so I dedicate Chapter Eleven to explore this fascinating thought. In all these previous chapters we have been looking backwards at events in the past up to contemporary times, but in Chapter Twelve we take a glimpse into the future, which is also followed up in Chapter Thirteen. Is the Bible true and authentic as it is claimed to be? For the hard-hearted who are still not convinced, I make an even stronger case in Chapter Fourteen that it is true and factual in every way. Finally, all of Christianity is pivotal on the truth of Jesus Christ, which I demonstrate in Chapter Fifteen that He truly is the Alpha and Omega of everything in our world and beyond, and that we are all without excuse not to make an effort to know Him and accept Him into our lives.

While other Christian books will provide the reader with a deeper, but narrower understanding of the Christian life, you will find this book attempts to string together a vast overview of man's relationship with God over these many centuries, and by doing so helps the reader gain additional insights into who God is, and what God expects of every human being that He has created. I also pray that this approach will touch the hearts of the non-believers in a way that will cause them to seek further help as they move forward with their lives.

Before you begin reading Chapter One I want you to imagine sitting in an automobile with two-sets of steering wheels, two gas pedals, and two brakes. Sitting next to you in the passenger seat is God, who speaks to you and says, "I want you to know that I love you and wish to have a close, personal relationship with you while here on earth, as well as in the next life, which is eternal. I will give you my full support; I will help you renew your mind so that you can experience joy and peace, and I will provide you with truth so that you will know what I have in store for you. All I ask is that you let me drive the car."

You now have a choice, because God has given you free will. You can drive the car yourself, or let God drive it for you. Remember, God knows where you are going, but do you? God then says, "If you drive the car, I will take my hands off the steering wheel, but I promise you that whatever you choose, I will never leave you or forsake you, even if you do drive down the wrong road. But don't you think it would be better if I drive the car? I know what direction your car (your life) needs to go in. So I ask you to trust me, but the choice is yours." Tell me, what decision will you make? As we look forward in this book, I ask that you strap on your safety belt, hold on to the wheel, and enjoy a ride that will hopefully change your life. But wait! Wouldn't it be much better if you allowed God to do the driving?

We all need to become true students of the one who created us, and who created everything that our finite minds can understand, and much more. The more we learn about God, the more we learn about ourselves and our fellow man, which leads to wisdom. We need to let go of our lives, and let God take over. If we do this, we will find the road forward to be a lot smoother, both for ourselves and our loved ones.

It was Mark Twain who once said, "The best days of our lives are the day we are born, and the day we find out the reason why."

CHAPTER ONE

A LITTLE PERSPECTIVE

In this chapter we will pull out our telescopes and take a good look at mankind through several different lenses, with the goal of creating a sharper perspective of who we are as human beings, and who we are individually. This is the 40,000 foot view.

LOOKING AT MANKIND THORUGHT THE LENS OF HISTORY:

Man's ability to acquire knowledge over the centuries has moved forward in bits and spurts, when in some cases it has moved very fast as in the 5th century B.C, with the explosion of knowledge brought about by the pre-Socratic Greeks, and then during the Dark Ages knowledge was basically dormant for centuries. Knowledge accelerated again during the Italian Renaissance of the 14th century due to the collapse of the Byzantine Empire, and a large exodus of scholars moving west into Europe. Again in the 17th century A.D. we witnessed a growth in knowledge due to the invention of the scientific method. With the beginning of the British Industrial Revolution in the 1740s, which later spread throughout Europe, we have witnessed such a rapid expanse in knowledge that one might make the case that knowledge has led to an out of control world that no man fully understands.

Think about this for a moment. When Jamestown, Virginia, was first settled in 1607, the pilgrims sailed from England on wooden boats no better constructed than those used by ancient mariners. When they farmed the land they used shovels, hoes, stick plows, and scythes to harvest their grain These farming instruments were not much improvement from those used in ancient Greece, Persia, China, and Egypt. They were still using ox and carts as their main form of transportation. Yet, in less than 400 years we have made such a quantum dash forward that our heads are still spinning from the new inventions. Here is just a partial list of inventions that have mainly come from Europe and North America during this very short time period:

17th Century: Refracting telescope /human powered submarine/the slide rule/blood transfusions/steam turbine/micrometer/adding machine/barometer/air pump/steam pump/calculating machine/pocket watch/bacteria under microscope/universal joint.

18th Century: Piano/tuning fork/fire extinguisher/atmospheric steam engine/ thermometer/ flying shuttle/electrical capacitor/ English dictionary/sextant/chromatic lens/spinning jenny/ steam engine/electric telegraph/flush toilet/submarine/spinning mule/bi-focal eyeglasses/parachute/hot air balloon/threshing machine/safety lock/power loom/ battery/ precision lathe/ smallpox vaccine/preserving food jar/steam boat/gas turbine/ gas lighting.

19th Century: Electric light/tin can/steam locomotive/ spectroscope/cement/matches/electro magnet/typewriter/

YOUR LAST CHANCE TO GET IT RIGHT! (A Journey from Darkness into Light)

sewing machine/mechanical calculator/revolver/radar/facsimile/Morse code/blueprints/fiber optics/pasteurization/washing machine/elevator/plastic/dynamite/air brakes/barbed wire/telephone/electric light bulb/tungsten steel/barbed wire/escalator/automobile/motorcycle/gramophone/diesel engine/vacuum cleaner/machine gun.

20th Century: Radio/lie detector/neon lights/airplanes/light bulbs/sonar device/Geiger counter/helicopter/cell phone/auto ignition system/tanks/television/robots/insulin/3-D movies/frozen food/loudspeaker/liquid fueled rocket/quartz crystal/glue/hydrogen bomb/ computer/watch/microwave/glue/Technicolor film/software/microwave oven/bar coding/atomic bomb/hydrogen Bomb/credit card/web TV/kidney dialysis machine/ballpoint Pen//synthetic pen/synthetic rubber/turbo engine/canned beer/tape recorder/stereo record/Polaroid photography/electron microscope/transistors/compact disc/VCRs/artificial human heart/printer/floppy disk/magnetic resonance imaging/human growth hormones/ /Internet/smart pill/Web TV/CD-ROM.

21st Century (so far): Artificial liver/self-cleaning window/solar tower/clouding/YouTube/ hybrid car/portable music/remote control surgery/Internet social media/smart phone/oil fracking/smart car/robotic enhancements/nanotechnology enhancements/virtual keyboard/translucent and smog eating cement/military combat robot/bionic lens/flying windmill/human camera pill/genetic creations/Segway technology/web inventions/robot vacuum cleaner/lab on a chip/flower sounds/Fovean camera chip/bug detective devices/free energy/surveillance gadgets the size of a fly.

The point of this exercise is to alert the reader to the fact that man has recently experienced a knowledge explosion that is greater than at any time since recorded written history more than 5,000 years ago. The Bible teaches there will be an acceleration of knowledge during the end times that will serve as a precursor to the return of the Lord. In Daniel 12:4, God says, " But you, Daniel, close up and seal the words of the scroll until the time of the end. Many will go here and there to increase knowledge." The New Testament alludes to a similar point in Matthew 24:8, when Jesus is talking about a great variety of signs – spiritual, natural, societal, and world political – and then He said that these signs would be like "birth pains." As a corollary to this, who can deny that during the last 50 years alone the speed of travel, and the rapid rate of knowledge, has surpassed the accomplishments of all previous ages?

At the same time knowledge has exploded, so has the human population. The following approximate statistics bear this out: [1]

Time of Christ		200 million
1650 years later		545 million
200 years later	1850	1.2 billion
100 years later	1950	2.5 billion
20 years later	1970	3.6 billion
10 years later	1980	4.3 billion
10 years later	1990	5.2 billion
10 years later	2000	6.0 billion
Latest figures	2015	7.0 billion +

These figures, which represent an exponential curve, would probably cause Thomas Malthus (1766 – 1834) to turn over in his grave. In his day, Malthus, was an expert on population growth, but in his wildest imagination he never would have thought that such population growth was possible due to the finite amount of food and potable water that was available. He actually thought the total weight of all the people would eventually be greater than the earth itself!

It is therefore very unfortunate to realize all this newly acquired knowledge that man has garnered during the last 400 years has not caused him to gain any real wisdom in the way he manages his life. Instead, judging by the negative direction society is moving in, it indicates that man feels God in his life even less. As St. Paul said in 2 Timothy 3:6b, "Man is always learning, but never able to acknowledge the truth." Modern man's secular-humanistic way of thinking, which we will address more fully in a later chapter, is a trend away from God that is best for us to have nothing to do with.

LOOKING AT MANKIND THROUGH A LARGER LENS:

Man has been called by many names over the centuries: Neanderthal, Cro-Magnon, Homo sapiens, human being, and about a dozen other names. He is certainly a separate and different creature from all the other animals in the world, and his intelligence is superior to all others. But the important key not to miss is the fact all men are manufactured by the God of all creation. Strip back the skin of any human and you find that we are all designed the same way. The only difference between one man and another, excluding natural attributes, is the color of their skin, the texture of their hair, their language, customs, culture, dress code and religion. By his very nature man is a self-centered creature who in times past thought he was the center of the universe, even though he lives on a very small planet, which is only one of eight identified planets in our solar system (excluding debatable Pluto), where the sun and our largest planet, Jupiter, make up almost 99% of the available mass.

According to scientists, the sun in our solar system is only one of an estimated 200 to 400 billion other stars that make up our Milky Way Galaxy. Scientists also tell us that there are about 170 billion galaxies in the known universe, with the number of stars estimated at a septillion, that's $10^{24(2)}$. These numbers not only stagger the imagination, but they must cause any right thinking person to concede the fact that only the God of all creation and of all ages, could be responsible for such a glorious and wonderful creation design that works in perfect union within its parts.

Consider for a moment the following from general knowledge:

The size of our Earth is Just Right:

If it were much larger it would hold too many gases and destroy life. However, if it were much smaller, its gravitational forces could not have retained any atmosphere at all. Therefore, our earth has just sufficient mass to hold around itself a blanket of gases that both supports life and shield life from the lethal rays of the sun.

The Earth's Rate of Revolution is Just Right:

The rate of revolution makes it ideal for the continuous renewal of the atmosphere for animal life. The stability of carbon monoxide depends upon alternating light and darkness, and consequently the plants have sufficient times of light and darkness to regenerate the air.

The Earth's Distance from the Sun is Just Right:

All living tissues are made of chains of carbon molecules, whose characteristics are retained only by a narrow range of temperature. If we were just two degrees closer to the sun or two degrees further away, it would be either too hot or too cold to maintain such tissue. In other words, life would not be possible.

The Earth's Seasons are Just Right:

Seasonal variations caused by the 23 degree tilt of the earth's axis, are vital for human life. If certain conditions did not vary, then some very harmful microorganisms would multiply beyond our control and destroy the human race. The variation of seasons controls such harmful microorganisms.

The Land-Water Ratio is Just Right:

The ratio of water to land on our planet is about 3 to 1. If we had more water the land area would be like a swamp; if we had more land it would look like a desert. As it is, the ratio produces rainfall to grow plants on the land.

The Earth's Satellite is Vital:

Our moon is the largest satellite relative to the size of its parent body. Therefore, the moon has sufficient mass to cause tides, and tides are very necessary in keeping the oceans fresh.

Tides flush the oceans and revitalize them, just as currents revitalize a river.

Using normal human reasoning, is it possible to think like atheists that God does not exist? What does it take to convince agnostics that God created our universe and everything in it? There is a tremendous body of evidence to support the fact that God is real, so when atheists and agnostics refuse to critically examine the evidence, I think it says more about their psychological hang-ups than it does about whether God is real. If this big picture perspective still fails to impress, then let's take a look at the evidence for design creation from God in one of the smallest places known.

LOOKING AT MANKIND THROUGH A SMALLER LENS:

In the year 2000, two American scientists found themselves in a race to break the genetic code for all life on our planet. One worked for the federal government, and the other worked in the private sector. In a salute to our private enterprise system, the private sector scientist won the day, and the genetic code, consisting of about three billion genes, was finally indentified. This discovery has tremendous implications for the future health of man, but more importantly it provided further proof for the existence of our creator, God.

According to the latest scientific estimates, there are about 37 trillion cells in the human body, [3] and each cell contains a nucleus. Try thinking of the nucleus as a library. Within the nucleus are membranes, which form the book-shelves. Within the membranes is DNA, which represents the books on the bookshelves. Finally, within the DNA we find genes, which represent the words on the pages of the books on the shelves in the library, that is in the nucleus of one single cell out of trillions in your body and mine. You see, DNA can neither be produced, nor its messages translated without precise enzymes, and the production of these enzymes in turn is exactly controlled by the DNA. This is a closed circle: The DNA won't work without the enzymes, and the enzymes can't be produced without the DNA. So the chance of life developing from random action, as Darwinists would have us believe, is simply nonsense.

Darwinism is one of the most pernicious theories ever developed by man, especially when you consider its effect on world society leading to Humanism, Communism, Fascism, and Nazism, which will be discussed in greater detail in a later chapter. Suffice it to say for the moment, however, that whether we look at the macro picture of man's existence, or the micro picture of just trying to figure out the creation of one human cell, we have to admit that a creator other than man was at work. The evidence is irrefutable. God created everything, and He deserves our love.

LOOKING AT MANKIND THROUGH A CONTEMPORARY LENS:

God has blessed me with the opportunity of visiting well over 100 countries on six continents, either while serving in the military, transacting international business, or for the sheer pleasure of life enrichment experiences. Throughout it all I have been constantly enthralled by the many people groups I have been in contact with, and to mingle among them was a thrill I will not soon forget. To observe with my own eyes exotic eco-systems such as vast deserts, tropical rain forests, savanna, grasslands, tundra, temperate and taiga forests, to say nothing of the magnificent mountain ranges of Everest and Kilimanjaro, has been stunning. And to cross the Pacific, Atlantic and Indian Oceans, and visit many island nations as well as exploring exotic coral reefs, are memories I will always cherish. These travel experiences have provided me with a deep appreciation for God's fantastic creation, which He designed for the benefit and enjoyment of mankind. If an atheist had travelled in my shoes, and saw the vast beauty of God's wonderful earth, there is no question in my mind that such a person would be awed by the wonder and power of God and His creation. Imagine further, if an atheist had an opportunity to traverse around the universe. Would he not be overwhelmed with God and His magnificent accomplishment?

Meanwhile, back on our small planet we find our huddled masses, all seven billion of us, living in some 200 countries, speaking about 6500 different languages, with just as many ethnic groups who all share different cultures and heritage. So the obvious question becomes, how do we create a worldwide system of law and order that will prevent man from entering into madness? Well, for starters we have a world-wide governmental body called the United Nations consisting of 193 member nations, but interestingly only five nations enjoy the prerogative of serving on the permanent security council. This privilege gives each of the five absolute veto powers, and by proxy nullifying the decisions of all other member nations.

As a consequence of this worldly set-up, friction and tension among nations and groups of nations is ever present. We have also enacted other worldwide agencies such as the International Monetary Fund (IMF), created to enact policies that effect exchange currency rates and balance of payments between nations by lending funds when necessary. There is also The World Bank Group, affiliated with the UN designed to make loans to struggling member nations.

Let us also not forget the military alphabet soup of acronyms that make up countless defense treaties designed to maintain peace among nations: UN, NATO, BALTRON, CSTO, SCO, COPAX, SADC, ANZUS, GUAM, ASF, PUNK, TAKM, RIO, PSC, CSDP, AL etc., just to mention a few of the many organizations that are designed to stop man from killing himself. But if that is not enough we now have nine countries that possess nuclear bombs that are capable of destroying every major urban center in the world many times over. And the largest international governing body, the United Nations, is restricted by charter from engaging in conflicts between two groups of combatants that are both located in the same country, except in very special circumstances. As a result we have anywhere between 30 and 40 wars being fought at any one time somewhere in the world. We are forever living on the brink of the next major disaster.

Imagine for a moment that you are an alien from outer space that is visiting earth for the very first time. What would you think? Would you be wondering if this was any way to manage a planet? What odds would you give humans of being able to keep up the madness without a major cataclysmic event taking place? I certainly would think that with all the greed and corruption within legitimate governments and private enterprises (not to mention the increasing number of rogue and gangster states), and the increase in crime world-wide, that our odds were not very good. Such is our current global situation today. The irony, of course, is that with all the knowledge and experience that mankind has gained over thousands of years, he finds himself living in a world today that is more dangerous than ever dating back to antiquity. What a sad commentary for man. The obvious question to ask is why? The answer is, I believe, that man has forgotten God, but fortunately God has not forgotten man. I will provide more elaboration later.

THROUGH THE LENS OF MANKIND'S HOPELESSNESS WITHOUT GOD:

Have you ever felt hopeless regarding your future? Have you experienced a moment in life when it felt meaningless to you? It was Socrates, the great ancient Greek philosopher, who once said, "An unexamined life is not worth living." Without developing a true purpose for your life it simply leads to more frustration, unhappiness and despair. Life is not like Alice in Wonderland, but the author, Lewis Carroll, did say, "That if you don't know where you are going, then you have already arrived." Take away a man's hope and you leave him with nothing.

Even prisoners in some of the worst prison systems have to hold on to their hope that one day they will get out, even if they never will. I once visited a lock-down ward for Alzheimer patients. As I sat at a table with my dear old friend along with four other patients, I listened intently to an elderly man in his 80's who discussed in painstaking detail how he was going to build a beautiful custom home when he got out. I listened patiently as he described in minute detail his elaborate plans for his dream home. He lived daily with the hope that one day he would be released even though I knew his situation was hopeless. Men need hope for the future in the most difficult of circumstances.

Therefore, it is important to have goals and a mission and purpose for your life. Even more important, however, is to ensure your future purpose is in lock-step with God's purpose for your life. Why try to go it alone when you can have God as your guide? After all, He has been down this road many times before, and is an expert in showing you the right way. You, on the other hand, are traveling down this dangerous road for the very first time. Life can only be understood backwards, but we must live it forward. Mark Twain once jokingly said how wonderful it would be if we could start life at 80 and work backwards! But it is what it is, so we need to take God's hand and let Him show us the way.

MANKIND THROUGH THE LENS OF JUSTICE:

By anyone's yardstick for measuring age, I am now classified as an older man, having lived my biblical three score years and ten in four different countries, with the opportunity of traveling widely. I feel I have been truly blessed by God in opening up my eyes to witness the plight of man on this planet, and the story, unfortunately, is not a pretty one. Mark Twain once said that bigotry, prejudice and ignorance are fatal to world travel, and I echo those sentiments.

In traveling the world you cannot help but notice the severe poverty of a large percentage of the people, and witness the tremendous inequitable distribution of wealth. The difference between the rich and the poor is startling. For instance, eight of the ten richest men on the continent of Africa, which represents 53 countries, prior to the "Arab Spring," were Egyptians, with wealth that runs into the billions. However, child mortality rates, malnutrition, and lack of access to medication in Egypt are the highest in the world. In Russia there are so many new millionaires in Moscow the government has lost count, but the growing ranks of alcoholics, homeless, and out of wedlock babies are skyrocketing. In the so-called communist society of China there are many billionaires today, while 300 million itinerant laborers who live like modern indentured slaves being moved from one governmental infrastructure project to another, where they live in make-shift shanty towns until the project is finished. As I travelled across China, I went days without seeing the sun due to the filthy pollutants from factories where workers move around on skates to save time, and women hold the distinction of having the highest suicide rates in the world due to their lack of hope for a better life.

In India, a country long defined by its immense poverty, now has about 158,000 millionaires, but only 42,800 claim on their income tax returns that they make more than 10 million rupees ($185,000) per year, resulting in only 3% of the population that actually pay taxes. [4] The rich are getting richer, and the government is so corrupt the vast majority of the 1.1 billion citizens are being left behind in abject poverty. To think that hundreds of millions of adults and their children go to bed each night around the world with very little in their stomachs is abhorrent. They have little access to the mere basic means of survival such as access to clean, drinkable water, medical supplies, and a steady supply of basic food. With little or no education, families find themselves in a perpetual cycle of poverty that transfers from one generation to the next. Their ignorance makes them like clay in the hands of their despotic leaders who have no intention of changing the status quo. They intend to hold on to power at any cost, even if it means starving children to death. They are unable to see the darkness within themselves. The world is replete with similar stories on all six inhabited continents. Unfortunately, it's not likely to change any time soon. Meanwhile, the latest Forbes 400 list of the world's richest people (March, 2014), now shows the minimum net worth required to get on the list is now $30 billion compared with one billion dollars 25 years ago. There are now more than 500 individuals in the United States alone that are billionaires. The gap between rich and poor continues to get larger.

So if you are looking for justice in this world that explains why the poor continue to rise in numbers, it is unlikely you will find it this side of the veil.

THROUGH THE LENS OF MANKIND'S FREEDOM:

When God created mankind, He certainly had plenty of options. He could have made man in the form of a robot that would obey His every command, but that would be a one way love, and God was looking for a reciprocal love. God then, according to the Bible, decided to create man in His own image, and separate man from all the other living species that God created. It can be argued that man and beast were provided with a body and a soul, but only man was given the power of God's spirit, which not only separated man from all other creatures, but also man was given dominion over them. The freedom that God gave to man came with a price, however.

First, God wants man to love Him, and follow His ways in order to enjoy a good, long life while here on earth. Also, in order to give man the freedom he needs, there had to be a set of laws that would provide that freedom. The laws of nature were created, including the law of gravity, and the first and second laws of thermodynamics. When man looked into the sky and said he wanted to fly like a bird, he invented an airplane, and then flew just like the birds. However, occasionally planes do crash, and passengers are killed. I remember standing at the memorial site in Lockerbie, Scotland, where almost 300 people died there when Pan Am 101 crashed back in the 80s. To view the bios of the passengers was stunning to the senses – all those wonderful, innocent people died so young leaving their families and friends behind. Some pundits cried, "Why God, did you allow this to happen?", but the simple fact is that man created the plane, and two men (terrorists) brought it down. However, God was there on the back end of the disaster, slowly working inside the lives of the bereaved to help them mend their wounded hearts and to move forward with their lives. Our loving God gave us what we wanted – freedom to do what we want to do.

Although God gave man ultimate freedom, man has been doing everything to take the freedom away from other men ever since. Today, in many of the countries I have visited they do not provide the seven basic freedoms Americans and British, for instance, take for granted: freedom to speak without fear the secret police won't arrive in the middle of the night and usher you away to a slave camp for simply expressing a particular point of view; freedom to practice your own religion without fear of being accused of apostasy resulting in prison time or even the death penalty; freedom for women, who often represent 50% of the population, so their rights under the law are equal to a man's rights; freedom to own real property with a valid legal title that no one government official can arbitrarily take away just because he wants it for himself or one of his cronies;

freedom whereby all citizens are treated equally under the law, with no one set of laws for the rich, and another for the poor; freedom from the despotic laws of government so that it cannot over-reach and abridge those freedoms that are firmly established by law, and finally a respect for the rule of law by all citizens and the government, which provides a consistent, steady application of the law from one generation to the next.

A good example of how freedom has progressed is to compare South America to North America over the last 500 years. The governments and leaders in the countries in the south have not respected many of the freedoms sighted above, and the people have consequently been economically held back by leaders who chose to line their own pockets rather than perform the common good that would have increased standards of living for all. Consequently, the comparison of the two hemispheres today is quite remarkable. Power, greed, and lack of a good relationship with God are at the heart of such matters.

THROUGH THE LENS OF MANKIND'S LIMITED TIME:

To be realistic we have to accept the fact we are all dying every minute of every day. Life is a terminal illness, and there is no escaping the death experience for any life form living on this planet. The average human life span is about 25,550 days, consisting of about 86,400 seconds per day that we get to live. In the last sentence the operative word was "average." The truth as we all know is that our lives can end at any moment, because life does not come with a minimum guarantee. We may have no time to say goodbye to loved ones, no time to correct our mistakes. Someone once pointed out that if the age of the earth represented the face of a clock, then man has only been around for only a few seconds, to put matters into proper perspective. There is a quote from Job 14:1 that says, *"Man born of woman is of few days and full of trouble. He springs up like a flower, and then withers away. Like a fleeting shadow he does not endure."*

If just one of our vital organs is taken from us, then our body simply collapses into dust, and conscious experience of this earthly existence is gone. We are history as far as this reality goes, and the perplexing part is that we have no time to put our life in order, to ask for forgiveness, or to pay penance for what we may have done to others. When your number is up, that's it!

Most people are just too busy and preoccupied with making a living, trying to get ahead in the world, or just trying to survive whatever current circumstances they find themselves in, to be thinking about what happens after this life is over. Some people may say this is a good thing, because to be worrying about what may or may not happen in the future is a fruitless exercise. I certainly do not advocate worrying about such matters, because 80% of the things we worry about never happen as we see them in the present moment. So, if I do worry and it doesn't happen, then I have worried for nothing. If by chance all my planning to avoid worry does in actual fact happen, then I will have worried twice about the same thing. All I ask is that you enjoy life to the fullest, but allow God to be in the driver's seat.

Why is it that millions of people living on earth today appear to pay little attention to metaphysical matters that ensure a life, if they accept it, long after this one has run out? Our loving, gracious God has promised all mankind a gift of eternal life provided they accept into their hearts and minds His only begotten Son, Jesus Christ. The problem we face is the influence of so many religions, cults, peer pressure, and the opinions of strong minded individuals who, although many times clueless, guide others down the wrong path.

The problem is that we have so little time in our mortal existence here on earth to get it right. With life being so short, we can easily get mislead down a bunch of fruitless rabbit trails that cause us to get even more confused than we already are. Think about this for a moment. We are all suffering with an unfinished education, and only a short class time to get it right. How can we hope to get a passing grade in understanding our Creator, if we don't start right now in becoming students of God?

The first man, Adam, lived for 930 years before he died. Try to imagine living that long. The Bible also tells us that during the time of the patriarchs men lived incredibly long times: Seth lived 930 years, Enosh 905 years, Kenan 910 years, Mahalalel 895 years, Jared 962 years, Enoch 365 years, Methuselah 969 years, Lamech 777 years, and Noah 950 years. On the other hand, if you look at some of the great men over the last 2500 years, men who made great contributions to the knowledge of man, they lived very short lives in comparison: Socrates (70) Plato (80), Aristotle (62), Confucius (72), Newton (84), Copernicus (70), Galileo (77), Pascal (39), and Einstein (76). We can easily see, therefore, that modern man is faced with a very interesting dichotomy. On the one hand, today's man lives in a very compressed time line before he dies, yet at the same time he has access to more information and knowledge than at any other time in man's recorded history. Because of this short life-span, it is tremendously important that we all get with the program quickly so that we can earn an "A" grade for this earthly experience thus allowing us to enter the right door into eternity. Continuing to disbelieve will inevitably cause you to enter the wrong door when you eventually shed your mortal body.

So, it has become rather evident that we in the present age have the unique challenge of trying to get a good grade for the way we live our lives, but also achieving it with so very little time to learn it all. Clearly we must begin the long journey now, and embark on the straight and narrow path laid out by God Himself in the Bible.

Life without God does not bode well for the future of America. Yes, we can muddle our way through this worldly existence, by getting a good education, getting married, having babies, chasing dollars, and trying to climb corporate ladders of success, but at the end of the day it is all hollow, all vanity that temporarily satisfies our ego ambitions, but none of it does anything to dampen our thirst for knowledge that explains the true purpose for our lives.

The Bible tells us we are always learning, but never able to come to the knowledge of the truth (2 Timothy 3:7). Vanity, vanity, all is vanity, said a wise king so many years ago. This ancient king named, Solomon, was allowed to choose one gift from God. He chose the gift of wisdom. Consequently, he became the wisest man in the world. He experienced all that life had to offer: fame, riches, power, and a thousand women at his bidding. In the end, however, he concluded his life was hollow because he had lost touch with God. All his accomplishments, which were many, were simply empty vanity as he looked back in old age, and all his worldly possessions were left behind for someone else to enjoy after he died.

Not too long ago, Hugo Chavez, the president of Venezuela died, and it was reported that on his death bed, he clung to the arm of his priest and said, "Please don't let me die, please don't let me die." Hugo had strayed from his Roman Catholic faith many years earlier, and as an avowed Communist, whose belief in God is questionable, he felt he had a lot to lose. The most powerful man in his country, who had millions stashed away in foreign bank accounts, was now worried as to where he was going after he died.

Now compare Hugo Chavez's death bed wish with that of a Christian friend of mine who died about the same time. She was asleep when her pastor paid her a visit. When she woke up she said, "Oh, it's only you." This was a little deflating to the pastor's ego, until she went on to say, "I thought that the next time I opened my eyes I would be looking into the face of Jesus." She died the next day with a smile on her face, for she knew exactly where she was going. My friend, just like King Solomon, knew that it is far better to build up treasures in heaven than to seek the fleeting approval and admiration of men here on earth.

It may be true that many people don't really care about their future; others just laugh it off to hide their ignorance or simply don't want to think about the subject. Many others, however, have a thirst for knowledge, which causes them to seek answers to life's basic questions, such as: Where did I come from? What is the purpose of my life? What happens to me when I die? How and when will I die? Why do I have to die at all? Why does life seem to be so unfair when we witness the death of infants, but many adults die of old age? Why do bad things happen to good people and good things appear to happen to bad people? Drawing closer to God who knows all things is a good start in trying to understand such matters.

THROUGH THE LENS OF MANKIND GROWING SPIRITUALLY:

At the expense of sounding simplistic I have to state the obvious, which is not all that obvious to some people. We grow physically automatically, from child to teenager and then adult. It is also true we grow automatically in an intellectual way. A child cannot add two and two, but an adult can calculate with great precision how to place a man on the moon. The third part of man's nature, however, the spiritual part, does not necessarily grow automatically like our physical and mental components. Our spiritual component may remain dormant within us for most or all of our lives unless it is prompted and cultivated by exposure to God's purpose for our lives.

What is so interesting to me is that intellect and good education are no guaranty spiritual development will follow. Some of the most educated people on our planet are spiritually lost, yet many lesser-educated individuals seem to get it, and subsequently are at peace with themselves and the world around them. America now has more than two million of its citizens behind bars in some 4500 plus prisons scattered across the country. These prisons are overcrowded with people who have never developed the spiritual side of their nature. As a result, they are committing themselves to a terribly hard life paying for some action they took earlier that went against the laws of either man or God. Separated from their Christian roots they are lost, like a ship without a rudder. They go through life without purpose, and then one day find their ship of life has hit a rock, and they begin to sink into a sea of self-deception, never knowing the right course to take to get to a safe harbor. I pray this never happens to you or someone you know.

LOOKING THROUGH THE LARGEST LENS OF ALL:

Besides the current seven billion people living on our planet, there are many more billions who have lived and died over the centuries. Have you ever wondered what God's master plan is for humankind? None of us know all the answers, but God has revealed certain information that causes logical human minds to attempt to put together some thoughts that I believe are well worth mentioning. So here is a sincere attempt to bring some clarity to a subject that never gets enough press considering the finite time we humans have to get it right with God. Good men and women may differ in their opinions, but my hope is that by shining some light on this subject it will cause more people to think and discuss the matter, and by doing so they will become more introspective regarding their own future salvation.

<u>Pre-Cross:</u> Long before Jesus Christ walked the earth as both fully man and fully God, we read that mankind had no idea who Jesus was, and therefore was unable to accept Him as Lord and Savior. God did, however, provide man with the General Revelation, that demonstrated the whole world, moon, sun, stars and planets, were designed by a creator who obviously was not a man, but in fact God, the creator of all things. Therefore, God judged man by his righteousness (his ability to follow his conscience to do the right thing in the way he conducted his life). An example of this thinking is

Abraham, the father of the Jewish faith, who never knew Jesus, but was considered righteous because he faithfully obeyed God's instructions. So Abraham was found righteous in God's sight. See Romans 4:3 where Abraham believed God, and it was credited to him as righteousness.

The Old Testament further tells us that all men died and went to Sheol (note that the Old Testament refers to Sheol (Hebrew) whereas the New Testament refers to Hades (Greek). Both are temporary holding places for the unsaved.) Sheol was divided into three compartments: 1) the place of torments, where the unrighteous were held 2) the great divide, and 3) paradise (also known as Abraham's bosom), which hosted the righteous. This is made evident in Luke 16:19 where Jesus talks about the rich man and the poor man, Lazarus, who are separated by a great divide.

The Cross: When Jesus was crucified by man at Calvary, we find in II Corinthians 5:21, "God made him who had no sin to be sin for us, so that in him we might become the righteous of God." This means that from that point forward, anyone who accepts Jesus as his personal Lord and Savior will receive eternal life with God. However, in Luke 11:23 it clearly states there is no neutrality on this subject. Either one accepts Jesus or rejects him. There is no third choice.

The Church Age: We are now currently living in the church age, or the age of the Gentiles. This time period began at Pentecost (50 days after the resurrection of Christ), and will continue until the Rapture, the next major prophetic event (explained later). Until then, people who believe and accept Jesus will be saved, and those who do not accept Jesus as their personal Lord and Savior will perish.

Further Prophetic Events:

In chapters twelve and thirteen we will discuss what the Bible has to say about the future of man as we advance through the rapture, the seven year tribulation period, and the one thousand year millennium. During these time periods many more people will be saved, but unfortunately many others will not. In this way you will also see how man's story has both a beginning and an end.

SPIRITUAL WAGER:

Blaise Pascal was an 18th century French Philosopher and Christian who, among other things, is remembered for the wager he once made, commonly referred to as *Pascal's Wager.* He talked about an argument between a man who believed in God, and another who did not. The Godly man said to the other, "If you are right and I am wrong, then we both have nothing to lose because, according to your statement there is nothing after we die. But if I am right and you are wrong, then I gain everything, and you lose everything."

The point Pascal was making is that in life we have to gamble. We are all constantly put in the position of making decisions with inadequate knowledge as to how the decision will work out. Do we make those decisions based on what we know now? Obviously, if we don't make the decision, we will never know if the new start-up business, or taking the new job, or getting married, will turn out to be successful. In the same way, Pascal was arguing the same case about God.

We can never understand everything about God in advance, because what happens to us after death is unknown to us in this reality. Therefore, we have to consider our options and make our wager. Pascal further states that we have two basic choices, and either way we must consider the risk of being wrong. For instance, if we have faith in God and we later find out He does not exist, then we have made a metaphysical error. However, if we reject God while in our mortal existence, and it turns out that God does exist, then our risk is greater as we are eternally separated from God. Based on the two possible outcomes, Pascal makes the case that it is less risky to have faith in God. The cleverness of Pascal's argument is that it forces the necessity of making a choice, because the wrong choice could invite the death penalty. This logic should cause agnostics some pause, because they refuse to make a decision about God when there is no option to abstain. By not making a decision, the agnostic actually makes a choice – a choice against God!

Now that we have completed this chapter, I hope that you are able to see the reality of our limited mortal life here on earth more clearly. Maintaining a healthy perspective of what is really important, from the less important matters of this world, is crucial in helping all of us find the one true way towards God.

CHAPTER TWO

DISCOVERING AND UNDERSTANDING CHRISTIANITY

Before we discuss principles of the Christian faith, I think it important for us to discuss certain foundational truths that are important to understand as they provide the support system for everything we will be discussing. We must first understand something about the spirit world, which includes: God, Jesus Christ, the Holy Spirit, Satan, angels, demons, heaven and hell. We have learned that spirits never die, they are eternal whether good or bad. Even we humans are also spirits, but we are temporarily trapped in our mortal bodies, which are designed to only last for a short time. Then we will return to the spirit world to be with God and live eternally like all spirits, provided we have accepted Jesus as our Lord and Savior. Our other choice is hell, where we will also live eternally. Our finest minds admit that mankind knows less than 10% of all the knowledge in the universe. Therefore, a strong case can be made that the other 90% we do not know about is in the spiritual world, of which we have limited knowledge.

After discussing the spiritual realm I will give my personal viewpoint on the importance of educating our children at a young age to the importance of Christianity, so that they don't spend a lot of time in adulthood searching down all the wrong paths as so many people have over these many years, including myself. Finally, we will discuss the core Christian principles that are fundamental to the Christian life, as they are a necessary prerequisite for coming chapters.

ETERNAL FOUNDATIONAL TRUTHS

WHO IS GOD?:

It is most difficult for man, with his finite mind and finite knowledge, to fully understand who God is. Someone once said, "That if God were small enough for our minds, then He wouldn't be big enough for our needs." We Christians do know that God has promised us one day we will know everything about Him and His character, as it will be made clear to us (1Corinthians 13:12). Until that day arrives, we will find everything we need to know about God in His Word, found in the Bible. Here are some examples:

We first need to know that God is Omniscient (all knowing); He is Omnipresent (He is everywhere at once), and He is Omnipotent (all powerful). We call these the three omnis. God, who created everything in the universe, knows even the smallest detail of our lives as mentioned in Matthew 10:29-31. Nothing escapes the knowledge of God.

God is in Control.

No matter how chaotic we think the world is in, God is always in control. (Romans 11:33-36)

God is Holy:

God's incomparable holiness is deserving of our worship. (Revelation 15:2-4)

God is Loving and Just.

At first glance, these two words appear contradictory. The Bible tells us that God is love, but His love is sometimes misunderstood. People think that because God loves us, He will not judge us. His love for us, however, does not abrogate the fact that He is also just. Therefore, even though He loves us, He must still deal with our sins.

The God of the Bible is the One True God.

While many religions around the world serve multiple gods, Christians believe that only the God of the Bible is the true, living God, and worthy of our praise and devotion (1 Corinthians 8:4-6).

God is a Personal God

There are numerous references in the Bible to demonstrate that the Christian God is a personal God. Examples include: Loving (1 John 4:16); Righteous (Romans 1:17); Jealous (Exodus 20:5-6); Angry (Exodus 15:7); Veracious – truth telling (Titus 1:2); Omnipotent – all powerful (Matthew 19:26); Omnipresent - everywhere (Psalm 139); Omniscient – all knowing (Romans 16:27).

How does God view Man?

God continually tests man's character, faith, obedience, integrity, love and loyalty. The testing of man appears in the Bible more than 200 times, and in each case we find God using these trials to reveal and build our character. We are all tested when we experience broken promises, betrayal, job loss, health issues, undeserved criticism, impatience, envy, jealousy, and unanswered prayers. Remember, though, that God wants us to pass the tests of life, so He never allows us to take a test that is greater than the grace He gives us to handle it. In James 1:12, it says, "Blessed is the man who perseveres under trial, because when he has stood the test, he will receive the crown of life that God has promised to those who love Him."

We have also learned that God also uses trust to test our character. The Bible demonstrates that all of our opportunities, energy, intelligence, relationships, and all of our assets, are all temporary gifts from God. All the assets we own are ours only for a short time, because God owns everything! (Psalm 24:1). However, while assets are in our possession, we are expected to use them wisely, and be good stewards in managing them. We can hoard them to ourselves, like Scrooge, or we can share our good fortune with the poor and destitute. In the parable of the talents (Matthew 25:21), we find Jesus stating, "His master replied, 'Well done good and faithful servant! You have been faithful with a few things; I will put you in charge of many things. Come and share your master's happiness.'" I remember the quote from Hudson Taylor, the great missionary, who once said, "Small things are small things, but faithfulness in small things is a big thing."

So God uses testing and trusting to determine how we will respond to these challenges. He also asks us not to judge each other. We find in Matthew 7:1, Jesus saying: "Do not judge, or you too will be judged. For in the same way you judge others, you will be judged, and with the measure you use, it will be measured to you." He also goes on to say, "Why do you look at the speck of sawdust in your brother's eye, and pay no attention to the plank in your own eye?" There are many more admirable wisdom quotes that God provides for us in the Bible, but it will be a good exercise for you to examine them for yourself.

WHO IS JESUS?:

More will be said about the Lord Jesus in future chapters, but meanwhile let's look at some of the attributes of Jesus that we need to be familiar with:

Jesus became a Man.

When Jesus conducted His ministry here on earth some 2,000 years ago, He was both fully God and fully man. He became the perfect example of God in human flesh. As a result, He experienced life as a human, not as a rich man, but a man of very modest means. He had no earthly wealth; He took the humble position of a slave, and wandered all over the Holy Land on foot. When He became a man the Scriptures tell us that He "gave up his divine privileges," but it did not mean that He ceased being God. He simply veiled His deity, but He never voided it. Jesus always was, and always will be God.

Jesus had a Specific Mission

Jesus came to earth as a man for only one purpose, which was to save man from his sins. Isaiah 61:1-2 elaborates a little further by describing in more detail the purpose for His mission. He came to preach the Good News to the poor, the poor of soul that is. Jesus ministered to all people, irrespective of their wealth or social standing. He gave sight to the blind, healed the broken hearted; He brought deliverance to those who were steeped in sin, and He brought liberty to the oppressed.

Jesus had the Power to Transform People

Jesus can change the lives of the most unlikely people, such as Paul who aggressively persecuted Christians, and was there when Stephen was stoned to death, but later was confronted by Jesus on the Damascus Road. From that point forward, Paul became a slave for Christ, and wrote 13 of the New Testament books (this is one of the best examples in the Bible to prove that anyone can be saved by Jesus irrespective of the sins they have committed, provided they want to be saved). Other notable people we need to include are the twelve apostles who all died a martyrs death ministering for Christ, with the exception of John (though once boiled in oil for his faith but who lived), and later died of old age.

Jesus made the Greatest Sacrifice

1 Peter 2:24 states: "Jesus himself bore our sins in his body on the tree, so that we might die to sin and live for righteousness; by his wounds you have been healed." As you will see in a later chapter, without Jesus paying for man's sins with His own blood, it is impossible to imagine what life would be like here on earth today.

WHO IS THE HOLY SPIRIT?:

The Bible tells us many things about the Holy Spirit, the third person of the Trinity (explained in the next chapter), including the fact that He is a person. Notice I used the word "He" and not "it." The Bible is very clear in John 14, 15, and 16, that the Holy Spirit is a person, and Jesus Himself never referred to "it," but rather "He," indicating that He is not just a force but a person. The Holy Spirit speaks (Revelation 2:7); He intercedes

(Romans 8:26); He testifies (John 15:26); He leads (Acts 8:29); He commands (Acts 16:6,7); He guides (John 16:13); He appoints (Acts 20:28); He can be lied to (Acts 5:3,4); He can be insulted (Hebrews 10:29); He can be blasphemed (Matthew 12:31, 32); and He can be grieved (Ephesians 4:30).

The Holy Spirit is also a divine person: He is God, therefore He is eternal, He is all powerful, He is everywhere present, He is all knowing, and He is the Creator. The Holy Spirit is alive in our lives today, but there will come a time in the future when the Holy Spirit will pull back His power, as I mention in Chapter 12.

WHO IS THE DEVIL?:

Many theologians agree that there can be no sound theology without understanding demonology.

Millions of people have an inaccurate understanding of who the devil is, mainly because in times past when people were less informed than they are today, the collective public thought was shaped by people like Dante (1265 – 1321) who wrote the *Inferno;* Milton (1608 – 1674) who gave us *Paradise Lost,* and Goethe (1749 – 1832) who wrote *Faust.* Each of these authors provided the public with shapes and images of who the devil was. They saw him as a man dressed in red, with horns, and carrying a pitchfork. Consequently, many have fallen into the trap of either underestimating or overestimating the power of the devil due to our ignorance of him. This is the devil's most effective weapon against us. As a result, some even question the very existence of the devil! When we read the Bible, however, we find that it clearly shows that the devil, who is also known as Lucifer, or Satan, is mentioned some 55 times by different names, and is an active and cunning fellow who is out to destroy as many souls as possible before the end of time. It is encouraging to know, however, that as the "Prince of this world," he does have limitations, and his ultimate demise is forecast in the book of Revelation. So the more we understand the tactics of this intelligent spirit, the more prepared we will be to fight off his attacks.

The devil once was a beautiful angel until iniquity and pride was found in him (Isaiah 14:12-15), and he was expelled out of heaven a long time ago. Also, in Ezekiel 28:11-17 we find that the devil was thrown out of heaven with one third of the angels, because of his pride, and his wisdom was corrupted because of his splendor. Since then he has roamed the earth (Job 1:6-12) and has been creating trouble for mankind ever since. Sometime in the future (Revelation 12:7) states he and his fallen angels (the demons), make war with the arc-angel, Michael, and his army of angels. The devil loses and is hurled to earth (thus no longer having access to God in heaven), and he continues to make war with mankind. But later, he loses the battle against Jesus and is thrown into the Abyss for one thousand years (Revelation 20:1-3).

The most important point to remember is that the devil is not as powerful as God, and he does not possess the three omnis like God does as mentioned above. Satan, the devil, is none of these things. He cannot be in Russia or Iran at the same time, but he can use his fallen angels (demons) to do work for him. It is also important to always think of God when you think of the devil. Maximize God and minimize the devil. Make God greater, and the devil smaller. It is easy to see what happens when we place a small quarter coin over our eye when we look at the sun. That small coin is capable of obscuring the blazing light of the sun, a star whose diameter stretches across a vast 865,000 miles. Satan operates in a similar fashion by helping us block out the vision of God. That is why it is important never to see or talk of Satan without seeing God.

Satan's strategy throughout the ages has been to kill and corrupt by any means: murder, rape, immorality, and sexual perversions. Unlike God, however, Satan cannot create anything! He cannot create matter ex nihilo that is out of nothing. But he can, and does, spread the many lies of occultism: reincarnation, esotericism, pantheism, relativism, and Hedonism. So it is very important to know what God wants and what Satan wants with our lives. In this life we are in training, which takes suffering, discipline, faith, and discernment. In the end, however, Christians are protected from the evil creature, Satan, because they are part of God's family. It is the unbelievers who have plenty of reason to worry.

WHO ARE ANGELS?:

Many people do not believe in angels, but the Bible mentions them some 273 times, so if you believe the Bible is God's Word for mankind, then you have to believe in angels. In December, 2011, the Associated Press conducted a survey that determined that eight out of ten Americans believe in angels; 46% believe they have a guardian angel, and 32% claim they have experienced an angelic presence at some point in their life.

Angels have not always existed (Colossians 1:16); they were created at the Creation of the world (Job 38); their purpose is to serve Christians (Hebrews 1:14), and they protect us from harm (Hebrews 1:14; John 7:30; John 8:20; Psalm 91:11). We are told in Hebrews 12:22, and Revelation 5:11, that there are thousands upon thousands of angels, but their numbers are fixed. Angels never die (Luke 20:34 -36), and they never marry or are given in marriage. It should also be pointed out that Jesus is superior to all the angels, but angels are superior to man while he lives in a mortal body. When man dies, however, he becomes a co-heir with Christ, and will be above the angels (Romans 8:17; I Corinthians 6:3).

We know that angels have personalities demonstrated by their intellect (Isaiah 28:17), their emotions (Job 38:7), Luke 15:10), and they have a will (Revelation 12:4). They also protect man from spiritual danger (Ephesians 6:12), and they also sustain and encourage us (Hebrews 1:14). Angels also escort us to heaven when we die (Luke 16:22). It is also important to point out that Satan can masquerade as an angel of light, as stated in II Corinthians 11:14:

"And no wonder, for Satan himself masquerades as an angel of light. It is not surprising then, if his servants masquerade as servants of righteousness. Their end will be what their action deserves." Also, Luke 3:5-7 demonstrates the earthly power of Satan. Looking at the horrible realities going on in many countries where Islam is the dominant religion, many people are expressing the thought that perhaps the angel, Gabriel, who gave Mohammed the words to the holy Qur'an, may have been impersonated by Satan himself. We have insufficient evidence, however, to make such a conclusion. When in doubt about anything that God or any of the prophets have said, it is always best to confirm with the clear words of the Bible.

In summary, it is always good to remember that angels have always existed, and to know that Jesus is superior to angels, as mankind will also be one day. Angels never marry, and therefore do not procreate. They have a personality, intellect, emotions, and a will. They also act as guardians, by protecting man from harm, as they have a purpose in serving him. Angels also sustain and encourage man, and they sometimes bring unbelievers to faith in God. Most importantly, man should not worship angels, because angels can sometimes be used by Satan to deceive us. But make no mistake – angels are all around us!

WHAT ARE DEMONS?:

Demons are fallen angels, who are out to serve Satan, and work towards man's destruction. It says in Revelation 12:4 that Satan took one-third of the angels with him to earth when he descended from heaven. The number of angels is unknown, but we do know that it is a very large number, which provides Satan with a highly organized force under his control. Most interesting about demons is the fact that they acknowledge the one true God, just as Christians do. This is well documented in Matthew chapter 8:29, when the demons say to Jesus, "'What do you want with us, Son of God?' they shouted. 'Have you come here to torture us before the appointed time?' " Obviously, these demons understood Jesus' power, and they were in fear of Him. What is important to recognize in this passage is the fact that many people in the world today do not believe in Jesus Christ, and even if some do believe that Jesus is the Son of God, these verses show that it is not enough to prevent one from ending up in hell, just like the demons in this story. Belief without accepting Jesus as Lord and Savior, and living in His light, is worthless. You will find that those who give less than a total commitment to Jesus may find themselves with the demons at the time of judgment.

It is important to underscore the fact that demons cannot harm people who have a genuine relationship with Christ. However, those who do not believe or accept Christ are "open season" for these servants of Satan, as evidenced in Acts 19:13-20, where a demon seized upon seven sons of a Jewish priest, and beat them thoroughly. To this day, many Christians fear Satan and his demons, yet everyone who has placed his trust and faith in Jesus Christ comes under God's protection. Job 1:10 tells how God placed a hedge, or wall of protection around Job. Even though it is true that demons have real power, we Christians have no need to fear them, but we do need to remember and appreciate the power Jesus has given us in the face of this awful enemy.

WHAT IS HEAVEN?:

Jesus, said: "No one has ever gone into heaven except the one who came from heaven – the Son of Man." – John 3:13. Also, Proverbs 30:4-6, states: "Who has gone up to heaven and come down? . . . what is his name, and the name of his son? Tell me if you know." We do know, however, that heaven does exist, and it is well documented by Jesus, and many other places in the Bible.

In Christian theology, heaven is the throne of God, and His angels. It is a place where all believers end up for a temporary stay before returning to earth with the Lord Jesus Christ. After the crucifixion of Christ, He ascended to heaven to sit on the right side of God, and He will return to earth with all His saints at the Second Coming. The Bible provides us with vivid descriptions of heaven, where streets are paved with gold, and there will be no more pain or suffering. There will be no fear, and no sorrow for the loss of loved ones like we experience in the present realm. As splendid as heaven is described to be, it is dwarfed by the splendor of being in the presence of God forever. This is the place we should all strive for as our one vital goal to attain.

If you would like to discover further descriptions of heaven, they can be found in the following Scriptures: 1 John 3:2; 1Corinthians 13:12; and John 17:24, where we see God as He is, and we share in His life. Our bodies in heaven will never experience hunger, thirst, death, or sickness – see Isaiah 4:4; 33:24; 35:5-6; 49:10; 65:20-24; Jeremiah 31:12-13; Ezekiel 34:29, 36:29-30; Micah 4:6-7; Matthew 13:43. Also, there will be peaceful conditions on earth during the millennial kingdom: Isaiah 2:2-4, 9:7, 11:6 - 9, 27:13, 32:17-18, 33:20-21, 60:18-22.

WHAT IS HELL?:

The Bible provides man with two options when he dies. He can either go to heaven or to hell. Interestingly, today we have the results of survey after survey disclosing that most people do not believe they will go to hell when they die. They seem to think that only hardened criminals, and people who commit evil acts will end up there. Jesus Christ Himself tells us otherwise, and there are plenty of Scriptural verses to support the fact that hell is a real place:

"Woe to the world because of the things that cause people to sin! Such things must come, but woe to the man through whom they come! If your hand or your foot causes you to sin, cut it off and throw it away. It is better for you to enter life maimed or crippled than to have two hands or two feet and to be thrown into eternal fire. And if your eye causes you to sin, gouge it out and throw it away. It is better for you to enter life with one eye than to have two eyes and be thrown into the fire of hell." These words were spoken by Jesus Himself in Matthew 18:7-9 to emphasize the horror of man ending up in hell.

Whenever hell comes up in a conversation, which is not too often, non-believers always have their pat objections: "I don't believe in hell." "How could a good God condemn a sinner to an eternity of torment?" "People are too weak to avoid sin; how could God condemn them to hell for doing what they cannot avoid?" "No one can be so bad to merit eternal punishment!" "Your notion of hell makes God into some kind of great monster who delights in tormenting people in hell forever." "You shouldn't scare people with all this talk about hell and eternal suffering."

These standard objections about hell often come from people who have never studied the subject, but like to ask glib questions or provide easy stock answers. They often have strong opinions about the subject of hell, but they usually want to keep the conversation light and funny, and if the conversation appears to be getting a little heavy, they usually try to change the subject. What these non-believers fail to realize is that the concept of hell is real, and to think otherwise is to doubt the infallible word of God. When we don't believe, we give ear to the words of humanistic, secular libertines. Those atheists who deny hell are like the African ostrich. When chased by hunters, it plunges its head into the sand and, standing still, believes it is secure from danger because it does not see the enemy. There are many other Bible verses to support the reality of hell, such as: Matthew 5:22; 8:11-12; 10:28; 11:20-24; 13:41-42; 25:30; Luke 12:47-48; 16:22-24; Mark 9:42-47, John 15:5-6; II Thessalonians

1:9; Revelation 2:11; 20:3-14; 20:10; 20:12-13. Read them all carefully, and be prepared to be scared. Some wise man once said: "If you are not afraid of sin, you will be afraid of death. If you are afraid of sin, you will not be afraid of death."

To eliminate confusion when you read the Bible, please understand that the world of the dead is mentioned 65 times in the Old Testament as Sheol, which translates into "hell," "the grave," and the "pit." In the New Testament the world of the dead is referred to as Hades, which appears 42 times. It is important to note that Sheol and Hades are not hell, because the Hebrew word Sheol, and the Greek word Hades both refer to the same temporary place, whereas hell is a permanent place (later mentioned as the lake of fire). Since Jesus Christ paid the price with His blood on the cross, all believers now go directly to heaven to be with Jesus when they die, and therefore do not have to go to Sheol-Hades. In Luke 23:43 we find Jesus telling the thief that "Today you will be with me in paradise." There are some people who believe that those in torment will be granted a later opportunity to be saved, but this contradicts Isaiah 38:18, which says, "Sheol cannot thank you, death cannot praise you; those who go down into the pit cannot hope for Your truth." Perhaps Pascal's Wager, as mentioned previously, makes more sense now that you know a little more about hell, a place to be avoided at all cost.

UNDERSTANDING THE CORE PRINCIPLES OF THE CHRISTIAN FAITH:

I mentioned earlier that I did not have the benefit of a Christian upbringing when I was growing up, and it caused me great pain later on when I made so many mistakes that may have been avoided had I been well grounded in the principles of Christianity. I suppose that is why I have such a high level of sensitivity when I see children not receiving a good Christian education. I can only pray that they won't make the mistakes that I made, or worse.

It is interesting to me as an Englishman that I should first be introduced to religion through Islam. After completing my military training in Southern England, which included obtaining my "wings" as a paratrooper, I was very quickly ushered off to the Middle East where I would spend the next several years as part of a British rapid deployment special forces patrol designed to maintain peace primarily in the Persian Gulf area under a UN peace keeping mandate.

One day at the Souk I heard a great deal of noise and wailing only to find that a pregnant Moslem woman had been run over and killed by a man on a horse and cart. He had apparently stepped off his cart to verify the woman was indeed dead, and then pointed to the sky with the words, "It must be the will of Allah," and then went on his way. His words were interpreted to me by an Arab fluent in English. This fatalistic idea that whenever anything goes wrong it must be the will of Allah is more prominent in Moslem society than most people realize. I also observed beggars who I was told, had deliberately blinded themselves by looking all day at the sun in order to gain sympathy. A similar fatalism prevailed when I was in India regarding their caste system. I will share more about this later.

I will discuss more on Islam in a later chapter, but suffice it to say that due to the poverty and ignorance I witnessed in the Moslem countries I traveled in, I was obviously not impressed with formalized religion, which appeared to be a man made system designed to subdue men, and their wives, into a particular way of thinking so that they could be more easily controlled by their leaders. It was also a religious system that enslaved women. Men were allowed to beat their wives with the full approval of the Qur'an (Islam's holy book), which was unbelievable to my young naïve mind. But to many a Muslim man's credit, he would usually beat his wife behind closed doors, which gave little comfort to his wife who was receiving the brunt of the pain.

I also could not understand why we troops were often solicited for sex, not by women, but by Moslem men! I was also told that female genital mutilation was done on the majority of young girls in Egyptian households. What kind of society was I being exposed to anyway? I wondered. Today, I can look back and realize I was in Satan's playground. But one lesson that was driven home to me in a big way was the fact that it is possible to be immersed in a particular religion, and still not really understand the true ways of God, the creator, no matter how religious a person becomes. It is also somewhat fascinating on one level how we become what we think. Although I was never an atheist, I could not help but sympathize as a youth with Philip Carey, the central figure in W. Somerset Maugham's 1915 classic, *Of Human Bondage*. Maugham went on to describe Carey as follows:

"Not knowing that he felt as he did on account of the subtle workings of his inmost nature, he ascribed the certainty he had reached to his own cleverness. He was unduly pleased with himself. With youth's lack of sympathy for an attitude other than its own, he despised not a little Weeks and Hayward (fellow students) because they were content with the vague emotion which they called God and would not take the further step which to himself seemed so obvious. He was free from degrading fears and free from prejudice. He could go his way without the intolerable dread of hellfire. Suddenly he realized that he had lost also that burden of responsibility, which made every action of his life a matter of urgent consequence. He could breathe more freely in a lighter air. He was responsible only to himself for the things he did. Freedom! He was his own master at last. From old habit, unconsciously, he thanked God that he no longer believed in Him."

How easy it is for young, impressionable minds, including my own, to be manipulated when they are denied, for whatever reason, the opportunity to learn about God's ways in their early education. This is what I experienced in England, a modern, enlightened state. It is still happening in the Middle East, and prayer was taken out of the schools in America after 1963. It is tragic that the evil doers in this world will do anything and everything to deny God, but to also deny God to children is particularly heinous. Consequently, today we find those same children have since grown up to become parents and grandparents who know nothing about God's ways, and are therefore unable to teach their own kids the basics of Christian Doctrine. I was one of the fortunate ones who was led to Christ at a later age, which proved once and for all that you can never be too old to accept Jesus into your life, and be saved for all eternity.

Now that we have a good background concerning the spiritual realm, and how man fits into the overall scheme of things, we can now see more clearly how the young can easily be manipulated into accepting religions that are far from God's calling if they never learn about Christian theology. With those thoughts in mind, we will now take a closer look at the core principles of Christianity as laid down by God Himself in the New Testament of the Bible. This section is important for a number of reasons: 1) First, I have to assume many readers will need this instruction because they may not have been taught it before. 2) Later, we will be comparing Christianity with other world religions, and 3) throughout the rest of this book there will be occasional references to Christian principles that will be easier to understand if they have already been explained. Of course, it goes without saying if the reader is already fully conversant with Christian theology then perhaps he or she may wish to skip this chapter.

I must point out from the start, however, if the reader has no exposure to Christian theology, some of the concepts may appear somewhat odd or peculiar. A person, for instance, sitting down and reading the Bible, the best-selling book ever written, a book that has done more good for mankind than any other book ever produced to date, may find it full of stories they may find incomprehensible based on their level of education, experience or basic background. You won't be the first educated person who does not immediately grasp the principles God is trying to convey to you. All you need is basic literary reading skills as many a less educated person has found out to their pleasure. You will find, however, it is not about education, but rather having the right "headset" on when diligently studying God's word. Reading the Bible is not like reading any other best-selling novel. It is a holy book, and should be treated as such. So keep on studying, asking God for guidance, and each time you read it with a sincere heart He will reveal more truths to you.

Remember, the inspiration of Scripture is not necessary for salvation to be possible. People were saved before there was a Bible, and some people are saved without ever having read the Bible. The Bible is, however, the only divinely authoritative foundation that makes the plan of salvation knowable. Therefore, I ask only that you demonstrate some faith in God's written manual for mankind as you read it, and temporarily suspend your opinion until the end.

CHRISTIAN CREEDS:

First we will look at the Christian doctrines that have served Christians extremely well over the last 2,000 plus years. The essential doctrines are contained in the Christian Church's ancient statements of faith called "creeds," which are like a short summarization of what the Bible teaches, that help clarify Christian beliefs. So let us now take a closer look at each of these core doctrines remembering they are all mentioned in the Christian Bible, which we will discuss more thoroughly in the next chapter. Almost all Christians who seek biblical faith agree with the following doctrines:

BASIC CORE CHRISTIAN DOCTRINES:

GOD'S UNITY:

Although many people around the world believe in many gods, a true Christian believes in only one God, the creator of all things. God has always existed, and will always exist. "I am the Alpha and Omega" says the Lord God, "who is and who was, and is to come, the Almighty." – Revelation 1:8.

Now this is eternal life: that they may know you the only true God, and Jesus Christ whom you have sent - John 17:3

I am the Lord your God . . . You shall have no other gods before me - Exodus 20:2-3

THE TRINITY:

Although Christians believe in only one God, He exists eternally in three Persons (Matthew 28:18-20). God manifests Himself to mankind in the Bible through:

God the Father (2Thessolonians 1:2)

God the Son, Jesus (John 10:30-33; John 20:28; Hebrews 1:8; Philippians 2:11)

God the Holy Spirit (Acts 5:3-4; 2 Corinthians 3:6)

So, although God is only one essence, He is three Persons. Moslems, Jews, Hindus, Buddhists, and many cultist religions do not believe in this concept. As soon as Jesus was baptized, He went up out of the water. At that moment heaven was opened, and He saw the spirit of God descending like a dove and lighting on Him. And a voice from heaven said," This is my Son, whom I love; with him I am well pleased." – Matthew 3:17.

"May the grace of the Lord Jesus Christ, and the love of God, and the fellowship of the Holy Spirit, be with you all" – 2 Corinthians 13:14.

HUMAN DEPRAVITY:

As mentioned in the previous chapter, God is a personal loving God who seeks a personal relationship with all of His human creations. Human depravity, which has come about by man's poor choices, means every human is spiritually separated from God, and totally incapable of saving himself. When Adam the first man sinned, he died spiritually and his relationship with God was severed. As a consequence, all of Adam's descendents are "dead in trespasses" (Ephesians 2:1). Without a new birth (which means being created anew) no one can enter eternal life (John 3:3). We are sinful, and cannot please God with our good works, because we can never "be good enough." When we try to deal with the problem of separation and death on our own terms we will fail, which results in eternal separation from God. As it is written: "There is no one righteous, not even one. There is no one who understands, no one who seeks God. All have turned away. They have together become worthless; there is no one who does good, not even one." – Romans 3:10, 11.

CHRIST'S VIRGIN BIRTH:

Mary, Jesus' mother, became pregnant without engaging in a sexual relationship (the Immaculate Conception). As a result, Jesus' birth over 2,000 years ago, was a miracle. Though this miracle was preordained prophecy (Isaiah 7:14), the reason it is essential is due to God's supernatural intervention. Our sin is not merely something we do, or don't do, it is who we are. Sin is inborn in all of us. Our depravity is passed on to us by our parents (Psalms 51:5; I Corinthians 15:22; Romans 5:12-15). Thanks to God interrupting the normal birth process, Jesus was able to enter this world sinless, and therefore did not inherit a sin nature. Jesus, therefore, not only did not sin, but had no inclination to sin even when tempted. He was in a word, perfect. This is how the birth of Jesus Christ came about: His mother Mary was pledged to be married to Joseph, but before they came together, she was found to be with child through the Holy Spirit. An angel said:

"Joseph, son of David, do not be afraid to take Mary home to be your wife, because what is conceived in her is from the Holy Spirit. She will give birth to a son, and you are to give him the name Jesus, because he will save his people from their sins." All this took place to fulfill what the Lord had said through the prophet: "The virgin will be with child and will give birth to a son, and they will call him Immanuel" – which means, "God with us."- Matthew 1:18-23.

CHRIST'S SINLESSNESS:

As mentioned above, Jesus did not suffer the effects of a sinful nature, and throughout His life He remained sinless. Because of man's sin, however, we cannot have a relationship with God, unless Jesus, as a sinless figure, is able to represent us (or stand in the place of us) before God.

"God made Him who had no sin to be sin for us." (2 Corinthians 5:21)

"For we . . . have one who has been tempted in every way, just as we are – yet was without sin." (Hebrews 4:15)

"He committed no sin, and no deceit was found in his mouth." (1 Peter 2:22)

CHRIST'S DEITY:

The sin divide between man and God meant the only way for man to be spiritually restored with God was for God to create a bridge across the gap of separation. This meant that God, in order to retain His full God nature, became a perfect man in Christ in order to connect the chasm of separation. If He is not both God and man He cannot mediate between man and Himself (I Timothy 2:5). Jesus Christ is the second Person of the Trinity.

"In the beginning was the Word, and the Word was with God, and the Word was God." (John 1:1)

"For in Christ all the fullness of the deity lives in bodily form" – (Colossians 2:9)

"But about the Son He says, 'Your throne, O God, will last forever and ever.'" (Hebrews 1:8)

CHRIST'S HUMANITY:

The biblical record indicates Jesus was also fully human. He got hungry and thirsty, and He got tired and had to sleep just like us humans. Without being fully human, He could not pay the price for human sin. Jesus also had to be divine in order to save us, and He needed to be human in order to adequately represent us. In other words, He had to be both divine and human. Therefore, we have to be fully confident Jesus is able to fully represent all mankind in atonement.

Christ Jesus . . . "taking the very nature of a servant, being made in human likeness." – Philippians 2:7-8

"The Word became flesh and made his dwelling among us." (John 1:14)

"Since the children have flesh and blood, he too shared in their humanity so that by his death he might destroy him who holds the power of death – that is the devil." (Hebrews 2:14)

GOD'S GRACE:

Our own human depravity causes us not to be able to save ourselves. It is only through God's grace that salvation is possible, and God is right in making humans accountable for their sin. As a result, undeserving people will be united in fellowship with God and avoid judgment. Without God's grace, it is not possible for anyone to enter into a relationship with God, which brings peace and joy. God's grace also brings man eternal life (John 17:3).

"If a man remains in me and I in him, he will bear much fruit; apart from me you can do nothing." (John 15:5)

"For it is by grace you have been saved, through faith –and this is not from yourselves, it is the gift of God – not by works, so that no man can boast." (Ephesians 2:8, 9)

"He saved us, not because of righteous things we had done, but because of his mercy" –Titus 3:5-7.

Many religions are based on doing good works in order to obtain eternal salvation. This is not a requirement of Christianity. Faith in Jesus Christ as your Lord and Savior is all that is necessary.

NECESSITY OF FAITH:

Having faith simply trusts that God can and will save us for all eternity. No one can earn salvation no matter how many good works they perform, because no one can ever repay the debt owed to God. But, by trusting fully in God, and demonstrating thankfulness in accepting His gift of salvation, we can be united with God. It is important to remember faith is an act on our part, but it is not a work. Faith is simply trusting in God to do what we could not do for ourselves. (Ephesians 2:8, 9; Titus 3:5). "And without faith it is impossible to please God, because anyone who comes to Him must believe that He exists and that He rewards those who earnestly seek Him." (Hebrews 11:6)

CHRIST'S ATONING DEATH:

Death for all of us is inevitable, but the penalty for sin is not only physical death (separation of the soul from the body), but also spiritual death (separation of ourselves from God). We owe a penalty to God, which was paid by Christ through His death on the cross. The acceptable payment had to be perfect, complete, and without fault. This is where Christ, as a sinless sacrifice, gave Himself in our place, so that whoever believes in Him will not die, either physically or spiritually, but have everlasting life. (John 3:16).

"For even the Son of Man did not come to be served, but to serve, and to give his life as a ransom for many." (Mark 10:45).

"For Christ died for sins once for all, the righteous for the unrighteous, to bring you to God." (I Peter 3:18)

CHRIST'S BODILY RESURRECTON:

Although the atoning death of Christ paid for our sins, we find the process was not complete until he had defeated death by being physically resurrected in the same body (John 2:19-21). As a result, Christ became the complete victor over death, and the prototype of a new, glorified physical body. This means all humans will also be resurrected and live forever in either heaven or hell.

"If you confess with your mouth, 'Jesus is Lord,' and believe in your heart that God raised him from the dead, you will be saved." God could not have made it any simpler for man to be saved for all eternity than reciting this simple commitment. (Romans 10:9)

"He was delivered over to death for our sins and was raised to life for our justification." (Romans 4:25).

THE BODILY ASCENSION OF CHRIST:

Some 40 days after Christ's physical resurrection, He was taken up bodily into heaven, and now that Christ has ascended to the Father, the Holy Spirit now guides us, showing us when we are wrong, and comforting us when we experience difficult times (Acts 1:9-11). The key point to remember is that the Holy Spirit now indwells in all believers, and helps us to make the right decisions for our life.

"But I tell you the truth. It is for your good that I am going away. Unless I go away, the Counselor (Holy Spirit) will not come to you; but if I go, I will send Him to you." – John 16:7.

THE INTERCESSION OF CHRIST:

When Christ's body ascended into heaven it allowed Him to serve as a mediator between man and God, and in God's presence He was able to pray continually on our behalf. Jesus acted like a lawyer in God's court of law, in defending mankind against the accusations of Satan (Revelation 12:10).

"After he had provided purification for sins, he sat down at the right hand of the Majesty in heaven." (Hebrews 1:3b)

"For we do not have a high priest who is unable to sympathize with our weaknesses, but we have one who has been tempted in every way, just as we are – yet was without sin."- Hebrews 4:15

CHRIST'S SECOND COMING:

After Christ was resurrected, He later left the world physically, and He will return in the same manner: "Men of Galilee," they said, "why do you stand here looking into the sky? This same Jesus, who has been taken from you into heaven, will come back in the same way you have seen him go into heaven." (Acts 1:11). His second coming is the hope of the world dating back two millennia, and the Bible tells us it will definitely be fulfilled. This glorious event is explained in greater detail in a later chapter.

"At that time the sign of the Son of Man will appear in the sky, and all the nations of the earth will mourn. They will see the Son of Man coming on the clouds of the sky, with power and great glory." (Matthew 24:30)

"For you died, and your life is now hidden with Christ in God. When Christ, who is your life, appears, then you also will appear with Him in glory." (Colossians 3:3, 4)

The above core Christian doctrines are absolutely necessary in order to call yourself a Christian, a follower of Jesus Christ. Obviously, I have covered a lot of material here, and further prayer and study will be required in order for you to be fully conversant with all aspects of these doctrines. Continually "bathing" yourself in the words of God will provide you with deeper insights into the richness of His glory, and the future He has in mind for you. Most importantly, if you have children, it is of tremendous importance that these precious little ones receive a spiritual education as well as a formal one. Educating children in the ways of the world without helping them to develop the spiritual side of their nature is less than half an education, and it can cause great trouble for them later in life.

It has often been repeated that we have two choices while living this earthly existence. We can either live once and die twice, or live twice and die once (Revelation 20:11-15). This is not a riddle. It simply means we can choose not to accept Christ in this life and then later die. However, if we make that choice we will also suffer a second death at the Great White Throne Judgment at the end of the millennium period (to be discussed in a later chapter). This is like living once and dying twice. Or, we can choose to die in Christ by surrendering our life to Him, (John 3:3), in which case when we die a physical death we will be with the Lord forever. This is like living twice and dying once. Each individual has to make this choice.

When a Christian dies, he or she knows exactly what will happen, and where they are going. Can a non-believer have the same certainty? In the last chapter of this book, I will demonstrate a step-by-step process on how to become a Christian, but in the meantime I realize for the hard hearted who still do not believe, I need to produce additional evidence.

CHAPTER THREE

GOD'S WRITTEN MANUAL FOR MANKIND

As I stood at the showcase looking at the oldest manuscripts of the book of Isaiah in what is known as the Shrine of the Book, a wing of the Israel Museum in Jerusalem, I could not help but be impressed with how well preserved the manuscripts were considering they dated back to the B.C. era. Isaiah, the evangelical prophet who promised the coming of a messiah (which happened more than 700 years later) was also known as Judah's greatest prophet. The Isaiah manuscripts also predicted the fall of Babylon to King Cyrus of Persia in 539 B.C., and the eventual restoration of Israel (which actually happened in 1948 after more than 1800 years of the Jews being in exile without a country). It was a very special moment for me. Every book of the Hebrew Bible was on display with the exception of the book of Esther, and they all gave increased credibility to the authenticity of the Bible itself, which is God's written manual for mankind for all times and in all places. Man's history is really "His Story," the story of mankind through the eyes of God.

I would suggest before reading the Bible, in order to receive the maximum benefit from it, that you first go to God in prayer, and ask Him to give you the wisdom and knowledge you will need to unearth the deep truths that He wants you to hear. For it is written in I Corinthians 2:14, "The man without the Spirit does not accept the things that come from the Spirit of God, for they are foolishness to him, and he cannot understand them, because they are spiritually discerned. The spiritual man makes judgments about all things, but he himself is not subject to any man's judgment." So read the Bible to become wise, believe it to be safe, and practice what it says in order to be right.

You will find the Bible uses a range of literary techniques to communicate with the reader. Some parts are purely literal, others figurative, symbolic, parable or metaphor. The important point is that we make an honest attempt to understand what God is telling us through this holy book. Arguments about literal, figurative or symbolic approaches tend to steer us away from the main goal, which is to understand what message God is personally conveying to each of us. I like the quote from a respected Christian theologian, Tim La Haye, who once said: "If the plain sense of what you are reading makes common sense, then make no other sense, lest you make it nonsense." I think it is also important not to read a Bible verse without reading the entire paragraph in order to gain context of what God is really saying. Let us also remember that the Bible is God's written instruction manual for mankind, and it should be held to the highest respect, and read with a reverence for the inerrancy of God's words to us. So don't be spooked by critics of the Bible who use certain passages to make a negative point. For instance, they like to refer to the early great Christian leader, Origen, who is said to have castrated himself based on a quote from Matthew 19:12, that says that some made themselves eunuchs for the sake of the kingdom of heaven. The Bible will always be criticized by non-believers, but as we grow in our faith we can more easily see how blinded such people are. It is up to each of us to read the Bible for ourselves, which I implore you to do before you make any evaluations.

THE PROTESTANT BIBLE:

Space requirements do not allow me enough time to discuss both the Catholic Bible and the Protestant Bible, which came about due to the Reformation period that took place in the 16th century in Europe that resulted in the reformed Protestant Bible, which is the one we will concentrate on in this chapter. The Protestant Holy Bible is actually made up of 66 books contained in two separate testaments. The Old Testament (OT), known as the Jewish or Hebrew Bible, contains 39 books, and the New Testament, (NT) known as the Christian Bible, contains 27 books, for a total of 66. It is said the Old Testament is the New Testament concealed, and the New Testament is the Old Testament revealed.

Dr. Charles Stanley once explained the Bible as the story of man's redemption with God, and from the very first book, Genesis, to the last, Revelation, you will find the redemptive story of man being played out over the centuries. The Bible is not about man seeking to find God, it is rather about God seeking to find man. It is truly a great story with a wonderful ending for man provided he follows the ways of the Lord. That is why when you study the Bible you will gain greater insights on how to more effectively manage your life today, and also gain a better understanding of where mankind is heading in the future. We are clearly in the end times of biblical prophecy, and we can expect the road to get very rocky before it's all over. But with the knowledge you will be given from God, you need not let your heart be troubled (John 14:27).

Most books, irrespective of how influential they later become, are usually written by a single author or a group of individuals working together over a brief period of time. On the other hand, the Bible was written by a wide variety of authors over a period of more than 1500 years! It was not, however, a single work, but in fact is a collection of sacred books including volumes of law, history, wisdom, and prophecy. Miraculously they all tie into a common theme: Love God!

THE OLD TESTAMENT (JEWISH BIBLE):

As you read the Old Testament, you will find the first five books (known as the Torah, and later as the Pentateuch) were authored by Moses, and are referred to as the Books of the Law. In Jewish tradition, when Moses received the first five books from God on Mount Sinai, he was also given a body of authoritative commentary, or guidelines, for interpreting the laws. For while God decreed no work should be done on the Sabbath, He did not specify what tasks could be done. These judgments were to be made by the religious sages from Joshua to the teachers and scholars of post biblical times.

For hundreds of years the commentary – known as oral law – was not set down in writing, yet the commentaries helped keep these five books a vital part of people's lives, since laws could be adapted to change. So the original Torah remained unchanged, but the body of oral law grew, and by about A.D.(Ado Domini – the year of Christ's birth), the body of commentaries had become overwhelming. It was then scholars began to systemize and write down these laws into what is known as Mishnah, the first codification of oral, Hebrew law. This is one of the most important documents in Judaism after the Bible itself.

The translating of the Torah into Greek came later, and is known as the Septuagint, and was achieved during the reign of Ptolemy, King of Egypt, who authorized 70 Jewish scholars from the twelve tribes to be the ones to make the translation. Thus 70 scribes accomplished the task and the world of the Jew was opened up to the Gentiles (non-Jews). The books of the Old Testament are full of inspiring stories of the Jews fighting their enemies, later rebelling from God, only to end up paying a terrible price for so doing. Great men and women lived and died, and the lessons they learned provide wisdom for all later generations. The OT is also replete with prophetic statements, by such great men of God as Isaiah, Ezekiel, Jeremiah, Zachariah, Daniel, and the 12 Minor Prophets. They provided hundreds of prophecies, many having to do with the coming of a Messiah, which did happen, but in a way that the Jews could not understand even to this day. About one half of these prophecies have already been realized, others will come true in the future, and none have proven to be false.

I will spend more time discussing Bible prophecy in a later chapter, but for the moment I simply want to point out that after hundreds of years of such prophecies being made by inspired men of God, there was suddenly silence for some 400 years after the last prophecies of Malachi (the last book of the Old Testament). Jewish life continued, of course, through the so called Maccabee period, but prophecy stopped, no biblical prophets wrote or spoke anything, and God was silent. It is referred to as "the period of silence."

Prior to this silent period, Alexander the Great had died, and his empire was divided among four of his generals. Egypt and all the eastern Mediterranean countries were ceded to his general, Ptolemy. Now the Syrian kingdom arose, and conflict erupted between Syria and Egypt, which resulted in Syria's King Antiochus Epiphanes, seizing Judea, and the persecution of the Jewish people began. The Jews were forbidden to worship in the Temple and were compelled to eat the flesh of swine, which was forbidden by Moses (Leviticus 11:1-8). Many Jews rebelled and were martyred. The cruelties of Epiphanes brought about the revolt of the Maccabees under the leadership of Mathias. The Jews defeated this despotic Syrian king, only later, in 63 B.C. to come under the subjugation of the Romans, which prepared the way for Jesus to be born.

THE NEW TESTAMENT (CHRISTIAN BIBLE):

Then, some 2000 years ago, God Almighty sent to earth His only begotten Son, Jesus Christ, to act as an intermediary between man and God, the Father. Life for man has never been the same since. Although Jesus was fully man as well as fully God, He only lived on earth into His mid-thirties, and then was crucified by man on a cross, only to become resurrected in His full immortal body three days later (Matthew 28:1-10), (Mark 16:1-7), (Luke 24:1-8). After His resurrection was witnessed by more than 500 people (1 Corinthians 15:6), Jesus ascended to heaven, and the Holy Spirit was released at Pentecost (50 days after His ascension). This event changed the direction of man's future significantly. Prior to Christ's arrival, men were worshipping pagan gods, and evil and corruption were systemic throughout society.

The Gospels, reciting the life of Christ, were written by four Godly men: Matthew, Mark, Luke and John. The first three are known as the Synoptic Gospels because they are not only striking in their similarities, but also in their differences. They were primarily written around the Galilee area, but John's gospel stands in a class by itself and covers Jesus' time in Judea. The Synoptic narrate Christ's miracles, parables, and address His message to the multitudes. John represents Christ's deeper and more abstract discourses, conversations and prayers. So the Synoptic describe Christ in action, but John portrays Christ in meditation and communion.

These three Synoptic Gospels have often been challenged over the centuries, but consider this thought for a moment. If four witnesses should appear before a judge to account for a certain event, and each person tells the exact same story in similar words, the judge would probably conclude that although their testimony would have some value, it would demonstrate the only event that was certain beyond a doubt was that they had all agreed to tell the same story. On the other hand, if each man told what he had seen, and how he saw it in his own words, then the evidence would be acceptable and very credible notwithstanding any differences. So, when you read these Gospels, isn't that exactly what the reader finds? The four men tell the same story in their own words in their own way, but with differences.

The four Gospels tell us when and how Christ came to earth. In Matthew, for instance, Christ is presented as King, and His genealogy is traced back to the Jewish King David. Therefore, it is written primarily for the Jews. In Mark, Christ is presented as Servant, and is written for the Romans. In this book there is no genealogy. Why? Most people are not interested in the genealogy of a servant. More miracles are presented in this book than the others as Romans were less interested in words, and more interested in deeds. Then we find in Luke, Christ being presented as perfect Man tracing His genealogy back to the first man, Adam. This book was focused on the Greeks. Finally, in John, Christ is portrayed as the Son of God, and written to all that believe, both Jew and Gentile.

After the Gospels we find in the Book of Acts the birth of the Christian Church (Acts 2:1-12), up to the power of Pentecost (50 days after the resurrection of Christ). We then read the Epistle Letters, written by St. Paul, which tell us why and for what purpose Christ came. Dr. William H. Griffith Thomas, provides us with four words that help us to link together the whole of God's revelation to mankind:

> Preparation: In the OT, God makes ready for the coming of the Messiah.
> Manifestation: In the four Gospels, Christ enters the world, dies for the world, and then establishes His Church.
> Appropriation: In the Acts and Epistles the ways are revealed in which Jesus was received, appropriated and applied in individual lives.
> Consummation: In the Book of the Revelation, the outcome of God's perfect plan through Christ is revealed.[1]

A clear reading of the Bible teaches that man cannot get into heaven based on doing good works like so many other religions and cult practices. The Bible tells us we are all full of the sin of Adam, (the first man), and it runs in the bloodline down through the centuries. Isaiah 64:6 states, "All of us have become like one who is unclean, and all our righteous acts are as filthy rags; we all shrivel up like a leaf, and like the wind our sins sweep us away." Therefore, only God can save us from spending eternity in Hell, provided we want to be saved.

You may now be thinking that being a Christian is as simple as accepting Jesus as your Lord and Savior. Fortunately for you that is not how it works. If you have a sincere heart, and truly want to be a follower of Christ, then you need to fully admit that you are a sinner and seek forgiveness for all your sins; then Christ will wash your sins away, and you will become a new person in Christ. You will die to sin, but saved in the spirit of God. You will then begin to enjoy the Fruits of the Spirit, which will be discussed in detail later in this chapter.

PRACTICAL BENEFITS OF READING THE BIBLE:

The Bible is a true source for learning how God wants us to live properly while alive on earth. It is full of good, practical recommendations to help make our lives easier by learning what it has to say. There is a lot of truth and wisdom God wants to share with each Bible reader, yet for some reason we find millions of people in the West never bother to read it let alone study it with a concentrated focus to learn the wisdom of the ages. Yet in many other parts of the world we find people going to great lengths, even risking death to get their hands on a copy. Such are the differing value systems around the world.

Below are some practical examples:

MONEY:

Money is not the root of all evil as some think, but it is the love of money that causes so many problems in the lives of millions of people. Money is a big thing to all of us, but it is not a big thing with God who is more interested in knowing what we do with this small thing, that makes a big difference in eternity. Whether we have a lot or very little money, God cares about our faithfulness, and is more interested in how we invest in His kingdom where we discover treasures that are far better than the temporary and insignificant riches of this world (Matthew 6:19-21). By being faithful to God with the money He entrusts us with, He will be faithful to us through financial turmoil that we will inevitably experience as we advance through this world. We have assurances from Jesus who once said: "Seek first God's kingdom and his righteousness, and all these things will be given to you as well." (Matthew 6:33).

When it comes to money management, we have to take the right approach to its management according to the principles laid down by God. By having the right "head-set" on we become more fully aware that "The earth is the Lord's and everything in it," (Psalm 24:1). Haggai 2:8 says: "'The silver is mine and the gold is mine,' declares the Lord Almighty." God is the owner, but we are His managers, and He has entrusted us to manage our assets wisely. The Bible demonstrates that faithfulness with the use of money will be rewarded. "His master replied 'Well done, good and faithful servant! You have been faithful with a few things; I will put you in charge of many things. Come and share your master's happiness!'" (Matthew 25:23). There is also a great quote in Luke 16:9-12, which says, "Whoever can be trusted with very little can also be trusted with much, and whoever is dishonest with very little will also be dishonest with much. So if you have not been trustworthy in handling worldly wealth, who will trust you with true riches? And if you have not been trustworthy with someone else's property, who will give you property of your own?" Many years ago, Billy Graham said:

"Give me five-minutes with a person's check-book, and I will tell you where their heart is."

For thousands of years, the Bible has taught man to understand the right ways to approach the use of money. Here are just a few examples:

Scriptures speak very clearly about cosigning a note for someone else. Proverbs 17:18 says it is poor judgment to countersign another's note, to become responsible for his debts. This truism was stated several thousand years ago, and yet it is as true today as it was then. A recent FTC study found that 50% of those who cosigned for bank loans ended up making the payments. 75% of those who cosigned for finance company loans ended up doing the same thing.

"Whoever loves money never has money enough; whoever loves wealth is never satisfied with his income." (Ecclesiastes 5:10)

Money - "be content with what you have, because God has said, 'I will never leave you; never forsake you.'" (Hebrews 13:5)

"A generous man will prosper; he who refreshes others will himself be refreshed." (Proverbs 11:25)

"For where your treasure is, your heart will be also." (Matthew 6:21)

The average person works 100,000 hours during his lifetime, so take heed from what is said in Colossians 3:23-24, "Whatever you do, work at it with all your heart, as working for the Lord, not for men, since you know that you will receive an inheritance from the Lord for your reward. It is the Lord Christ you are serving."

"The house of the righteous contains great treasure, but the income of the wicked brings them trouble." (Proverbs 15:6)

"If you love your neighbor as much as you love yourself, you will not want to harm or cheat him, or kill him or steal from him . . . love does no wrong to anyone." (Romans 13:9-10)

OTHER PRACTICAL ADVICE FROM THE BIBLE:

Money problems are not the only challenges we face in life. There are many other daily issues that we need to face, and the Bible can provide the answers. Here are a few more practical ways to solve the many problems that enter into our lives, which you can look up for yourself as an exercise in making good use of the Bible:

FACING CRISIS: Read 2 Timothy 1:7; Hebrews 4:16

SICK OR IN PAIN: Matthew 26:39; 2 Timothy 2:3; Hebrews 12:1-11; James 5:11-15; 1 Peter 4:12, 13, 19

NEED OF PEACE: Psalms 1:1, 2; 4:8; 85:8; Romans 5:1-5; Romans 8:6; Colossians 3:15;

FRIENDS FAIL YOU: 41:9-13; 55:12-23; Luke 17:3, 4; Romans 12:14, 17, and 19

WHEN DISCOURAGED: Psalm 23, 37:1-17; Philippians 4:4-7; Isaiah 42:1-4; Ephesians 3:10-13.

DISASTER THREATENS: Psalm 34, 118:5-9, 121; Jeremiah 17:17-18; Proverbs 3:25-26

WHEN BEREAVED: Luke 6:21b; 1 Corinthians 15:20-23; 1 Thessalonians 4:13-18; John 14:2

WHEN AFRAID: Psalm 27:1; Matthew 6:25-34; Romans 8:15-16; 2 Corinthians 12:9; John 14:27; 1 Peter 3:13-15

WHEN IN TROUBLE: Psalm 16:1; 31:7-8; 32:7; 37: 39-40; 38, 40: 2 Peter 2:9

The above is just a partial list of the many pearls of wisdom found in the Bible. All we have to do in order to enjoy a full, abundant life is to study them, and take them to heart.

THE BIBLE'S BIG BONUS:

Besides providing excellent advice on how to manage money, bouncing back from failure, facing a crisis, discouragement, seeking peace, working through bereavement, avoiding temptations, and managing fear, the Bible has even more benefits for those who have accepted Jesus Christ as their Lord and Savior. We call them Spiritual Gifts that come from the Holy Spirit. There are at least 28 Spiritual Gifts that mature Christians can receive, including the gifts of: Administration, Apostleship, Celibacy, Deliverance, Discerning of Spirits, Evangelism, Exhortation, Faith, Giving, Healing, Helps, Hospitality, Intercession, Speaking in Tongues, Interpretation of Tongues, Knowledge, Leadership, Leading Worship, Martyrdom, Mercy, Miracles, Missionary, Pastor, Prophecy, Service, Teaching, Voluntary Poverty, and Wisdom. No one is given all these gifts, but some may have more than others. The Holy Spirit distributes spiritual gifts as He wills; they are freely given, and cannot be purchased. For further elaboration on this subject, I suggest you read several passages in the Bible: I Corinthians 12, Romans 12, Ephesians 4, and I Peter 4:10.

FRUITS OF THE SPIRIT

I must point out that the Spiritual Gifts mentioned above are not the same as the Fruits of the Spirit as mentioned in Galatians 5:22-23. The Fruits of the Spirit (mentioned below) are aspects of Christ's character, which every Christian should strive for, to promote, and to develop. This can take a lifetime. The fruits of the Holy Spirit are attributes of redeemed nature, and just like fruit they can be cultivated, and when they are displayed by a Christian they represent a manifestation of the Holy Spirit. The Fruits of the Spirit are: Love, Joy, Peace, Patience, Kindness, Goodness, Faithfulness, Gentleness, and Self-Control. Against such things there is no law. Let us look at these virtues a little closer:

LOVE: We find that love seeks the highest good for others. Love is not based on emotion or feelings, but rather it is a decision to be committed to the well being of others without any condition or circumstances. John 3:16 tells us, "God so loved the world that he gave his one and only Son, that whoever believes in him shall not perish but have eternal life." And Jesus went on to say in John 15:9, "As the Father has loved me, so have I loved you. Now remain in my love."Also, in John 15:12-14, Jesus further went on to say, "My command is this: Love each other as I have loved you. Greater love has no one than this, that he lay down his life for his friends. You are my friends if you do what I command." Love is the all encompassing fruit of the Spirit – the rest are expressions of the same thing in different forms. When we speak about love as a fruit of the Spirit, we often refer to the Greek word, *agape,* which refers to a mindset as much as a feeling.

JOY: Happiness is not joy. Happiness is being given a new car or home, but joy is gladness that is not based on circumstances such as financial gain, good health, or popularity. To experience true joy a believer in God must obey God's will, receive His forgiveness, then participate in fellowship with other believers, minister to others, and share the Gospel. In John 16:22-24, Jesus said, "Now is your time of grief, but I will see you again and you will rejoice, and no one will take away your joy . . . ask and you will receive, and your joy will be complete." Knowing Jesus, who knows what life is like for us, grants in us a reservoir of joy never to be depleted, even amid our difficult circumstances.

PEACE: God does not want us to worry, but to have peace, which is a state of assurance. With this assurance we tend to lack fear (an acronym for False Evidence Appearing Real), because it provides us with a sense of contentment. You might say this sense of peace frees us from worry and negative thoughts. Romans 14:19 states, "Let us therefore make every effort to do what leads to peace and to mutual edification." It is also stated in 1 Corinthians 14:33, "For God is not a God of disorder but of peace." This peace is not an absence of conflict but the assurance that no matter what life brings, God knows and cares for our world, and our lives are in His hands.

PATIENCE: Most of us lack patience, but what is it really? Patience is a slowness in avenging wrongs. It is the quality of restraint that prevents believers from speaking or acting hastily in the face of contention, opposition, or sometimes persecution. Patience is bearing pain without complaint, knowing that right will eventually be done. Proverbs 14:29 tells us, "A patient man has great understanding, but a quick tempered man displays folly." And I Thessalonians 5:14 states, "And we urge you, brothers, warn those who are idle, encourage the timid, help the weak, be patient with everyone." Patience allows us to understand that we all make mistakes, which allows us to demonstrate good will when others exasperate us. The word *patience* is most often used in the New Testament when speaking about God's attitude toward us. We all fail to live up to His standards, yet God is patient and forgives us as we should forgive others.

<u>KINDNESS:</u> The Bible tells us kindness is merciful, sweet and tender, and is an eagerness to put others at ease. It is a sweet and attractive temperament that shows friendly regard towards others. Proverbs 11:16, 17 tell us "that a kindhearted woman gains respect, but ruthless men gain only wealth. A kind man benefits himself, but a cruel man brings trouble on himself." God also states in Jeremiah 9:23, 24, " Let not the wise man boast of his wisdom or the strong man boast of his strength or the rich man boast of his riches, but let him who boasts, boast about this that he understands and knows me, that I am the Lord, who exercises kindness, justice and righteousness on earth, for in these I delight, declares the Lord."

<u>GOODNESS:</u> This is the virtue of having a selfless desire to be open hearted and generous to others above what they deserve. In Ephesians 5:8-10, it demonstrates an example of how the fruits of the spirit are supposed to work, "For you were once darkness, but now you are light to the Lord. Live as children of light (for the fruit of the light consists in all goodness, righteousness and truth) and find out what pleases the Lord." And we find in Titus 3:4-7, the following admonition: "But when the kindness and love of God our Savior appeared, he saved us, not because of righteous things we had done, but because of his mercy. He saved us through the washing of rebirth and renewal by the Holy Spirit, whom he poured out on us generously through Jesus Christ our Savior, so that, having been justified by his grace, we might become heirs having the hope of eternal life."

FAITHFULNESS: Having a firm commitment in your faith in God, demonstrating loyalty to your friends, and being dependable in carrying out your responsibilities, are all outward manifestations of faithfulness. Having faithfulness is also demonstrating conviction that even now God is working and acting on one's behalf. "Righteousness will be his belt and faithfulness the sash around his waist." (Isaiah 11:5). "Let love and faithfulness never leave you; bind them around your neck, write them on the tablet of your heart." (Proverbs 3:3)

GENTLENESS: The quality of gentleness does not come from weakness or passiveness, but rather from a position of strength. It is a humble and non-threatening demeanor. Jesus was gentle and humble at heart as is demonstrated in Matthew 11:28-30, "Come to me, all you who are weary and burdened, and I will give you rest. Take my yoke upon you and learn from me, for I am gentle and humble in heart, and you will find rest for your souls. For my yoke is easy and my burden is light." We also find Paul saying: "What do you prefer? Shall I come to you with a whip, or in love and with a gentle spirit?" (1 Corinthians 4:21)

SELF-CONTROL: To be in harmony with God, one must restrain personal emotions, actions and desires. Demonstrating self-control is doing God's will, not living for one's self. Titus 2:11, 12 goes on to say that, "For the grace of God that brings salvation has appeared to all men. It teaches us to say 'No' to ungodliness and worldly passions, and to live self-controlled, upright and godly lives in this present age…" "Like a city whose walls are broken down is a man who lacks self-control" (Proverbs 25:28). And "A fool gives full vent to his anger, but a wise man keeps himself under control." (Proverbs 29:11)

All nine of these wonderful gifts become available to people who become believers in Jesus Christ, and they can have a tremendous impact on their lives.

Prior to accepting Christ I had no idea of such gifts. I had a restless, empty heart, where material gain and ambition to get ahead trumped everything. At that time I was ignorant of all these wonderful gifts, which are now worth more to me than any wealth, which I will not be able to take with me when I die.

As a Christian today who is enjoying the Fruits of the Spirit, I must admit that as a young man I would have been clueless if someone had mentioned these spiritual gifts to me. As a youth, I never realized I was living in darkness without the benefit of God in my life. I can only recall my strong, unbridled ambition, which was bent on becoming rich and never repeating the life of being poor. I was going to succeed financially no matter what risks I had to take, mainly because I had the innate feeling within me that I could accomplish it.

MY OWN PERSONAL TESTIMONY:

When I first arrived in America, I had no family here, no friends, no job, no business contacts, no networking system, and $150.00 in my pocket. The job I hoped to get was taken, and so I found myself sleeping in my car, which was no big deal as I had done it before many times. In fact I had slept on rocks and sand when I was in the military in the Middle East, so the back seat of my car was a luxury in comparison. In the darkness of the moment, however, I swore never to repeat the experience, especially now I was in America, the land of great opportunity. Every day, I stomped the pavements looking for work, any work, until I finally got a job. I worked in a finance office wearing the same set of clothes every day for the first three weeks until I received my first pay check. I remember co-workers, especially the women, joking about how "Alan is here again with the same old suit on!" I did not call my parents for help, although I thought about it. I had made this "bed," and I was bent on sleeping in it whether I had a pillow or not. I decided there and then that being poor was no fun, and I intended to change my circumstances regardless of how hard I was going to have to work.

My blind ambition caused me to be obsessed with saving money, because I thought that money was the answer, and I had no fallback position except to live on the streets. But I was now living in the greatest country in the world, and it was up to me to make the most of it. I instinctively knew that America was giving me an opportunity I could never have achieved back home in England, where good job opportunities and a higher education were far more difficult to achieve for a working class lad like me who went to work full-time at the age of fifteen (at this time I would also like to thank America for providing me with a university education in Business, which came later).

True, I worked exceedingly hard in order to accelerate promotion, which included long extra hours working by myself without pay in order to learn, but I achieved great results. I passed all my exams, and was soon managing a finance office for a major corporation, which provided an excellent salary and bonuses. My insecurities, and strong work ethic (which I credit to my parents), were paying off handsomely as the drivers of my ambition. It was at this time I was able to reunite with my estranged wife and son in Los Angeles, who had earlier returned to England from Canada.

In a very short time my beautiful wife had started a very successful business, and I kept my job with the finance company. Then we purchased a dairy retail store, and we began to acquire rental properties from surplus savings. Working in the finance office during the day, and managing the store in the evenings and weekends, while my wife managed her business, caused us to be like shadows passing in the night. Although we were well on our way to an early retirement, it gravely affected our marriage, and she ended up filing for divorce. I was devastated.

The next thing I remember was seeing much of our hard earned money, which we had sacrificed so much time and effort to accumulate, going up in flames in payments to attorneys and taxes. This was the lowest time in my life, because I had stupidly sacrificed my family on the altar of the almighty dollar. This was truly the biggest mistake I have ever made, before or since, and it still pains me after all these years.

Where had I gone wrong? How could I have been so ignorant? Success in the eyes of men is one thing, but to fail in my marriage proved how far off the mark I really was. You see, it was all about me, and never about God. I don't want to excuse my ignorance, but I truly was a very misguided person who thought that if I made plenty of money, then I would be classified as a "winner," and would enjoy the esteem of other men. How foolish I was to think this way. If only I had known about Philippians 2:3, which says: "Do nothing out of selfish ambition or vain conceit, but in humility consider others better than yourself." The spiritual part of my education I had never received was now catching up with me, and I was reaping the whirlwind.

So with a huge hole in my heart that desperately needed to be filled, I began a quest to search for real meaning in my life, a meaning that talked to where I lived. A meaning that would transcend through my future in this world, and my life beyond this mortal existence as well. I knew there were answers out there, but where to look? I visited many churches, but spiritual matters did not begin to come together until I met my second wife, who was a strong, very attractive Christian lady. It was then that a sinner kissed an angel, and my life began to change. She taught me a great deal, not only during our courtship, but throughout our very successful marriage. Some of my sophomoric attitudes began to be replaced with a character that was more fitting of the man that God had always wanted me to be.

I took Jesus up on His offer as laid out in Matthew 7:7, which reads: "Keep asking, and it will be given to you. Keep searching and you will find. Keep knocking and the door will be opened to you. For everyone who asks receives, and the one who searches finds, and to the one who knocks on the door it will be opened." For the first time in my life I began to understand what one Christian once said when he explained the experience of moving from darkness into light, from death to life, from bondage to freedom, from gloom to glory, from fear to faith, from defeat to victory, from failure to success, from guilty to not guilty, from hatred to love, from grief to joy, from weakness to power, and from I can't, to I can. The light was getting brighter in my life.

With the support of my loving wife, I humbled myself in prayer realizing for the very first time in my life that I could leave all of my troubles at the seat of the Cross, where the shed blood of Jesus Christ would wash away all my sins. I cannot adequately describe the liberated feeling I experienced. It was as if a huge weight had been lifted from my shoulders. I imagined what it must be like for a prisoner to experience freedom for the first time after many years behind bars. Now at last I could see things far more clearly. It is as if I had been blinded to my own faults, but now I had a chance at a new life where my emphasis would be more on serving others as well as Almighty God. I came to realize God did not want a religious relationship with me. He wanted a personal, loving relationship. All the religiosity in the world comes up short of having a personal relationship with God. Christianity proved to me it was the only way I could enjoy that personal relationship, and I will speak on this subject later. I also confirmed in my own mind that as a Christian I had the responsibility of discussing my faith with non-believers, and it is not an easy task. It is almost like trying to explain love to someone who has never been in love. But the effort is well worth it if someone can be saved from hell.

As my marriage continued to grow stronger, and my faith more mature, I looked forward to a long life together with a wonderful partner with whom I had shared so much personal history. Then, quite unexpectedly at the young age of 47, she died. As I sank into a deep hole of self-pity and depression, I thought my life was over. Looking to the future, all I could see was darkness. There was no light, no hope, no reason whatsoever to do anything. What was the point of living?

What reason was there to carry on without her to share my life with? It was then that God began to pick-up the pieces of my life, and slowly put me back together again. It took a long, long time, and quite frankly the grieving process was hell. I never imagined that grieving for a loved one could be so unbearable. It is though part of me was missing. I felt like half a man. I would much prefer to experience physical pain and torture rather than go through that experience again. All experiences provide lessons for us to learn, however, and I began to realize that it is times like this that God works His miracles. My faith in God grew stronger, and I love Him more today than ever. I now know quite clearly that He is the main purpose for my existence, and my job is to simply please Him with the way I conduct my life. The Fruits of the Spirit propel me in the direction of always wanting to please Him, and to help others less fortunate than myself. What joy there is in living according to God's laws and not mans.

I share my story with the reader to point out that we all take different paths through life, and we make lots of mistakes until we get it right. No one has an easy ride. There are lots of bumps along the road, and only our faith in Jesus will get us through this life where we yearn for justice, but never find it without Jesus. One day, though, we will live a perfect life, and that's the one I look forward to.

CHAPTER FOUR

A SEARCH FOR THE MEANING OF LIFE

At the heart of man's yearnings over these many years, has been his attempt to find not only true meaning for his life, but also to find the one God that brings joy and peace into the hearts of all His believers. This quest for life's meaning affects all of us throughout our lives, and is well worth examining closer, simply because billions of people are still searching for illusive meaning in their lives to this very day, despite the increased knowledge that God has provide us since the days of Christ.

Although the size of earth has not changed since the dawn of man, it nonetheless appears to have become a much smaller place. With advances in transportation delivery systems that can transport us to the far corners of our planet within days, plus the technological advances in communication such as the Internet, which allows us to communicate with anyone in the world within seconds, and it becomes understandable for us to think that the world's people groups have come closer together. Compare, for instance, that prior to 1850 it took two months to transmit a message from New York to Tokyo, and before 1900 a journey from Philadelphia to Paris would have taken ten days.

Globalization, technological advancement, knowledge explosion and language trends, are homogenizing a shrinking world.

Only a few generations ago we believed people in far off lands were much different than ourselves, and they obviously thought the same about us. We distrusted these people because of their differences, and they distrusted us. To us they were foreign heathens, strange and peculiar, and they were our potential enemies. You might say our attitude towards them was based on ignorance and misapprehension, and a great deal of misunderstanding. Our level of awareness was not at the level it needed to be. Ignorance and lack of education is a terrible thing. Today, of course, we are far more enlightened, and the world has become flatter in the sense that satellite communication, and the speed of travel have opened up dialogue with almost everyone on the planet. We have learned that the more we are different the more we are the same – all creatures manufactured by the same creator.

Today there are approximately two hundred countries in the world, that envelope some seven billion human souls. At the end of the day, however, the one basic thing we must try to understand is the faith by which these people live. All else is elaboration. Right from the beginning of man's existence he has always known God. Unfortunately, over time man has moved further and further away from his close relationship with God, only to find himself mired in more and more complicated forms of worship, which have become so complex that today they defy any attempt to explain them. So looking at the past will assist us in trying to understand ourselves better, and the world we live in today. In our search for meaning we have to look backwards in order to look forward.

BACK TO THE BEGINNING:

As far back as human history will take us, we find man searching for positive meaning for his life, and attempting to figure out what human life is all about. Initially we find early man eager to set the date of the world's creation. The very first account we read about in practically every religious literature is a description and an explanation of how the world was created, and when man was given dominion over everything on earth. According to some older writings, the world was created exactly 4004 years before the Christian era, or just over six thousand years ago. The Jewish calendar begins in the year 3760 BC, and other religions, although not so specific, claim the world was created much earlier. Take the Jains of India, for example. They claim the first religious leaders appeared on earth one hundred trillion palyas ago. "What is a palyas?" you ask. It is the length of time that it would take a bird to empty a well, one mile square, filled with fine hairs, if it carried away a single hair every hundred years! So how old are the Jains?

Primitive man was interested in gaining answers to many questions about his life. We find that he ate, drank and slept just like the other animals. He wished it was hot when it was cold, and he feared for his life just like the animals. But unlike them, he asked questions. *Why* was among the very first words he used, and he used this word constantly. Why did the sun shine in the daytime and not at night? Why does the moon grow fat and round from night to night? Why does it always thunder after lightening? But most importantly, who made all these things in the world? Asking 'why' was a good thing in that it helped man to progress, but at the same time it caused man to move further from God. Not only did he ask questions, he also tried to answer them. Of course, asking questions is one thing, but answering them was quite another. If he could not come up with an answer he imagined it, and then claimed that was the answer. This was the beginning of story-telling.

WORSHIPPING NATURE AND IDOLS:

Soon the story-teller was explaining the sun was a Wheel of Fire on which the Sun Spirit took a ride each day across the skies to see the world. At night the Sun Spirit put the Wheel of Fire away in the Hall of Darkness and went to bed. But the next day if the Sun Spirit was lazy he may not take his ride, and the sun would not shine. So man began to worship the Sun Spirit, and soon he began to worship other things such as the Moon Spirit, and later he began to believe the stars were other lesser spirits to worship. Over time man began to worship hundreds of spirits, and Nature Worship became the first religion of mankind. Before long there were thousands of images that people began to worship. There were images made of wood, clay and stone. And there were little images that looked like wolves, bears, lions, crocodiles, frogs and fish. The people were now no longer worshipping the Nature Spirits, but instead were worshipping many images called, idols, and idol worship was born.

These idols, so the people believed, if flattered enough by prayers and sacrifices, had the power to do good for the people who believed in them, and to harm their enemies. If a man quarreled with his neighbor, he would go and pray to his favorite idol in order to make his neighbor's cow give bloody milk, or try to hurt him in some other way. But the neighbor had idols too, and so while a man was trying to punish his neighbor he also had to worry about his neighbor harming him. In order to protect himself against the power of the evil spirits that fought on the side of his enemies, man began to wear little images of his idols around his neck called amulets or talismans, in the belief they would protect him from harm. Some people actually thought using certain amulets could open the Gates of the Future and see what was going to happen. With these beliefs spreading among the people, they began spending much of their time trying to perform magic, and plotting to harm their enemies through sorcery and witchcraft. This form of religious worship is still being practiced around the world today. We call in Animism, which is explained in a further section.

Formalized religions became a natural outgrowth of idol worship, and all the rituals and prayers that had been established. The religions that men created changed over time as the people changed. Some of the past religions no longer exist today, just as some nations of the past no longer exist. Of the modern religions, some are so old we don't know when they began. Others are so young that people living today can remember when their religion first started. Out of this shaping of societal groups came the first ancient civilizations that created the major world religions.

ANCIENT CIVILIZATIONS:

As the population of humans continued to grow, and evil and violence abounded everywhere, there was a need to unify large groups of people in order to protect the land, and provide a semblance of law and order to avoid chaos. From this development came various religions designed to unite the people under powerful kings, countries and great empires, and to provide meaning for the everyday lives of its citizens.

It was famed archaeologist, James Henry Breasted, who first coined the phrase, "The Fertile Crescent," in his 1906 book, *Ancient Records of Egypt.* He made the case that various bygone kingdoms (great civilizations) evolved in a crescent-shaped region of lush lands in western Asia and north east Africa where they could use the soil and water to nourish their growing populations.

Good fertile land had long been the case in the area historically known as Mesopotamia (Iraq), the land between and surrounding the Tigris and Euphrates rivers, where it so happened the people already had a head start with their invention of writing, glass and the wheel. Thus the term, the "Fertile Crescent," came into being, and it is also referred to as the "Cradle of Civilization." This region of the world today consists of the modern states of Iraq, Iran, Kuwait, Syria, Lebanon, Jordan, Israel, the Palestinian Territories, Turkey and Egypt. All of these countries at one time worshipped nature, idols, and animal and human sacrifices, plus multiple gods. The one exception was the people of Israel, who were the only ones to worship a monotheistic God.

Almost all ancient peoples mention a time in their history when there was a great flood, which killed off most of mankind. The Bible is no exception to this belief, and it goes on to describe how God became disgusted with the behavior of man and decided to give a 120 year notice before the flood took place. Meanwhile, Noah and his wife, three sons and their wives, were chosen by God to build a great ark and supply it with two of all the animals. Despite God's warning, man continued to live a sinful lifestyle, and appeared to be incapable of reform. Consequently, Noah and his family, along with all the animals, were the only survivors of this world-wide disaster. Noah's three sons, Japeth, Ham and Seth, became the ancestors to a long line of peoples that later populated the Middle East, Africa and beyond. In Genesis 10 you can read in the Table of Nations who begat whom right down to the time of Nimrod, the great hunter warrior who reputedly founded Babylon and Nineveh (modern day Mosul), which were two great rival capitols that sat at the heart of the Babylonian and Assyrian Empires. Genesis 10, along with the assistance of great scholars from many scholastic disciplines, have put together a wonderful account of how various bloodlines developed over the ages.

MAN'S ANCESTRY

After the great flood, we find Noah's three sons: Shem, Ham and Japeth creating families of their own. Shem was the father of the Semitic race – Shemites. His five sons produced the following peoples: Elam, became the father of the Elamites, the Persians (Iranians); Asshur fathered the Assyrians in northern Iraq; Arphaxad produced the Chaldeans, Hebrews (Jews), Arabians, Moabites, Jordanians, and Palestinians. Lud became the father of the Lydians, Chubs and other related groups. Finally, Aram created the bloodline of Arameans/Syrians, Lebanese, and other related groups. It is Shem's bloodline that is traced to Abraham, Isaac, and, Jacob's twelve sons that founded the original twelve tribes of the Jews. Then from one of the tribes, Judah, came King David of whom Jesus Christ was a direct descendent. It may be of further interest for you to read Luke chapter 3:23, which describes in detail the genealogy of Jesus Christ dating all the way back to the first man, Adam, who was created by God.

Ham, literally interpreted means hot, burnt or dark, and was the father of Mongoloids and Negroid races – Hamites. He was the progenitor of: Canaan who produced the Canaanites, Mongols, Chinese, Japanese, Asians, Malaysians, Amerindians, Eskimos, Polynesians, and Pacific Islander groups. Cush "black" produced the Nubians, Ethiopians, Sudanese, Ghanaians, Africans, Bushmen, Pygmies, Australian Aborigines, New Guineans, and other related groups. Mizraim is the father of the Egyptians (Copts), and Phut started the bloodline of the Libyans, Tunisians, Berbers, Somalians, and other North African groups. So we find that tribes in other parts of Africa, Arabia and Asia, aboriginal groups in Australia, native Pacific Islanders, American Indians and Eskimos were birthed from descendents of Canaan, Cush, Mizraim, and Phut.

Noah's other son, Japeth, had seven sons. Gomer, became the father of Galic, Galicia, Galatia, Gaul, Crimea, Calendonians, Picts, Milesians, Umbrians, Helvetians, Visigoths, Goths, Vandals, Scandinavians, Jutes, Teutons, Franks, Burgundians, Armenians, Germans, Belgians, Dutch, Angles, Saxons, English, Cornish, Irish, Welsh, French and many other groups. Magog became the father of Scythians, Alans, Ulans, Rosh, Samaritans, and other related groups. Madai created the bloodline of the Medes, Aryans, Persians, Caspians, Kurds, Turks, East Indians, and the peoples of Afghanistan, Pakistan, Azerbaijan, Khazachstan, Turkmenistan, Uzbekistan, Tajikstan, and Kyrgystan and other groups. Javan is the father of the Tarshish, Xuthus (Grecians, Greeks, Elysians, Spartans, Dorians, Britons), Italics, Romans, Valentians, Sicilians, Spaniards, Portugese and other related groups. Tubal created the Georgians, Albanians, and other related groups. Meshech is the bloodline that produced Moscow (Muscovites, Latvians, Lithuanians, Romanians), and other related groups. Finally, the son, Tiras, became the father of the Norge (Trojans, Etruscans, Pelasgians, Scandinavians, Varangians, Vikings, Swedes, Norwegians, Danes, Icelandics), and other related groups.

Jewish sources tell us that there is a time period of about 4,000 years from Adam, the first man, until the arrival of Jesus Christ. We also know, based on the Book of Matthew 1:17, that there were 14 generations from Abraham to King David; 14 generations from David to the Babylonian exile, and another 14 generations from the exile until the arrival of Jesus Christ.

THE MIDDLE EAST:

The creation of civilizations has demonstrated, particularly since recorded history some 50 centuries ago, that a large part of mankind's creativeness had gone into inventing many new ways of killing and torturing other human beings. It had been proven that the threat of pain or death had been found to be the best, and perhaps the only successful method of control in ruling large numbers of peoples. In Mesopotamia, Egypt, Persia, India and China, empires had been established to rule over large areas of land and millions of subjects, and these rulers gave their people law and order, which created a level of peace and security against their enemies. Unfortunately, they provided no security against the rulers themselves. In this chapter we will discuss two of the oldest civilizations: Mesopotamia and Egypt in order to obtain a sense of how man developed from knowing a personal loving God into creating religious systems that took him further from God.

MESOPOTAMIA – THE LAND BETWEEN THE RIVERS:

They say that in the beginning all roads lead to Sumer, which until recently was the earliest recorded civilization (currently the oldest document ever recovered gives Egypt that distinction, which we will discuss later). Sumer is the name given to a historical area in the southwestern area of Mesopotamia, and located between the Tigris and Euphrates Rivers that lead to The Persian Gulf. It is here the first non-Semitic peoples created a great civilization consisting of five major cities (Eridu, Bad-Tibira, Larsa, Sippar, Shuruppak), and numerous minor cities. Sumer is an Akkadian term meaning, "Land of the civilized kings," and is believed to date back to 5000 B.C., although historical, written records only date back to 2900 B.C. These people are theorized to have migrated from the Samarra culture of northern Mesopotamia. The Sumerians provided us with the potter's wheel, which evolved later into mill wheels and wheeled vehicles (interestingly, the wheel was not known to the Inca when the Conquistadors arrived 500 years ago, which is a good reference to point out how knowledge spread in some countries but not in others). They also created cuneiform writing, arithmetic, geometry, irrigation systems, boats, lunisolar calendar, bronze, leather, hammers, braces, nails, pins, hoe, knives, swords, water-skins, bags, chariots, sandals, and beer. This is quite an amazing legacy when you think about it.

WARS WITHOUT END:

It was during the third millennium BC that a close relationship began with the Akkadians, a Semitic speaking people who later subjugated the Sumerians under their control. The Semitic language was used throughout the empire, though the Sumerian language continued as a sacred language. Later, the Akkadians were conquered by the Amorites, who founded Babylon, and as the Babylonians grew in strength, they eventually overthrew their oppressors. This allowed the Babylonians to secure their power in the southern areas of Mesopotamia, while at the same time the Assyrians were gaining strength in the north in their capitol city of Nineveh. For hundreds of years these two great empires would fight each other, and much blood was spilled between them

The people of Babylonia and Assyria were Semitic speaking, and this language spread to include Eblaites, Ugarites, Canaanites, Phoenicians, Hebrews, Ahlamu, Arameans, Chaldeans, Amorites, Moabites, Mandaeans, Hykos, Ishmaelites, Nabateans, Maganites, Shebans, Sutu, Ubarites, Dilmunites, Bahranis, Maltese, Syriacs, Amalekties, Arabs, Sabians, and Palmyrans. This list points out the fact that Arab and Jew are both Semites, which is interesting when you think about the word anti-Semite, which usually only refers to Jews and not Arabs in today's parlance.

BABYLONIAN AND ASSYRIAN RELIGIONS:

Throughout this period of the Sumerian civilization, polytheism was rampant. The people worshipped multiple gods, and the leaders and their priests soon began to use religion as a tool to control their own interests. The temple priests soon maneuvered themselves into a societal position of interpreting the equally absolute and despotic will of the gods, accompanied with the temporal rulers to keep the people under submission to their will. The people submitted because they had very little choice in the matter. They realized the strong did what they wanted, and the weak had to suffer. In those days there was no arbiter, and the strong always won the day.

Many Babylonian deities, myths and religious writings are singular to that culture. For instance, the uniquely Babylonian deity, Marduk, replaced Enlil as the head of the mythological pantheon. The ritual care and worshipping of the statues of deities were considered sacred, with the gods residing inside the statues and in the temples. An elaborate ceremony of washing the mouths of the statues was used to gain favor with the gods. Astrology and magic were also pervasive in society, and the kings would often turn to their priests and other holy men for advice based on what the stars were telling them. They worshipped everything but the one true God. Assyrian religion coexisted with Babylonian religion for about 1300 years, from the 18th century to the 5th century BC. Each belief system was in competition with the other, and each was somewhat similar in their world view of humans, of society, and of cult practices. The main difference was the gods they revered: in Assyria it was Ashur, and in Babylonia it was Marduk.

Historical documents tell us far more about Babylonia than Assyria. In Babylonia we know they had a system where salvation by works replaced salvation by faith, which we discussed. Consequently, for 2,000 years there were almost constant wars among the Sumerian city-states, which only added to new military technology and techniques that created even more bloodshed.

Babylonia was overthrown by the Kassites in the 17th century BC, and they ruled for 576 years, until 1157 B.C. The Kassites originated in the Zagros Mountains of what is today Western Iran, and theirs was an isolated language perhaps belonging to the Hurrian language of Asia Minor. Babylonia regained its independence under King Nebuchadnezzar I (1124 BC to 1103 BC).After this period, Babylonia suffered repeated incursions from Semitic nomadic people such as the Arameans, Chaldeans and Suteans, and was taken over again by both the Assyrians and the Kassites. In 612 BC, however, the Babylonians, with the help of the Medes, finally defeated the Assyrians. In 605 BC, Nebuchadnezzar II became king, and you can find a fascinating biblical account of this king in the Book of Daniel.

Eventually, Babylonia was taken over by the Medo-Persian Empire, which was later subjugated by the Greeks under Alexander the Great. The final great empire, the Romans, eventually overthrew the Greeks, and then became the greatest empire the world had ever known up to that time.

The Book of Daniel also provides a prophetic story that describes well in advance the fall of all the above mentioned great empires. In Daniel 2:31-35, Daniel is interpreting a dream that King Nebuchadnezzar had of a very large image of a man. The image's head was of fine gold (which represented the Babylonian Empire); he had breasts and arms of silver (Persian Empire); he had a belly and thighs of brass (Greek Empire); he had legs of iron, and his feet part of iron and part of clay (this represents the Roman Empire including its split into a western empire in Rome, and an eastern empire in Constantinople), which came about when Emperor Constantine decided to move the seat of power from Rome to Constantinople (modern day Istanbul). Daniel had confirmed with accuracy the rise and fall of these empires as foretold to him by God.

Alan W. Hayden

EGYPT:

The earliest civilizations grew up in major river valleys of Africa and Asia, and Egypt was probably the first of them all. Records take us back to the creation of their calendar, which dates back to 4242 BC thanks to the discovery in the early 19th century of the Rosetta Stone that broke the hieroglyphic code. From that point forward archeologists were able to open the great secrets of the past of ancient Egypt and all its splendid glory and achievements. Egypt existed as a semi-independent state until conquest by the Romans in 30 BC. For 30 centuries Egypt kept a great secret; they feared and hated change. As a result they managed to progress very little over their history. In a somewhat perverted way a hatred of change bore a certain wisdom in that any change for a tyrant was usually for the worse. So change for the sake of change was problematic in their eyes. Maintaining law and order, and as a result their own power, was what they cherished most.

The country was organized on hierarchical principles by having their gods sitting at the top, and below them were the large body of the dead. At the bottom of the hierarchy lay humanity i.e. the Egyptians. The Pharaoh held a powerful and unique position standing between humanity and the dead above him. Although a Pharaoh was human, he was also considered more than human by the people who feared, adored and obeyed him. Not to do so was to call everything into question, including social order, and the regularity of the Nile flooding, which cleansed the temples of evil spirits. In such a conservative society order was of the essence.

Pharaohs often married their own sisters or daughters in order to keep the bloodline pure, but they also kept abundant harems. This attitude spread to the people, and as late as the second millennium after Christ it was found that two-thirds of the people of the city Arsinoe practiced the custom. Men often married their sisters, not out of romantic love, but in order to share their inheritance (because all estates passed down through the female line i.e. mother to daughter). Blood ran warm along the Nile, and girls were nubile by age ten. Ordinary people of modest income, however, usually lived a monogamous relationship with their wives, and it was not until much later in their history those morals began to decline.

Why ancient Egypt was so conservative and tradition bound is open to speculation. We do know that in keeping with their extreme conservatism the Egyptians were in love with death. Egyptians lived but to die, and they spent their entire lives and fortunes preparing for the inevitability of death. Death to an Egyptian, however, was not the same as we see it today. The dead were all around them, in the air, in the ground, in the waters of the Nile. Thinking of the dead gave these ancient peoples a certain comfort as they went about their lives.

It has been said we cannot understand the Egyptian until we understand his gods, for beneath and above everything was their religion. We see its influence in its literature, in government, art and everything except morality. They believed that in the beginning was the sky, and the sky plus the Nile were Egypt's main divinities. The heavenly bodies were not mere bodies, but represented external forms of mighty spirits, gods who manipulated all the movements of the sky. The moon was a god, perhaps the oldest worshiped, but in the official theology the great god was Ra, the sun god, the creator, the fertilizer of the land and the flooding of the Nile.

The Egyptians worshipped many things including plants, but they had a particular preference for animal gods, which included the Nile crocodile, bull, hawk, cow, goose, goat, ram, dog, and the cat. All of these animals were allowed to roam freely in the temples, much like in India today. The goat and the bull were particular favorites owing to their alleged sexual creative power. Beautiful women were offered in coitus as sex mates, the bull in particular, as the incarnation of Ra, and in Mendes, women were offered in coitus to the divine goat. When their gods became human they still retained their animal doubles and symbols: Ra as a bull, Horus a hawk, Osiris as a ram, Sebek as a crocodile etc.

At last the gods had become human, or rather men had become gods. Pharaoh became the chief priest of the faith, and led the great processions and ceremonies that celebrated the great festivals of the gods. It was through this divine lineage he was able to rule so long and with so little force. Thus, the priests became necessary props of the throne, and the secret police of the social order. With faith becoming so complex, a class had to arise to be adept in magic, so their skills became indispensable in approaching the gods, thus securing their positions. The office of priest passed down from father to son, though not officially, and so a class grew up that through the piety of the people, and the generosity of the Pharaoh, became in time richer and stronger than the royal family itself. This priestly power became common among all the earliest civilizations and their empires.

When I traveled to Egypt for the second time a number of years ago, it was easy to be reminded of this great civilization that has lasted for seven millennia. Seeing the Great Pyramids, The Sphinx, the bustling city of Cairo, and then traveling up the

Nile to Luxor, Aswan, and visiting the Valley of the Kings, and the Valley of the Queens, along with numerous other towns and villages, brought ancient life before my eyes. On both sides of the river I could see temples that had been torn down and re-assembled by engineers to accommodate the building of Nasser's Aswan Dam by the Russians. Egypt does not change very easily, and parts of the country have not changed very much in several thousand years. In fact, in some parts of the south, if you could imagine suspending your sense of reality for a moment, you could easily feel you had lived in this ancient land so many centuries ago.

Ancient Egyptians deliberately built their temples by the edge of the Nile in order to cleanse the temple's evil spirits during the annual flooding. This however, presented a problem for the government in that all this antiquity would be flooded once the new Aswan Dam was officially opened. To prevent this from happening, the engineers cut the temples into thousands of large blocks, and then rebuilt them on higher ground. At Abu Simbel, for instance, which is the most famous site south of Aswan, where lie the magnificent temple and large statues of Ramses II and his favorite queen, Neferteri, the engineers cut 1,000 eleven ton large blocks, and moved them to higher ground. For the benefits of posterity I was able to see the new site close to the Sudanese border, which sat more than 200 feet above its original location, looking as though it had sat there since ancient times. To see such a great society pillaged and plundered over the years by so many invading forces was sad, but also to be expected. Then, after Christ was resurrected, the Egyptians gave up their pagan ways, and became Christians. The great Coptic Christian Church was formed, but after the

7th century A.D. the Moslems invaded and took power across all North Africa. There is still a minority of Coptic Christians in Egypt today, but their future is tenuous.

THE RISE AND FALL OF EMPIRES:

Civilizations and empires come and go, but God is always there to listen to the hearts of men who want to find meaning in their lives, and worship the one true God. It is of interest to note that Sir John Glubb wrote about the rise and fall of empires in his 1976 book, *The Fate of Empires*. He pointed out that empires do not necessarily begin and end on a particular date. There is normally a gradual period of expansion and then a period of decline. With the exception of Babylonia, which existed for only 74 years, and Egypt, which was constantly being conquered by outside forces, most of the empires recorded below lasted between 200 and 250 years:

		Duration in years
Assyria	859BC-612 BC	247
Persia	538BC-330 BC	208
Greece	331BC-100 BC	231
Roman Republic	260BC-27BC	233
Roman Empire	27BC-180AD	207
Arab Empire	634AD-880AD	246
Mameluke Empire	1250-1517AD	267
Ottoman Empire	1320-1570AD	250
Spain	1500-1750AD	250
Romanov Russia	1682-1916AD	234
Britain	1700-1950AD	250

Although the above dates are somewhat arbitrary and subject to criticism, they help to point out that man builds from a village, a town, a city, and then a multiple city state until huge chunks of real estate are under the control of one ruler using religion as a weapon not only to justify war, but to subjugate his population. Later the expansion may continue into other countries where the indigenous peoples are subdued under the control of the empire. In the end, however, in every case the empire eventually falls into decline, and none appear to have lasted for 300 years or more, which is insignificant in relation to man's time on earth.

What were these empire builders trying to accomplish? What possible meaning were men searching for to quench their empty hearts? What was the purpose of gaining great power if they became more disassociated from God? This attempt to find meaning for their life, and to discover the one true God, has haunted man almost since the beginning. This search for meaning in all the wrong places has cascaded down through the centuries causing millions of people to become lost. Yet the General Revelation (see next paragraph) that God gave to all men has always been there, yet many men never heeded it.

PURSUING MEANING IN YOUR LIFE:

Ancient man and modern man have much in common in their pursuit for the true meaning of life. Although ancient man did not have the benefit of Jesus visiting him to show him the way, he was aware of the General Revelation of God: "Since what may be known about God is plain to them, because God has made it plain to them. For since the creation of the world, God's invisible qualities – his eternal power and divine nature – have been clearly seen, being understood from what has been made, so that men are without excuse."(Romans 1:19b, 20).

Modern man does have the knowledge of the special revelation of Jesus Christ, and therefore has no excuse not to accept Him. Over these many years, man has continued to make many circuitous routes to find meaning for his life, which we will discuss in greater depth in the next chapters, but unfortunately many men have been searching in the wrong direction. That is why it is important for Christians to continually get the word out in the best way they can, to put men back on the right relationship for a successful future with God.

A dramatic story that demonstrates the power of faith and the pursuit of meaning for one's life, despite horrible, evil circumstances, comes out of the annals of World War II. Viktor Frankel was a Jewish doctor who had the great misfortune to spend four-years in a Nazi concentration camp, along with his family. The thought of once again being reunited with his family kept him alive, giving him something he could look forward to beyond his terrible present condition. Unfortunately, although he survived this terrible ordeal, he learned after the war that his wife, mother, father and brother had all died in the gas chambers.

After the war, he wrote a book about this miserable period of his life, and he titled it, *Man's Search for Meaning.* In having experienced along with his fellow prisoners, hard daily work on meager food rations, and witnessing cannibalism, prisoners losing all hope, and deliberately running into the live barbed wire fence as the most popular form of suicide, Frankel learned a great deal about the human condition. He found men would do anything to survive including betrayal, lying, cheating, and even acting as Capos or Sonderkommandos (Jews hired by the Nazi) that required Jews doing the dirty work that Germans did not want to do. Prisoners were completely dependent on the mood and the whims of the sadistic prison guards, and daily life included the perpetual fear that they might be the next one to die. Auschwitz – Birkenau, for instance, functioned after the pattern of an industrial plant, with all the elements you would typically find there: machines, production lines, workers, managers, senior managers etc., Only two major differences existed between a regular factory and a Nazi death camp. The raw materials in the death camp were human beings, and the only product produced was human ashes.

Frankel came to realize his fellow prisoners represented two types: those with a strong will to live, and those that did not. Some prisoners looked to the future believing one day they would be free again and reunited with loved ones. Or, they had a special talent they wanted to share with the world. Many also had a strong religious faith that caused them to think of a much better life once this one was over, because they knew their life on earth was temporary, and there was much to look forward to beyond this one. In other words, they had something to look forward to outside of themselves by putting their fate in the hands of God as a method of survival. However, the prisoner who had lost faith in the future, or had no religious faith, no matter how big or strong he was, sealed his own fate and was doomed. Suddenly, and without warning, this type of prisoner would refuse to get out of bed one morning despite the beatings, and would simply lie in their own excreta until carried away and gassed.

In later life therapy sessions, Frankel would counsel patients who were so messed up with their lives they could no longer cope with their situation. Frankel would ask them, in a point-blank manner, why they had not committed suicide. The answers he heard over and over again validated what he had heard in the concentration camp experience. They had a purpose for living beyond themselves, and a religious conviction their lives would somehow get better. Although Frankel was not a particularly religious man he did acknowledge that love is the only way to grasp another human being in the innermost core of his personality.

A personal story out of my own life concerns my friend, Jeff, who represents a wonderful example to me of a man who has a strong will to live due to something he believes in beyond himself, namely Jesus Christ. Jeff's strong Christian faith has been of immense value to him as he struggles with serious problems that would cause many a man to simply give up on life, but not Jeff. He married at age 20 to his 19 year old bride who died less than a year later. Despondent, he joined the military and spent many years abroad serving in special ops. After being shot in the back in Vietnam, and other health issues, he retired at age 36. Jeff was diagnosed with diabetes, which has caused him to lose fingers and toes. Then, about eight-years ago, at age 50, he came down with renal failure, and has been on kidney dialysis three times per week ever since. In March, 2014, a heart attack caused Jeff to be removed from the kidney transplant list, which destroyed any chance of him being able to enjoy good health, and a normal life ever again. After the heart operation, Jeff was put into an induced coma due to his erratic body gyrations, and he could not be revived to a conscious state for about a month. By his own admission, he felt that he died three distinctly different times, only to come back to life.

Today, Jeff is back living in an adult care facility, where he continues to receive therapy in order to be able to walk without falling. Despite being flat broke, experiencing terrible health problems, not having any wife, children, brothers or sisters for support, and only a few friends, you will find Jeff today still enjoying a strong faith that the Lord will take care of him no matter how tough life gets. He knows that his life is temporary, and he has no fear because God is by his side, and has promised him that the next life will be full of joy and peace, and he will experience no more pain, sickness, loneliness or despair. Jeff is aware that, in the words of C.S. Lewis, "All that is not eternal, is eternally useless."

Now the question I pose is simply this – could Jeff have endured this type of hardship with no solutions to rectify his problems, and no way out of the dilemma, without a strong faith in something he believed in outside of himself? That something, for Christians and especially for Jeff, is a belief in Jesus Christ as his Lord and Savior. Obviously, Jeff's life story is well worth telling, and he stands as a role model for all those people out there that are experiencing financial, health, or relationship problems. Jeff does not just have one of these problems, he has all three! That is a burden weighty enough to drag anyone down. Nonetheless, Jeff is still standing tall knowing that God is in his corner.

Jeff, like many Christians, has become aware that identity is central to their lives. "Who am I?" we ask. "Where did I come from?" "Where am I going?" Bound up in this drive for identity are our needs for unconditional love and acceptance, and to gain meaning and purpose for our lives. These questions have plagued man right from the beginning, because they are all part of basic, spiritual needs, and the answers we decide to adopt, determine the direction of our lives. Do we identify our lives in the "flesh" or in the "spirit?" Whatever a man depends upon for his identity (or self-image), and meaning and purpose for his life, will eventually control him Do you remember in the Introduction when I mentioned well educated Nazis identifying themselves with the evil of Hitler rather than obeying the commandments of God?. Control comes through dependency, because if I am dependent on what you think of me, then you control me. If I depend on my job for my identity, then my job will control me, and so forth. Therefore, it is only when we depend on God for our needs that we can truly be free. It is then that we can focus on the real purpose for our lives, which is learning about Christ. You will find that our relationship with God carries over into our human relationships, which helps us to accept people as they are. It is also true that we will ultimately treat others in exactly the same way we think God treats us.

The story of Victor Frankel and my friend, Jeff, serve as real testimonies to advocate looking outward towards God for answers to the meaning of life, rather than looking inward into ourselves. Jesus is the clear answer, offering us unconditional love, unvarnished truth, and an unconditional promise that He will be our guide through life, provided we believe in Him. We find in the Christian faith, God cares more about two of His commandments to us than any others:

Love your God with all your heart, soul, mind and strength, and love your neighbor as you love yourself.

PURPOSE FOR YOUR LIFE:

Every man's life is driven by something, according to Thomas Carlyle, who went on to say that "A man without a purpose is like a ship without a rudder – a waif, a nothing, a no man." It was also Socrates that once said, "The unexamined life is not worth living." As mentioned earlier, with only about 25,000 plus days on earth to get it right, with no minimum guarantee, and without having a solid purpose that moves us closer to God, we have to wonder about the very purpose of our existence. The best and only way to discover meaning for our lives is through the Scriptures. So, why not try letting God transform us into new people by changing the way we think? "Do not conform any longer to the pattern of this world, but be transformed by the renewing of your mind. Then you will be able to test and approve what God's will is – his good, pleasing and perfect will." (Romans 12:2). We also have a verse from Colossians 1:16 that says, "For by Him all things were created: things in heaven and on earth, visible and invisible, whether thrones or powers or rulers or authorities; all things were created by Him and for Him. He is before all things, and in Him all things hold together." In other words, everything got started with God, and finds its purpose in Him. Even Bertrand Russell, a well known atheist, once said, "Unless you assume a God, the question of life's purpose is meaningless."

You perhaps may not realize it now, but God really does have a purpose for your life, and if you follow these steps you will discover what that purpose is:

First of all, we must all realize that we gain our whole identity, our completeness, by developing a relationship with Jesus Christ, which is absolutely essential for gaining purpose in this life, but also to develop an understanding of the next one as well. Secondly, it is important to know that God created a purpose for your life long before you were born. You can choose a lot of things in this life, but you cannot choose your purpose. That is God's job. Thirdly, your life fits into a much larger frame-work of cosmic forces of which we are not aware. Only through God can we gain the insight we need to make progress with our life's mission. So let's take a moment now for me to ask you a question that I would like you to ponder. The Lord reached out to me many years ago to open my eyes to grasp the Good News, and show me the purpose for my life. Is He perhaps reaching out to you now as you read this paragraph?

CHAPTER FIVE

EASTERN BASED RELIGIONS (ORIENTIAL)

So far, we have explored the origins of man's spiritual development as he started out asking numerous questions *Why,* which led to original story-telling, idol worship, and the eventual hi-jacking of religion by the few to gain power over the many. We have also learned about paganism, polytheism, and the whole pantheon of inanimate objects that have been worshipped over the centuries. We have seen that throughout man's history we find religion not too far away from man's presence. As a result of grappling to understand the spiritual side of his nature, man has been down many religious roads in attempting to seek truth and meaning for his life, and the birth of the great religions of the world is part of the result.

At this point you might ask yourself the question "Why should I learn about other religions?", and the answer is they represent manifestations of man's attempt to find meaning in his life, just like we are attempting to do in the West. Today we live in a world that seems to be getting smaller and smaller, and therefore it is more important now than ever before to learn what our world neighbors think. By studying these other religions you will be able to sharply focus the contrast between them and

Christianity, which will then provide a basis for clearer thinking and understanding. This is something the world desperately needs right now, especially when we look at the religion based turmoil in the world. Considering that almost five out of seven people today are not Christians, we have an obligation to reach out and try to understand these people in a more loving light, so that we can bring them out of darkness into the light of Christ.

Travel to any large city in any country in the world today and you will find a cosmopolitan melting pot of people from all over the planet. You will find yourself working side by side with them in the work place, living next door to them, and sharing the same city conveniences. Religious ignorance cuts both ways, but if the barrier can be lifted, we should make the attempt.

WHY DOES MAN PRACTICE RELIGION?

Contemporary statistics combined with historical data, tell us that billions of people grow up with some form of religion, while others grow up without any exposure to religion at all. This causes many to wonder, on some conscious level, if they have missed out on something very important to their overall education. We know that when we analyze a person's religion to their neighbors religion, the religion of their culture compared to the religion of another culture, and the way they interact with each other, we find they all play an important role in shaping their worldview. Each person's worldview helps to crystallize their understanding of the world, and their place in it. This understanding also helps each of us to do a better job of interacting both collectively and individually with other people whose thinking is much different from our own. If all peoples of the world adopted this view, there would be a much greater level of understanding between them.

The best definition I have been able to research to define religion is to say it is a belief in a divine (superhuman or spiritual) being(s) and the practices (rituals) and moral code (ethics) that develop from that belief. Beliefs give religion its mind, rituals give religion its shape, and ethics give religion its heart. These belief systems teach people the concept of salvation, or enlightenment, truths about life, suffering and hope, and what happens after death. Peoples' beliefs give meaning to their lives, and help them to sustain hope in times of loss or sorrow. [1] A religion's teachings or doctrines are known as its theology, and this theology is its handbook of beliefs (although it must be pointed out that some religious theologies are not written down). Some religions such as Christianity and Islam have a long tradition of theology, whereas other religions, such as Judaism and Hinduism use stories, not systematic theologies to convey their beliefs. This is why getting a clear understanding of Judaism and Hinduism is much more difficult to grasp. Whether a particular religion uses theology or story-telling as a way of teaching their beliefs depends on their history, and how they define membership. We find though, when stripped to their bare essence, all religions include prayer to express thankfulness for life's blessings, to repent of sins, to forgive other people, and to apply the universal principles of the Golden Rule of doing unto others as you would have them do unto you.

Alan W. Hayden

THE GREAT RELIGIONS OF THE WORLD

As civilizations continued to develop, we find that the acceptance of a particular religious faith manifested itself in a major way across multiple provinces and countries. We will now explore these religions as they are practiced today, in order to create a greater understanding of people's faith walk for the better understanding of all.

Before we begin our investigation of great religious systems, however, I should point out the following material is provided to the reader without judgment or opinion, although some facts will be explained further in order for the reader to gain greater insight into these religious practices. I also reserve the right to criticize despotic governments that suppress their people and are their biggest enemies. Any opinions regarding the religions themselves are left up to the reader. One additional point to mention is that these other religions are discussed from a Western perspective. Muslims, for instance, contend Islam is not a religion, but is a way of life. Taoism is also considered not to be a religion, but is "The Way." Similarly Buddhism, which does not serve a god, believes in "The Path." And finally, some Christians say Christianity is not a religion, but a person, that person being Jesus Christ who is central to the faith. Keep these thoughts in mind as we begin to take a closer look at various religious systems.

In a discussion on world religions it should be mentioned no one really knows the true number of religions in the world, but the best estimate I have come across is about 4000, give or take. What appears to be very apparent is the vast majority of people across the globe who often find themselves seeking out some type of belief system that helps them maintain hope for their future, especially in times of stress and sorrow, and that also gives meaning to their lives. That's why the French philosopher, Voltaire, once said, "If God did not exist, it would be necessary to invent him!"

Due to limited space, and not wanting to get off focus, we will restrict our main focus on the five major world religions, with a discussion of some of their offshoots, and a section on Animism. By concentrating on this handful of religions we actually capture a very high percentage of people living in the world today.

We will first discuss Eastern religions that include Hinduism, along with its break-away religions of Buddhism, Sikhism, and Jainism. Then, after also discussing briefly Taoism, and the Japanese religion of Shinto, we will move to a review of Western religions, which include Judaism, Christianity and Islam, even though these religions were technically born in the Near East. They will be presented according to historical chronology. Our final segment shall be a discussion of Animism, a pagan nature religion, that as a world-wide phenomenon has managed to permeate itself into many of the great world religions, and touches six continents.

HINDUISM

Hinduism was founded in North India about 1500 BC, but Hindu scholars have attempted to trace the religion to its roots from the Indus River civilization (3,000 B.C.). Today, about 80% of the population of India practice Hinduism, which places their number around 800 million people. Although Hinduism is primarily practiced in India, it is a religion that can be found today in Nepal, Sri Lanka, and in communities stretching from the Caribbean Islands to North and South America, Thailand, South Africa, and, of course, Great Britain who controlled the sub-continent for over 300 years, and gave India many of its laws and form of government. Hinduism is pervasive in India manifesting itself into ethical issues, politics, social issues, and nationalism.

As we study Hinduism we find that this religion has no original founder as noted in many other great religions, and there is no single tradition or platform upon which a unifying philosophy can be interpreted by the average Hindu, let alone a Westerner trying to develop a deeper understanding of this faith system. The religion appears to have progressed over many years through a blending of religious influences that were not well suited to each other. The main central theme, however, is *Brahman,* or world soul, who, in the Hindu mind is one universal spirit, that is timeless without beginning or end. This world soul, called *Trimutri,* is expressed as three gods, who are personified as: 1) *Brahma,* the Creator; 2) *Vishnu,* the Preserver, and 3) *Shiva,* the Destroyer. *Brahma,* so the Hindus believe, created the first man, named *Manu;* and then he created the first woman, named, *Shastarupa,* and from them sprung all people. Over the centuries millions of gods have developed, but all of these gods are manifestations of the universal spirit. It is not unusual for a family to worship a personal deity, a village deity, a regional deity and a universal deity. It has been stated that over the years that Hinduism has evolved from polytheism to pantheism (all is God), which teaches that the divine is all things, and that all things are divine.

KARMA AND REINCARNATION:

Hindus, besides worshipping many deities, are also very concerned with people's actions, and particularly how those actions impact them when they die. This is to be expected considering that their religion instructs them that their life is a continual cycle of birth, death, and rebirth, that are all controlled by the *Doctrine of Karma.* This doctrine states that if a man lives a good life, he will be given a better life in the next reincarnation (note that when a Hindu dies, his soul immediately enters a new born baby). On the other hand, a man who lives a life of sin, selfishness, and self-indulgence, will lead to his reincarnation as a lower being, perhaps as low as an animal in the next life.

This belief in reincarnation causes Hindus to think that there is a lack of spiritual maturity among the average people. So, as they attempt to lead normal lives, they pursue the development of a closer connection to the full rejection of the personality. It is considered normal and proper to create wealth and enjoy love of the opposite sex during a certain season of life, but when Hindus become old they often separate themselves from their worldly possessions in order to seek the life of an itinerant monk. Giving up their accumulated possessions is considered a supreme law of morality in Hinduism.

Many Hindus attempt to be sensitive to the illusory nature of this earthly existence while progressively denying themselves material possessions, and even emotional and spiritual gifts. History informs us that the belief in reincarnation and karma have been used as tools to give legitimacy to the wicked Indian Caste System (explained below), which has subjugated millions of people to experience lives of poverty, misery, and hopelessness.

VENERATION OF ANIMALS:

Due to beliefs mentioned above, it is somewhat easier to understand why Hindus worship and protect animals. The cow is perhaps the most worshipped of all animals, and slaughtering them is banned throughout India. While it provides about 20 different benefits to the family, it can never be killed without very serious public outrage and penalties. As a result, most Hindus are vegetarians. If a cow dies on the owner's property, then a very complicated religious ritual must be enacted in order to purge the sin of such a great offence to society as a whole. As such, when a cow gets old, and stops producing milk, the owner will often release the cow into the community where it is fed by the people until it dies, often by the roadside. It was not unusual, as I traveled through the villages of India, to see cows wondering all over the place, causing traffic jams, and preventing customers from trading. The Dalits (otherwise known as untouchables) have the duty, when the cow dies, to skin it and sell the skin for a few rupees. The rest of the cow is consumed by dogs and wild pigs.

Many other animals are considered sacred, but in some of the rural areas you will find that some animals such as buffalos, goats and chicken are sacrificed to local deities. In the Karmi Mata Temple in Rajasthan, rats rule the temple. I was told that it was an honor for a villager to walk into the temple and have a rat jump onto his shoulder! In another village, monkeys are considered sacred, and have freedom to roam anywhere including one's living room!

MAJOR SACRED WRITINGS:

There are literally hundreds of Hindu scriptures, but the earliest and most important collections are The Four Vedas

(1500 – 1000 BC). Veda means "knowledge," and they consist of the *Rig Veda,* the *Sama Veda,* the *Yajur Veda,* and the *Atharva Veda.* Each Veda is also divided into four parts: the *Mantras* (these are the verses sung in rituals); the *Brahmanas* (used to explain the verses); the *Aran yakas* (thoughts regarding their meaning), and the *Upanishads* (they represent mystical interpretation of the verses). These scriptures are all called *shruti,* meaning that which is heard. Besides primary scriptures, there are also secondary ones that include epics such as: *Ramayana* ("Rama's Way"), and *Mahabharata* (known as "the great story."). You will also find the most popular of all Hindu scriptures within the *Mahabharata,* the *Bhagavad-Gita).*

THE CLASS AND CASTE SYSTEMS OF INDIA:

Inextricably intertwined with Hinduism are both the "class and caste" systems. Almost from the beginning of Hinduism there were four different types of people, and they all came out of one man, *Manu.* Out of his head came the best and holiest people in India, the priests and the Brahmins. Out of his hands came the kings and warriors. Out of his thighs came the craftsmen and merchants, and out of his feet came the laborers or lowest class. There was also a special category of an even lower class established for the labor class, who became the "untouchables," also known as Dalits, the lowest of the low in all Indian society. Since independence from the British in 1948, and the creation of an independent constitution enacted in 1950, the Indian government, as the largest democracy in the world, outlawed both the class and caste systems.

Although the class system no longer functions as in the old way, you will find, as I did, that the caste system is still very much alive in many parts of the country. As recently as 2011, when I was last there, I recall a British journalist who visited the village of Shahabpur, accompanied by a young Brahmin interpreter. They were hosted by an untouchable named, Sarju, who lived with his wife, Sushila, and two children in a small hut at the edge of the village, because they were not allowed to live in the village itself. Sarju had two occupations: he repaired shoes in the bazaar, and also had the job of disposing of dead buffalo, cattle and goats. Working leather had been Sarju's family profession for centuries as Hindu had ordained. His family is of the Chamar, or tanning caste, one of dozens traditionally dedicated to low, menial or "unclean" occupations, and therefore considered Untouchables. Sushila is the village midwife who performs another unclean task. It may seem odd, but conservative Hindu women who are about to give birth, actually despise women who deliver their babies, mainly because they come in contact with the afterbirth. It is believed this type of discrimination is suffered by one in five Indians to this very day. Apparently some 60 plus years after the caste system was outlawed, it appears not to be enough time to eradicate centuries of evil discrimination that acts like a cancer eating away at the heart of this society.

HINDU SALVATION:

The average Indian is extremely poor and uneducated, whose only hope is to find a permanent resting place that allows him to be finally relieved of the cyclical nature of numerous births and rebirths. Living a life that is devoid of anything but the basic necessities to stay alive, Indians yearn for a time when they can finally break the repeatability of life, and find peace in the loving arms of Brahman. While alive in this existence, however, they strive to accept self-denial by slowly refraining from material and emotional benefits as their way of preparing themselves for eventual death and rebirth to a much better life than the one they are currently experiencing.

In order to reach full emancipation, and freedom from the endless cycle of life and death, Hindus seek a form of liberation that achieves not only freedom from these many incarnations, but also allows them to seek self-realization and self-knowledge. This goal is called *moksha,* which allows a Hindu to concentrate all of his soul towards a total commitment to the celestial. This idea of self mastery is generally achieved through various forms of yoga, which allow Hindus to achieve their goals through both physical and spiritual exercises that concentrate all of their will towards creating a more robust soul that can avoid the distractions of everyday life.

The practice of yoga is thousands of years old, and manifests itself in many forms across India. However, there are six main types of yoga practiced today. The way of knowledge, which uses philosophy to help understand the universe, is called *Jnana yoga*. In order to achieve a form of selflessness, Hindus practice *Bhatki yoga*, which helps them in their devotion towards celestial glory. *Raja yoga*, referred to as the "royal road," concentrates on many meditative techniques. There is also *Karma yoga*, where action is the operative word. With this type of yoga, the adherent is steered toward achieving the goal of a right attitude toward action. There are other forms of yoga including *Hatha* and *Kundalini*, which emphasize both physical and spiritual disciplines.

HINDU RELIGION AND PRACTICE:

There are three major denominations of Hinduism: 1) *Shaivism*, which is a tradition with multiple expressions, with the most significant one being (*Shaiva Siddhanta*), which tends to be more theistic rather than impersonal. 2) *Vaishnavism* emphasizes the worship of *Vishnu*, and understands *Brahma* in terms of more personal manifestations. Examples would be *Ram* and *Krishna*, who are heroes of the *Bhagavad Gita*. 3) *Shaktism* pays particular devotion to *Shakti* or the *Devi* (the divine mother) as the ultimate expression of godhead.

Since a Hindu god is both singular and plural, Hindus have a magical and legalistic notion that one can attain spiritual "points" through contact with holy objects or people. Among many you will find an image of a family god, which is kept in a prominent place in the home. Villages also have an accepted local icon to worship, and as mentioned above, animals are particularly sacred, and certain rivers, especially the Ganges River, are also considered holy.

While on the Ganges I was able to witness the ritualistic burning of dead bodies by the Dalits (who appear to have the franchise), and ashes are then disbursed into the water. Sometimes, however, it is not unusual to see dead bodies floating nearby while bathers use the waters to improve their karma. This is particularly the case in the vicinity of the holy city of Varanasi, which borders the Ganges. You will also find that even among more intellectual Hindus, certain portions of scripture are memorized and chanted; sacred stories are acted out in plays and songs, and gods are prayed to in an ecstatic manner. Holy men are highly revered, and in serving them the people hope some of their holiness will be passed on to them as credit towards salvation.

As I crossed India I experienced mind boggling poverty; garbage piled as high as 20 feet on the sides of the roads, and dead bodies waiting to be picked up before the wild pigs arrived. Part of the problem is due to the fatalistic attitude of the people towards life in general, which gives them little incentive to improve their condition. The way things are is the way it is meant to be in this particular incarnation. They believe karma has dictated their current life based on sin committed in a previous life.

K.P. Yohannan, who founded Gospels for Asia, has experienced tremendous success in teaching young Hindu men and women the ways of Jesus Christ, and consequently millions of Indians are being converted to the one Almighty God of the universe. Indians are being taught God is a loving, compassionate God who expects all mankind to seek the very best life they can create for themselves, which is counter intuitive to the reincarnation principles Hindus are taught. K.P. states there are a million villages in India, and each practice faith to their own deities. Ignorance and darkness pervade, and when K.P. sends his young seminary trained men and women among the villagers to turn them to the teachings of Christ, they are often attacked and sometimes killed. K.P. tells his seminary graduates before they enter a new village, they must first dig a hole, which is to serve as their grave if serious conflict emerges.

Some Indians are now tearing down the artificial mental barriers that have subjugated them to poverty for generations, and finding out it is okay to strive for success, to own their own homes, to get the very best education for their children, to pull themselves up out of the slums and seek a much better life for themselves and their communities as a whole. These are concepts that have long been lacking in Indian society, but it is now beginning to change. Let's hope and pray these wonderful people will someday learn the true plan God Almighty has planned for their lives in a Christ centered life based in love for God, and love for their neighbors.

SIKHISM

By most world standards, Sikhism is considered a somewhat new religion in that it was not created until about 500 years ago in the Punjab region of northwest India, and modern day Pakistan. Like most man-made religions, Sikhism was developed and created by its founder, Guru Nanak, who lived between 1470 and 1540 AD. He believed in one omnipresent God known only to those who are spiritually awakened through a meditative process. Sikhism also happens to be pantheistic by considering the universe itself to be part of God, which provides for no clear distinction that separates God from the created.

In 1947, the Sikhs found their population being separated as the new country of Pakistan was formed, thus splitting the Sikhs into two autonomous countries. This was yet another event that proved troublesome to these great people. They had already experienced a bloody history of fighting the Mughals, the Moslem rulers of India through the late 19th century, and continuous fighting with Hindus over many years. At the same time, they fought against the British when they controlled the sub-continent. Today there are about 19 million Sikhs, who live mostly in the Punjab area, and consider Amristar, in Pakistan, their holy city.

Sikh means "follower" in the Sanskrit language, and they worship a monotheistic God called *Waheguru* (great teacher). Some scholars believe Sikhism evolved as a reform movement with a mixture of Hinduism and Islam, but Sikhs take exception to this. In order to obtain a better understanding of Sikhism it becomes important to learn something about the ten gurus who each in turn made major contributions to the development of Sikhism, which took place in the 16th and 17th centuries. A number of these great gurus were tortured by the Mughal leaders, which in turn caused the Sikh to take on a warrior mentality. Results of this attitude included men carrying a comb in their hair, wearing a sword, a steel bracelet, and a kachch (short pants for use in battle). The sword and pants are generally only worn in battle. Today, however, Sikhs are a peace-loving people who live by highly moral principles, and there is much to learn from these unique people of India and Pakistan.

SACRED WRITINGS:

In 1604, the *Sri Guru Granth Sahib* was completed, and it condenses about 6,000 *shabads* (hymns), which were composed in nine languages by the first nine Sikh gurus, with the help of other Hindu and Muslim holy men. The *Sri Guru Granth Sahib* is worshipped by Sikhs and regarded as their 11th and perpetual guru. Other holy books include:

The *Dasam Granth*, a varied compilation of writings
The *Varan Bhai Gurdus*, which contains commentary
The *Rahatnamas*, which is a code of conduct, and
The *Sau Sakhi*, representing a compilation of prophecies

At the heart of Sikhism is the discipline of purification, and the overcoming of the five vices: lust, greed, false pride, anger, and attachment to material things. Sikhs have a strong belief in reincarnation, and when they die they believe their good and bad conduct will be weighed, and the result will determine the family, race and character of the person being reborn.

The concept of heaven and hell is not believed by Sikhs, but they do believe that a person who has been cruel or selfish while living in this life will be punished in the next life. On the other hand, those Sikhs who are honest, compassionate, and show mercy in this life will be honored in the next. Each reincarnation develops the soul until it reaches maturity and becomes one with the infinite one. Due to their reincarnation beliefs, Sikhs spend little time mourning the dead, because they believe the person is now in a new body. As you spend time with Sikhs you will find men are particularly noted for their handsome, character lined faces, with meticulously trimmed beards, and colorful turbans. Also, due to their citizen relationship with Britain, you will find many of them working or running businesses in Britain today, especially in the larger urban centers.

JAINISM

Another religion indigenous to India is Jainism. Some scholars claim Jainism and Buddhism are reform movements that broke from Hinduism, and Jainism was at one time organically connected as a sect of Brahmanism. Jains deny this claim and state they have always been a separate religion. Jainism is an ancient community in western India that practices their own religion and philosophy. They enjoy distinct worship and rituals, social customs, and cultural traditions. They claim to be followers of *"Jina"* the conqueror, the spiritual victor over all worldly passions and desires. A *Jina* is a human being who has obtained omniscience through his own efforts.

In the whole history of Jainism there *have* been only 24 *Jinas*, of which *Mahavir* (599-527BC) was the last. Jainism is an ethical belief system that concerns itself with the moral life of the individual. The faith has similar elements to Hindu and Buddhism in that they all share the concept of karma, and each has an extensive literary heritage. Jains also have a history of asceticism, belief in reincarnation, and they worship images. The goal of Jainism is the complete purification of the soul, which Jains can seek through liberation and detachment of their bodies, which inevitably purifies their karma. Jains believe all actions are attached to their souls, and through reincarnation their souls are bound to new bodies. Jains also practice the principle of non-violence or ahimsa, which means "compassion" and a belief not to injure. This duty is seen as the most essential religious duty for everyone. For this reason, you will often find their elderly leaders walking about naked. They have nothing but a broom to sweep the road in front of them, and a small towel to cover their nose and mouth to prevent ingesting small creatures.

SACRED WRITINGS:

Jains apply the teachings of Mahavira and the other *Tirthankaras* (a person who has conquered *samsara,* the cycle of death and rebirth, thus creating a bridge for others to follow).They also have saved sacred literature that includes commentaries on texts and other religious works such as *Tattuartha Sutra*, *Klpa Sutra*, *Utteradhyam Sutra* and recent works by *Atmasiddhi Sarta*.

Today there are about five-million Jains who live mostly in the west India areas of Marathavada and Maharastra. However, because Jains are considered to be excellent tradesmen, they have travelled and settled in many major cities throughout the world. Like many other religions, one can learn a great deal from these wonderful people who portray two major traits: non-violence, and a unique ability that makes them excellent international tradesmen.

BUDDHISM

Buddhism was founded in the 5th century BC by Siddhartha Gautama (563 – 483 BC), who is now known as Buddha, or awakened one. Born into a rich family, Buddha was protected from the misery and squalor of the human condition that lay outside the palace where he lived. As an adult, Buddha, went on a pilgrimage of inquiry and meditation, which later caused him to give up his worldly possessions and begin teaching a new way, called the Dharma – the underlying order and truth of existence.

It was once said that Buddhists spend their whole lives studying themselves. By studying themselves, Buddhists believe they are able to forget themselves, and by doing so they are somehow awakened to all things, and this awakening continues throughout life.

It is possible to study Buddhism as an external object, but mainly it comprises of an internal exploration to better understand yourself and the world around you. Buddhist believe that the main obstacle facing man in obtaining salvation is ignorance rather than sin. By believing that the self exists, it allows the illusory wheel of existence to keep on perpetuating itself, and only by eliminating this belief can it alter the flawed existence of this life.

Buddhism has become the fourth largest religion in the world with about 500 million followers, mainly in China and South East Asia. Buddhists lay claim to having created the world's first printed book, the first monastic order that included women, and created the first martial arts. Adherents claim that their religion helps them to ascend to the highest portals of the mind, while at the same time descending to the most fathomless parts of the heart. They further claim their religion is full of harmony and love, and that it brings transparency and peacefulness to the soul.

One could make the claim that anything is Buddha, if it wakes you up, mentally or spiritually, as well as physically. We are talking here about really being awakened. This experience could be achieved by simply smelling a flower, listening to the sound of a bird, observing the playful antics of a child, or just gazing into the eyes of a loved one. Buddha once said, "If you want to really see me, then look at my teachings." We find then that Buddhism is a cycle of teachings, which of course are taught and accomplished by man alone. This approach makes Buddhism an atheistic religion that has no concept of the God of the universe.

BUDDHIST DOCTRINE:

The whole of the Buddha's teaching is summed up in the Four Noble Truths, the Noble Eightfold Path, and the Five

Precepts. These truths lay out his doctrine for each person to understand. The path outlines the discipline for each person to practice.

FOUR NOBLE TRUTHS:

The Four Noble Truths consist of: 1) Life is basically all about suffering. 2) The origin of that suffering lies in craving and grasping. 3) The end of suffering is possible through the ending of craving, and 4) the way to end all craving and to escape continual rebirth is by following Buddhist practices known as the Noble Eightfold Path.

NOBLE EIGHTFOLD PATH:

This path includes: 1) Right View – gaining knowledge and understanding of the Four Noble Truths. 2) Right Thought – always being aware of the effects of thoughts and actions. 3) Right Speech – always telling the truth no matter the outcome. 4) Right Action – acting out of love and not causing suffering by our acts. 5) Right Livelihood – earning a living that does not cause harm to others. 6) Right Effort – maintaining a positive attitude as one pursues the path. 7) Right Mindfulness – being aware and fully attentive to things as they are, moment by moment. 8) Right Concentration – using meditative techniques to gain powerful concentration.

FIVE PRECEPTS:

The Buddhist laity is urged to follow the Five Precepts, which prohibit killing (including animals), stealing, sexual immorality, wrongful words (including gossiping) and drugs or alcohol. Laity is also expected to support the community of monks. A number of years ago I witnessed an early morning procession where the villagers in Burma stood in a long line feeding the monks from a local monastery as they passed by holding out their baskets. I was told these monks were not allowed to cook for themselves by perchance they kill the tiniest organs of life. Monks and nuns follow a path of moderate asceticism, including strict celibacy, and the loss of all personal property.

MAJOR SACRED WRITINGS:

The oldest and most authoritative scriptures, which are most important to the *Theravadan* form of Buddhism (explained below), are the massive *Pali* Canon or *Tripitaka* ("three baskets"), an oral tradition of the life and sayings of Buddha committed to writing some 500 years after his death. It can be divided into three main sections:

The *Vinaya Pitaka*, known as the "basket of discipline," is a code of ethics for monks and nuns. The *Sutra Pitaka* known as the "basket of threads," accounts for the Buddha's teachings. The *Abhidharma Pitaka*, known as the "basket of scholasticism," are philosophical works. Other sacred writings include: The *Dhammapada*, which is a sort of anthology of Buddhist proverbs; the *Siksha Samuk Samukhya*, that presents sutras (scriptural words of Buddha), and The *Mahayana* Texts, which teaches the Tibetan Book of the Dead, the translation of the words of Buddha, and the Lotus and Heart Sutras.

BUDDHIST LEADERSHIP

Some Buddhist leaders separate themselves within their monasteries, contacting the public only to gain funding. Other

Buddhist leaders are often involved in education and charity work, and they are not above having well thought out positions on politics. In Myanmar (Burma), I remember the tremendous outburst of peaceful dissent in the capitol Yangon (formerly Rangoon). It happened at the Shwedagon Pagoda (also known as the Golden Pagoda or the Golden Glory), which happens to be the most sacred shrine in the country). It is possibly one of the most eye-catching sights in the world, with its dazzling colors, and the rays of the sun bouncing off its glittering displays of gold. The protests started over high gas prices, which placed an undue burden on the poor people, so the monks took on a leadership role. It turned out to be a real tragedy, as government forces moved in and killed an untold number of monks, and ushered many off to the local Inseine Prison. Some of them may very well be still serving prison sentences.

In a suppressed nation like Burma, you will find Buddhism is the only fall back support the people have against the hardships imposed upon them by their renegade government. Everywhere I traveled, from Yangon, up the Irrawaddy River to Began, and up to Mandalay, I witnessed the most abject poverty, and a government that was only too happy to allow their people to own their so called religious faith as long as it did not interfere with the status quo i.e. allowing the powerful military junta to live in luxury on the backs of their people. My Burmese guide told me how much his people hated the government, and that their only solace was their Buddhist beliefs, which helped sustain them.

TYPES OF BUDDHISM:

Buddhism can be traced back to the 5th century BC, and founded in modern day Nepal and India. It is a reformation of Hinduism not unlike the Reformation that separated the Protestant Church from the Catholic Church in the 16th century. There are today three main forms of Buddhism practiced with many sub-sets within the overall religion. The three main branches are:*Theravada Mahayana*, and *Vajrayana*.

Theravada Buddhism, which started in the beginning, places emphasis on the individual monk working through self-control and a series of meditative practices that progressively leads a person to lose a sense of craving. *Theravada* teaches that Buddhists can help others only by showing them an example of dedication and self-denial.

The *Mahayana* School, on the other hand, teaches compassion, and takes the position that the ideal of a monk striving only for his own salvation was selfish and did little for the majority of humanity. Mahayanists eventually came to suggest that a large number of Buddhas and Bodhisattvas, classified as "heroes of the faith," attempt to reach the point of nirvana (literally meaning "blowing out", as the flame of a candle). Bodhisattvas reach a transcendent, permanent state of enlightenment, but refuse to enter it until the rest of humanity can be brought along with them. In various ways, these heroes can graciously assist others through the diamond way.

The third branch, *Vajrayana,* merges elements of *Theravada* and *Mahayana* with a Buddhist adaption of an old ancient Hindu yoga called *tantra*. It is considered the most complex form of Buddhism, and the most complete.

BUDDHISM IN NEPAL:

One unique form of Buddhism can be found in Nepal, located north of India in the Himalayas. The Buddhists, as well as many Hindus, worship a "living goddess," who is a pre-pubescent girl carefully selected as a manifestation of the divine female energy or Devi that is found in both Buddhist and Hindu religions. She is called *Kumari* or *Kumair Devi*, and is generally chosen to be worshipped during certain festivals. She is generally believed to be the incarnation of the goddess *Taleju* until she menstruates, or bleeds for any reason. This causes the goddess to leave the girl's body, and the girl is then returned to her own family. In anticipation of this event the monks have already begun their search for a replacement by searching the country for a young girl that has a neck like a conche shell, a body like a banyan tree, eyelashes like a cow, thighs like a deer, a chest like a lion, and a voice that is soft and as clear as a duck. Former *Royal Kumaris* later experience difficulty getting married due to the traditional belief that their husbands will cough up blood and die within six-months of the marriage ceremony.

I had the pleasure of seeing the actual "living goddess," through a special invitation arranged by my Nepalese guide. The event took place at the *Kumari Ghar Palace* in the center of Kathmandu. As I waited with a group of people from all over the globe, I could not help but notice the many snipers located on the roof of the palace, and in some windows. Finally, the *Royal Kumari* was displayed through an upstairs window, where she made her presence for all to see for about ten-minutes Then she disappeared.

BUDDHISM IN TIBET:

Tibetan Buddhism draws on the teachings, techniques, meditation, and ordination vows of Theravada, as well as the philosophy and cosmology of Mahayana. However, you will also find the third school of Buddhism, Vajrayana, also being preserved with most of the distinctive qualities of Tibetan Buddhism is to be discovered in its Vajrayana history.

Today in Lhasa, the capitol of Tibet, you will find Buddhist monks being forced by the Chinese government to act as guides to foreign tourists as they are escorted through the Potala Palace, Jokhang Temple, and other sacred places, in order to provide hard international currencies to the banks in Beijing. The monks complain such long hours spent with tourists takes them away from their meditative studies, and negatively affect their spiritual life. As a result, many have rebelled in recent years, even committing self-immolation in the public square in front of hundreds of onlookers.

In general, though, I found most Tibetans to be very friendly people who just wanted to be free from the Han Chinese, and lived their lives in freedom. They yearn for the return of the Dalai Lama to the Potala Palace, (who lives in exile in India), and yearn for a time when they can pursue their religious vows without constant interruption by government officials from Beijing. If a sovereign nation is characterized as a group of people living in a particular landmass, who speak the same language, apply the same dress code, worship their own religion, and culturally think as one, then Tibet today is very much a country in everything but name. This is yet another example of how religion can be used to suppress people by corrupt governments.

WORSHIP:

In many cases, what appears to be worship is actually the paying of respect. The Buddha is revered as an example of a saintly life and as the originator of the teachings of Buddhism. Buddhists are taught they must personally overcome the obstacle of ignorance. Meditation, for instance, can focus on one's breathing, which is important because it is halfway between voluntary and involuntary action; one's own attitudes, such as mindful meditation, is where a person tries to be clear at all times as to one's motive in removing craving and a sense of self. In some sects it is believed a Bodhisattva can transfer his merit to another person and help them achieve nirvana. In those cases the Buddhist becomes very much like a worshipper petitioning for grace and mercy.

THE ATHEIST NATURE OF BUDDHISM:

The important point to remember about Buddhism is the fact that Buddhists, as a general rule, do not believe in a monotheistic God that created the universe and everything in it. This idea was a foreign concept to the Buddha, for in his world there were many gods. There is also nothing in the teachings of Buddha that suggest how to find God or worship even the gods of India in his time, as his teachings were non-theistic. The Buddha was more concerned with the human condition: birth, sickness, old age, and death. The Buddhist path is about coming to a place of acceptance with these painful aspects of life, and not suffering through them.

Buddhist have reinvented themselves many times over the years, and so today it is not unusual to visit temples, as I found in Vietnam, Cambodia, Laos, Thailand, and China, where you will find a Buddha statue in a Taoist temple, and some Taoist rituals being practiced in a Buddhist temple, all carefully sprinkled with the right amount of Confucian principles (which is technically not a religion), and local folk religious practices, including honoring the dead, so that there is a little something for everyone. It is also true that as Buddhism migrated from India into China and Southeast Asia in general, that as the religion migrated, it also metastasized causing some Buddhist today to actually believe in a supreme, monotheistic God. Unfortunately for these great people, the larger majority do not.

TAOISM:

The concepts of Taoism, also known in the English language as Daoism, are important to understand in gaining insight into Asian cultures, mainly those of China, Taiwan, Japan, Korea, and Vietnam. In the words of the Asian scholar, Wing-Tsit Chan, "No one can hope to understand Chinese philosophy, religion, government, art, medicine, or even cooking, without a real appreciation of the profound philosophy taught in the *Tao Te Ching,* written in the 3rd century BC. No other Chinese classic of such small size has exercised so much influence." [2]

Tao Te Ching, is also known as "The Way" and its power. It is also known as the Lao Tzu. The *Tao* is a force that makes the universe work the way it does. Taoists consider the *Tao Te Ching* the most essential guide to living a full spiritual and ethical life. It is a short book made up of about 5,000 characters and is divided into 81 very brief paragraphs of advice about life, and some poetic on the nature of the universe. This religion advocates simplicity and selflessness in conformity with the Tao, the central or organizing principle of the universe.

According to the law of Tao, everything moves from a state of non-being to being, and back to non-being.

Taoist believe that no one person wrote the *Tao Te Ching*, although some say it was written by Lao Tzu, who has been worshipped by some as a god. It is generally believed to be a collection of proverbs and sayings of many anonymous people over the centuries. Another important book is called the *Chuang Tzu,* which was published after the *Tao Te Ching*, although its compilation began earlier. The *Chuang Tzu* is credited to Chuang Tzu (Zhauangzi), which is considered a collection of the wisdom of many people.

Taoism, which has no founder and no founding date, although Laozi ("the old man") called Lao-Tzu (600 – 530 BC), has had some considerable influence on its movement. Later, Zhauangzi, (370 - 301 BC) popularized the Tao, defining it as the spiritual process of constant flow or give and take. It is a polytheistic religion, with worship of deities such as the Jade Emperor, and Laozi himself came to be venerated as a deity, along with many other "immortals." Our history books tell us that Chinese ancient tradition of philosophy and religious belief, are deeply rooted in Chinese customs and worldview. Although Taoism is translated as "The Way," it is hard to say exactly what this means. We do know that one of their firmest concepts is that of non-action or allowing the natural course of things. It is a direct link to the yin and yang (explained below). The Tao is the ultimate creative principle of the universe, and therefore all things are unified and connected to the Tao.

YIN AND YANG:

Think of the Tao as a religion of two opposites, the negative and the positive, but unlike Western dualism these two opposites, yin and yang, are in perfect harmony. The yin represents the negative traits of darkness, coldness, and is feminine, whereas the yang represents positive traits of light, warmth, and masculinity. It is said that yin is the breadth that created the earth, and yang formed the heavens. Followers say that when the materialism of this earth gets in the way, the balance of yin and yang is unbalanced. This principle states that the world is full of complimentary forces – action and non-action, light and dark, hot and cold, ad infinitum.

The Tao is not god, and is not worshipped. It includes many deities worshipped in Taoist temples, and they are part of the universe that depends, just like everything else, on the Tao. Although Taoists do not worship God the creator, because the Tao is not God, they do worship many deities that have been borrowed from other cultures. Although Taoism today is practiced mainly in China, it has spread to other Asian countries, which makes it somewhat difficult to determine the number of followers. Also, the number of people practicing Chinese folk religions in general is not tracked by the government as they are not part of the five accepted religions. Therefore, the best considered estimate is above 200 million, who also embrace certain Taoist concepts.

My own experience in visiting a number of countries in Southeast Asia where Taoism is practiced has caused me to understand why people, especially Westerners, can get confused when visiting a Taoist temple where you find in front of the main entrance a large container full of joss sticks. When they are lit, the rising incense becomes a representation of the people's prayers to the heavens. On either side of the containers are dragons, which are also found on the roof of the temple, which exemplify energy, strength, and life force. There are also many conflicting deities that have been borrowed from other cultures, especially folk religions, which are designed to attract large numbers of adherents. In the process, however, it creates a religious environment difficult to interpret.

The Taoist philosophy can be summed up by a passage from Chuang-Tzu who once said, "To regard the fundamental as the essence, to regard things as course, to regard accumulation as deficiency, and to dwell quietly alone with the spiritual and the intelligent, herein lie the techniques of Tao of the ancients." Today, we find Taoism is still somewhat of a regional, Asian religion.

CONFUCIANISM

Confucianism is mainly practiced in China, although in recent years it has spread beyond the borders of China into South East Asia. The core values of Confucianism – harmony, education, and respect for elders and ancestors – have been upheld in China for thousands of years. Today, these same core values continue to influence the culture in China, and the wider world.

The actual roots of Confucianism date back many hundreds of years before the birth of Confucius in 552 BC. History tells us many of the values promoted by Confucius actually date back to the Shang Dynasty (1766 – 1050 BC), especially at the imperial court. The emperors placed a high value on members of their courts who were well educated, trained in correct rituals, and motivated by virtue. However, in the 6th century BC the power of the Zhou emperors began to break down. Various scholars put forth ideas about how to rebuild the order, and one of these scholars was Confucius, whose ideas gained the most support.

CONFUCIAN TEXTS:

Confucius compiled a number of books known as the Five Classics to teach his students. The first, the Book of Changes, covers the metaphysics of the cosmos, and humanity's relationship with the universe. The Book of History provides examples of ideal government. The Book of Poetry contains a treasure of early Chinese verse on all aspects of life. The Record of Rites is a handbook of correct actions, and finally the Spring and Autumn Annals is made up of a series of judgments about good relationships. Successive students over the centuries have continued to apply Confucian methods up to the present day.

THE FAITH AND THE STATE:

Confucianism is not so much a religion as it is a way of behaving correctly in an orderly society, although they do worship deities as part of their doctrine. We find under the Han Dynasty (206 BC - 220 AD), the imperial court promoted Confucian methods in a dramatic way by creating a belief system that survived for 1700 years. The Han rulers gave Confucianism an organizational structure, establishing a university, re-editing the Classics, and setting up a system of competitive examinations for civil service positions based on Confucian principles. We have discovered that during the Song period (960 AD – 1279 AD), the Neo-Confucian movement elaborated on Confucian ideas. It focused on the role of the individual and self-development. Confucian values remained at the heart of Chinese life until the end of the imperial period in the early 20th century. The communist take-over of China caused Confucian values to be side-lined by the government, but the people still valued the virtues of harmony, respect, and balance, and the people see Confucianism as fundamental to the Chinese character. Some in China today even credit it with the great economic leap forward China has experienced during the last 50 plus years.

CORE BELIEFS:

At the very heart of the Confucian belief system is the concept of harmony at every level of society, from the individual person to the entire universe. This fundamental concept is pandemic in all areas of personal morality, government, history, and even the gods. There are two different concepts of god. First, there is an ultimate reality called Taiji. This is an absolute, unknowable force that controls the universe. Followers believe it is possible to achieve a type of unity with Taiji, through discipline, meditation, contemplation, and scholarship. On the other hand, the other concept of god, which is more accessible to ordinary Chinese, is the host of lesser gods, the deities or spirits, and their immortalized ancestors who live in heaven. These are seen as inhabiting a heaven similar in social structure to imperial China, with a ruling immortal called the Jade Emperor, and ranks of godly civil servants that administer his realm. We find this was particularly important to the emperors who saw the correct worship of these deities as a way of validating their own rule.

ETHICS, MORALITY AND LAW:

Moral values in Confucianism focus on various ways to achieve harmony at a personal level, and also at the levels of government. The Chinese people are expected to conduct themselves in a cultivated and humane manner, and to observe and respect modes of behavior that are in harmony with Confucian methods. Harmony can be achieved in two ways: *li* (the ritual of protocol), and *ren* (applying humane conduct). *Li* can be achieved by applying the behavior of the ancients in the Five Classics. It requires a mixture of manners, ritual, and ceremony. The other approach to achieving harmony is to apply *ren*, which encompasses love, goodness, humanity, and generosity. *Ren,* according to Confucius, should be the guiding spirit in all dealings with other people. Above all, Confucius stressed satisfying the needs of others, rather than thinking of self.

FAMILY VALUES:

Confucius was very concerned about implementing a system of family values to create harmony in family relationships. He laid out the nature of correct relationships between parents, children, husband and wife, elder and younger brother, friends, ruler and subject. He stressed filial piety above all, and he insisted children should respect and honor their parents, and always obey their elders. Harmonious family values, Confucius believed, helped to build a harmonious state.

There are about 1.3 billion Chinese citizens today, and as their economy continues to grow, and their affluence increases, they are now traveling the world. They will connect with us even more in the future, and so it is important we understand how they think. The major religions of China are basically atheistic, but they search for true meaning in their lives just like the rest of us. Despite oppression from the Chinese Communist Government, Christian missionaries have made great strides in penetrating the heart of these ancient people. In fact, China now has the fastest growing population of Christians in the world, despite a government effort to prevent it.

SHINTO

Japan is an island nation of some 120 million basically homogenous people who demonstrate great unity in their societal customs and practices. Their religion is called Shinto or (*kami no michi*), which means the "way of the gods," and is rooted in Japan's national history, and inextricably intertwined with its culture. The religion has no founder and no sacred scriptures (but they do have about 800 myths, some of which have been enshrined), and it is dovetailed into many of its rituals with Buddhism. They believe *kami* exists in gods, human beings, animals, and even inanimate objects. The Buddha, for instance, is thought of as a *kami* or another nature deity.

SHINTO CHARACTERISTICS:

Shinto is an optimistic faith that believes all people are good, and all evil is simply caused by evil spirits. Therefore, you find their rituals are directed towards trying to avoid evil spirits through religious rites of purification, offerings and prayers.

They believe all of humanity is *kami's* child, and by default all life and human nature is considered sacred.

One of the strong tenets of the Shinto faith is loyalty, which is demonstrated throughout society in loyalty to the family, superiors in the work place, and toward others in general by treating them with respect and consideration. Japanese society emphasizes community, and even the Japanese language contains conventions for speaking to those above, at, or below one's social standing.

WORSHIP AND PRACTICE:

There are no scheduled, regular religious services in the Shinto faith. Rather, people make up their own mind when they want to visit any one of the 80,000 shrines scattered across the country. Local people look after the small shrines, although there is often a priest on premises in the larger shrines. Although the new Constitution eliminated the nationalism of the pre-war era, traditional Shinto continues as an aspect of contemporary Japanese life. Only about 1.5 million Japanese out of 120 million declare themselves to be Christian, but about 112 million say they adhere to Shinto. You also find that many Japanese follow several religions because we are also aware that about 93 million Japanese also call themselves Buddhists!

To complicate matters further we also find that about 70% of Japanese claim that they do not follow any personal religion. These facts appear to make religious allegiance somewhat nominal. On the other hand, the Japanese will often state that to be Shinto is to be Japanese. In one shrine that I attended, I found myself surrounded by Japanese who were all clapping to wake up the Buddha from his sleep so he would hear their prayers. This scene was instructive in helping me further understand how Shinto manifests itself into society as a whole.

My experiences in Japan left me with the clear impression the Japanese are thoughtful, gentle people who are well educated, while also highly superstitious. They do worry about earthquakes, North Korea, their relationship with China, and their balance of trade issues with other countries. Above all, however, they live in fear of losing face, and will do almost anything to prevent it from happening. One final thought is to point out that because of their homogenous nature, and their sense of conformity to the rules of their society, they generally resist most of the other major world religions, including Christianity.

We have so far covered the major religions of the Far East, and several with much lower population figures, but significant nonetheless. My travels in Burma, India, Nepal, Thailand, Cambodia, Laos, Vietnam, Japan, China, Tibet, and Singapore, have made me realize that about 50% of the world's atheists live in this part of the world. That is a staggering number of people who are still living in darkness, and need the light of Christ to touch their hearts. These people did not choose the mother's womb that would give them life, and they are clearly raised with cultural norms and traditions that date back thousands of years, and are difficult to break from. Nevertheless, great achievements are being accomplished in this part of the world by dedicated missionaries who are assisting in winning millions of people for Christ, but there is still much work to be done to break through the barriers of darkness.

CHAPTER SIX

WORLD-WIDE WESTERN RELIGIONS (OCCIDENTAL)

In this chapter we will discuss the twin sister religions of Judaism and Christianity, the religions that created the Judeo-Christian principles upon which Europe and America were founded. As I mentioned earlier, the Old Hebrew Testament, and the New Christian Testament are joined together to tell God's story of mankind. We will first begin with Judaism.

JUDAISM

Every Christian should, at some point in his life, attempt a pilgrimage to Israel, just as one of Islam's Five Pillars of Faith requires all Moslems to take the Hajii, a pilgrimage to Mecca, in Saudi Arabia. To walk in the footsteps of Jesus, born a Jew, especially when He carried the cross down the Via Delarosa, is a very emotional experience. Visits to Golgotha, Jericho, Bethlehem, Capernaum, Nazareth, and the Sea of Galilee where so many of Jesus' travels took place, vividly recaptures a very special piece of history.

Although Judaism is a relatively modest sized religion, with approximately 15 million adherents, it is nonetheless a significant religious belief system that also serves as the historical foundation for two other much larger world-wide religions, Christianity and Islam. These three religions are the great monotheistic religions of the world.

Most Jews today live either in the State of Israel, where they are a majority, or in North America. The rest are scattered throughout many countries, and so is their influence. It can be said hardly a day goes by that Jews are not mentioned in the news, and it would be fair to say that they truly are at the center of the world's stage. As a group, they have made contributions towards the advancement of mankind way beyond their numbers, yet they are also the most hated of all people groups. They are one of the oldest people alive, and yet have created one of the youngest countries in modern history. Mark Twain once said, "All things are mortal but the Jew; all other forces pass, but he remains." Twain's words ring strongly when we consider the Romans destroyed Jerusalem and huge numbers of the Jewish people in the 1st century AD, and they were without a country for almost 1900 years. Yet they reclaimed their country of heritage in 1948 as proclaimed in their Hebrew Bible prophecy! The Jews are the only people group ever to achieve such a miracle! So follow me as we try to develop a better understanding of God's people.

WHAT IS A JEW?:

It is somewhat ironic that some ten-years after Israel became a new sovereign state, their government, which had passed legislation called the Law of Return Act, had still not determined who was a Jew. The matter was finally settled in the courts, as follows: "A Jew is anyone declaring in good faith that he or she is a Jew, and who does not profess to any other religion, shall be registered as a Jew." [1] So there we have it. Or do we? A couple of years later the courts modified the language again: "For purposes of the Law of Return Act, a Jew is someone born to a Jewish mother, or converted to the Jewish faith, and is not a member of another religion."[2] Of course the next obvious question is: "How was your mother determined to be Jewish?"(Jokingly, it has been said that a Jewish mother could take care of 100 children, but 100 children could not take care of her!).

It is believed that what they had in mind was Jewish identity is first decided by ancestry. Jews are descendents of common parents, and are the children of Abraham, Isaac and Jacob, instead of being simply the sons of Adam and Eve. By having a unique set of ancestors, it sets Jews apart.

ARE JEWS A RACE?

It should be emphasized that Jews are not a race. This idea of a Jewish "race" is a myth created by Adolf Hitler during the 1930's. His policy was to exterminate anyone who had the slightest trace of Jewish blood. But Jews are not a race of people. Although it is true they belong to the Mediterranean sub-division of the Caucasoid race, they have over many centuries migrated to many other parts of the world, and this has caused them to develop a multitude of different physical characteristics due to their cross-breeding with locals wherever they lived.

ARE JEWS A NATION?

Jews, interestingly, are not a nation. To make this point clear, it helps to recite the story of Napoleon who, after the French Revolution, decided to grant Jews equal rights with all other

French citizens. However, he had one major concern: Could Jews indeed be considered Frenchmen if they themselves thought they possessed a different national identity? A special commission was established, which asked a series of questions: 1) Do Jews think of Frenchmen as different from themselves? 2) Are Jewish citizens patriotic enough to defend the country? 3) Would Jews be bound to obey all the laws of France? The conclusion of the commission was that there is no Jewish nation, but only Frenchmen, Germans, Spaniards or Englishmen, who declare their faith in Judaism.

All sovereign nations have their own independent government, and own their land. The Jews, however, have survived with neither for almost the last 1900 years. During all of this time, they have conducted themselves as good citizens in countries where they have lived. Yes, it is true that the Jews now have control of the State of Israel, but less than half the world's population of Jews actually live there. Israel is also home to several million Arabs, a significant number. Finally, it should also be mentioned that when Jews speak of themselves as a nation, they mean it in a different sense than the rest of the world. For them, they are a nation in spirit. They are referring to same ideas, values and ancestry that supersede any land or government.

JEWISH ETHNICITY AND CREED:

It should also be pointed out Jews are not an ethnic group having their roots in many people groups across the world, and they prefer to refer to themselves as a religion of deed, and not a religion of creed. The only real doctrine is found in Deuteronomy 6:4, that affirms and teaches the unity of God, called the Sh'ma, which proclaims: "Hear O Israel, the Lord our God, the Lord is One."

JEWISH BEGINNINGS:

Judaism traces its origins to Abraham who, more than 4,000 years ago established a covenant with God (Genesis 12), by living righteously in great faith. He accepted God's terms to begin a new people, the Jews, who would be God's chosen people. He was told by God that he would be the father of many nations, and that his son, Isaac, and later grandson, Jacob (who would sire 12 sons forming the 12 great tribes of Israel), would carry on his legacy. Many years later, another great Jewish leader, Moses, would find himself liberating the Jews from 400 years of enslavement in Egypt. Moses was given the Ten Commandments from God on Mount Sinai, and Judaism began to take shape. The Exodus from Egypt and the Mosaic Law are foundational to the establishment of Israel as a nation. Here are the Ten Commandments from God that form the underpinnings, to the two great faith systems of both Judaism and Christianity:

> You shall have no other gods before me.
> You shall not make unto yourself any graven image.
> You shall not take the name of the Lord your God in vain.
> Remember the Sabbath day, to keep it holy.
> Honor your father and your mother.
> You shall not kill.
> You shall not commit adultery.
> You shall not steal.
> You shall not bear false witness against your neighbor.
> You shall not covet anything that belongs to your neighbor.

The Old Testament of the Bible, also referred to as the Hebrew Bible is replete with Jewish history, with a tendency to state the good, the bad, and the down-right ugly. Nothing is spared; sex, adultery, rape, murder, lust, romance, passion, conquest, wars and bloodshed on a massive scale. These themes have the making of a great book, right? No wonder the Bible is the number one best-selling book of all time.

The destruction of Jerusalem in 70 AD, and the subsequent destruction of the Temple, caused the deaths of more than 600,000 Jews, and an equal number were taken away as captives. The old priestly system and animal sacrifice practices also disappeared. The scattering of the Jews around the world is referred to as the Diaspora, and it created a decentralized form of Judaism that developed around synagogues and rabbis (teachers). The *yeshivot* (the religious academies for training of rabbis) were also created. With no new revealed scriptures for the previous 500 years, the rabbis began to think and debate about how to preserve the law under these new circumstances. Their collective writings created the *Mishnah*, and were compiled around 200 AD, although it should be remembered much of their content had existed in oral form for centuries. Further rabbinical writings with more application in nature were compiled over the next several hundred years, and they became the *Gemarah*. The combination of these two great writings became known as the Talmud, which, along with the Old Testament, serve as the basis for modern Judaism.

The Destruction of the Jewish Temple and the Diaspora, caused many Jews to migrate to other countries, especially Russia and Eastern Europe. The Hebrew language was essentially lost and replaced with local languages. Yiddish in

Europe comes to mind. Jews were kept separate from gentile populations, and had to live in ghettos. This separation and alienation caused Jews to be blamed for many things of which they were innocent. The Catholic Christian Church forbid its members from charging interest on loans, but the Jews had no problem in charging their customers interest. The Jews prospered and were inevitably envied as a result.

A SHORT MODERN JEWISH HISTORY LESSON:

In 1948 when the Zionist State of Israel was officially ratified by the United Nations, some 600,000 Israelis faced the anger of some 80 million hostile Arabs. More than 600,000 Arabs attacked and fought against 60,000 Israeli soldiers (a ratio of 10:1 in favor of the Arabs). The slogan of conquest by the Arabs was, "First the Saturday people, then the Sunday people."(This is a reference to the elimination of the Jews whose Sabbath is on Saturday, and then the elimination of the Christians, whose Sabbath is on Sundays). The Jews easily won the war. Again in 1956, Israeli, British and French soldiers had to use force to re-open the Suez Canal when President Nasser of Egypt tried to close it to their shipping interests. Then in 1967, an unprovoked attack on Israel by the combined forces of Egypt, Syria, Jordan and Lebanon, along with Iraq, Algiers, Kuwait, Sudan and the whole Arab nation, resulted in an embarrassing defeat for the Arabs in only six days. The Jews took the Golan Heights away from Syria, the Sinai Peninsula from Egypt(which was returned to Egypt in 1979 based on a historic peace agreement), and recaptured East Jerusalem from Jordan, and also the Gaza Strip, which the Jews disengaged from in 2005.

Then, in October, 1973, during the Jewish Yom Kippur celebration (a day of atonement, fasting and prayer), when Jewish citizens were in their synagogues, some 80,000 Egyptians over-powered some 500 Israeli soldiers on the Suez Canal border. Meanwhile, Syria sent 1400 tanks to sweep down on only one Israeli tank to oppose them. The Jews were taken totally by surprise, yet defeated all their enemies in 19 days. In 1982, under constant attack from Hezbollah in Lebanon, the Israelis were forced to counter-attack and move into Lebanon reaching as far as Beirut, the capitol. Since the Jews pulled out of Gaza, Hamas has broken ties with Ramallah, and has since become a bedrock of terrorism against Israel.

Some 2500 years ago, God said to Zechariah, "I am going to make Jerusalem a cup that sends all the surrounding peoples reeling. Judah will be besieged as well as Jerusalem. On that day, when all the nations of the earth are gathered against her, I will make Jerusalem an immovable rock for all the nations. All who try to move it will injure themselves." (Zechariah 12:2). The Bible is replete with many examples to demonstrate the fact that the Jews are God's chosen people, and even in these modern times, God remains faithful in preserving Israel against all attacks until the end of time. God's promise has been proven true many times over the years.

JEWISH PERSECUTION:

The history of Jewish persecution is very revealing. They were exiled from England in 1290 for about 400 years for practicing "Blood Libel," the utterly groundless charge that Jews were murdering Christian children to use their blood in making the Passover matzot. In the 14th century they were blamed for the Black Plague outbreak in Europe when about 50% of the continent's population died, but the Jews died less frequently due to adhering to their hygiene and sanitation laws given to them by Moses. They were accused by the Catholic Church of piercing wafers! Let me explain. Under the Catholic doctrine of trans-substantiation, Catholics believe drinking the wine of the sacrament is considered literally to be the blood of Christ. Also, by eating the holy wafer, it is considered to be partaking in the body of Christ. Catholics went on to accuse Jews of "piercing the holy wafer," which was symbolic to mean that the Jews were killing Christ once again.

Beginning in the 13th century, the gentile nations of Europe (all non-Jews) began separating the Jews from the gentile people, and the Jews were forced to carry a yellow badge to identify themselves. These Jewish ghettos (neighborhoods) existed until the end of World War II. From being accused as Christ killers, exiled from England, Spain and France, and later Russia during the pogroms, Jews were, from the 13th century onward, constantly being tortured and killed by the gentiles because Jews held to their faith. Often gentiles forced Jews with a sword to their throat, to accept Christianity or die. Some Jews did convert, and they were called "*Maranos*," which meant swine or pigs, although they secretly continued to practice their religious faith.

THE WORST PERSECUTION OF ALL – THE HOLOCAUST:

As I stood outside the old Nazi headquarters in the Berlin suburb of Grossen-Wannsee, I was reminded very vividly this was the place in January1942, where 15 Nazi bureaucrats discussed what they euphemistically called the "Final Solution." The meeting was headed by SS Obergruppen-fuhrer, Reinhardt Heidrich, and included Adolph Eichmann. It was agreed to evacuate every Jew in occupied Europe and move them to camps in the East. The purpose was to exterminate most Jews upon arrival, but to retain some for labor battalions. Death would soon come to the workers through starvation and hard work. This "Final Solution" was implemented ruthlessly by the Nazi with great efficiency. Death camps like Auschwitz, Birkenau, Treblinka, Chelmno, Majdanek, Sobibor, Belzec, and many others were used by the Nazi in the extermination of six million Jews, along with countless Gypsies, Slavs, and homosexuals. It was one of the darkest chapters in man's history, and to this day the Jew, and the world, is still asking why?

Why is there such hatred towards the Jews, even today, after some 2,000 years since the crucifixion of Christ? The only reason I can conclude is that some Jews, despite their tremendous handicaps and persecutions, have against all odds become successful, wealthy, and powerful in many countries over the centuries, which has caused envy. As minorities living among gentile populations, they were an easy target for any despotic ruler experiencing problems, and looking for a scapegoat. It is interesting to compare the Jews to the United States, which is a very wealthy and successful nation, yet is reviled and envied all over the world. Success does appear to breed envy and resentment by others.

TYPES OF JUDAISM:

Before the 18th century there was only one form of Judaism, but since then a number of branches have come into being.

These branches are not equivalent to our understanding of Christian denominations where one's identity is tied firmly to a particular denomination. The branches of Judaism are more like voluntary associations, with classifications according to cultural and doctrinal formulas, but with a commitment to a particular branch that is often governed by personal preference, such as how close is the nearest synagogue, or the particular style of the rabbi's teachings. This might also partially explain why the largest group of Jews world-wide, including Israel, are non-observant Jews, who do not follow Jewish religious practices at all.

ORTHODOX JEWS:

The largest official group is the Orthodox branch that strives to keep all 613 mitzvot (commandments) of the Mosaic Law (these represent the original Ten Commandments, and others that have been added over the years), and was the form of Judaism prior to the 18th century when the other branches began their formation. Please note that the 613 commandments represent one commandment for each letter of the original ten commandments of Moses plus the seven rabbinical precepts of the 7 Noachide laws (laws prescribed by the Supreme Court in Solomon's Holy Temple). Today, Orthodox Judaism is characterized by an emphasis on tradition and strict observance of the Law of Moses as interpreted by the rabbis. They are as a group the fundamentalists of the faith, and their total adherence to the Torah goes all the way back to Mount Sinai. Although they represent less than ten-percent of Jews in America, you will find that Orthodox Judaism is Israel's official religion.

REFORM JEWS:

This is a progressive form of Judaism that is in accordance with reason and recognizes only those moral laws that elevate and sanctify life, and also rejects those laws that are not adapted to the views and habits of a more modern civilization. You will find Reform Jews embracing modern scientific discoveries and lifestyles, and are generally less strict in their observances than Orthodox Jews. They represent about 35% of American Jews.

CONSERVATIVE JEWS:

As mentioned earlier, all Jews practiced the same religion until the 18th century when Reform movements began to take hold. When the Reform Jewish movement arose, some Jews felt they went too far in rejecting the traditional tenets of their faith. In 1887, a number of rabbis decided to establish the Jewish Theological Seminary that would preserve the knowledge of historical Judaism as laid out in the Hebrew Bible and the Talmud. This form became known as Conservative Judaism, which accepts human progress, while also upholding Biblical laws. This branch of Judaism represents about 33% of American Jews.

JEWISH ACCOMPLISHMENTS:

As I mentioned earlier, the Jewish people have accomplished many great things for the very small size of their population (about one fifth of one-percent of the world's population), and their deeds are far too lengthy to be described here. However, I will provide you with just three examples out of the many outstanding achievements of the Jewish people:

My first example concerns five poor, European Jewish men, who did not know each other, yet all independently migrated to Ellis Island, New York, in the late 19th century, along with their large families. Each later enjoyed great wealth and fortune, and their lives became very connected. In no particular order we have Benjamin Warner from Poland; Adolph Zucker from Germany; Louis B. Mayer from Russia, William Fox from Hungary, and Carl Laemmle, also born in Germany.

With their large families to feed, none of these men were above washing dishes, shoe shining, peddling notions, chimney sweeping, and cobbling. Yet in later life they moved out to California where Benjamin Warner created Warner Brother Studios; Adolph Zucker built Paramount Studios, Louis B. Mayer developed Metro-Goldwyn-Mayer; William Fox founded Fox Film Corporation, and finally, Carl Laemmle, created Universal Studios. Hollywood was virtually built on the backs of poor, uneducated Jews from small villages in Europe, who came to America with just the clothes on their backs, and took America by storm! What an incredible story!

A second example concerns the issuing of Nobel prizes. Prior to the death of Alfred Nobel, the inventor of dynamite, he established the Nobel Prize Foundation that has given Nobel awards for outstanding contributions for the advancement of man in many areas of human achievement. Since its inception in 1900 through 2013, we find that of all the Nobel prizes issued, 23% have been awarded to Jews! [3] This is an achievement of historic importance considering their small population. What other people group have ever accomplished so much with so few?

Finally, there was the invention of the Atomic Bomb by three Jewish men. This tiniest particle of matter, just like the tiny population of the Jews (compared to other world-wide religions), changed the course of history. Albert Einstein, considered by many to be the greatest scientist of all time, is the father of the atom bomb. His revolutionary concepts of time and space, as explained in his "Theory of Relativity," caused man to take a giant leap forward. By explaining the entire relationship of mass, gravity, space and time, Einstein set the course for others to "climb on his shoulders," and keep the "ball" moving forward. Then along came Neils Henrik David Bohr, considered to be the other "father" of atomic energy, who revolutionized the concept of the structure of an atom. He solved the problem of atomic theory and discovered U-235, a rare uranium isotope, as the source for splitting a uranium atom. Also, there was J. Robert Oppenheimer, who headed the famous "Manhattan Project," which produced the world's first atomic bomb that brought the war with Japan to an end. These three Jewish men forever changed the course of man's history.

CORE VALUES:

Above all, the Jews believe in the primacy of the Torah, which promotes Judaism's central values, such as upholding the sanctity of life, the ideal of generosity, the importance of justice, and the emphasis on education. They are a people of deeds. It should also be mentioned for the record, that Jews do not generally accept Jesus Christ as their Messiah, and they are still looking forward to seeing Him one day. This position is in sharp contrast with the Christian position that Jesus Christ is the Messiah, and was both fully man and fully God.

You will also find that all three branches of Judaism do not believe in original sin. They take the position that sin is caused by breaking Jewish commandments. Finally, on the subject of life after death, you will find Reform and Conservative Jews have no concept of personal life after death. It is said a person lives on in the accomplishments or in the minds of others. Some are even influenced by Eastern mystical thought where souls merge into one great impersonal life force. Orthodox Jews, on the other hand, believe in a physical resurrection. The righteous will live forever with God in the "World to come," but the unrighteous will suffer. There is still some disagreement over what happens to their ultimate destiny.

It should now be obvious that God has chosen the Jews to be his people, and all the prophecies in the Hebrew Bible (Old Testament) either have come true or will in the future. Unfortunately, the Jews have still not accepted Jesus as their Messiah, and therefore are not followers of the New Testament. From a Christian perspective, however, we see a definite symbiotic relationship with Jews, and we believe that both the Old Testament and New Testament are all the work of the one true God. It should be pointed out, however, that many Jews have come to accept Christ, and they are referred to as Messianic Jews. So it will be of great interest to see how many Jews convert to Christianity in the future.

CHRISTIANITY

Once considered a minor sect in a small corner of the Roman Empire some 2000 years ago, Christianity has since developed into the largest religion in the world with some 2.1 billion believers (as of 2010). This figure comprises 1.1

billion Roman Catholics, 600 million Protestants, and about 270 million Eastern Orthodox, with the rest made up by other independent groups. The faith is hugely influential in Europe, and North and South America, and is making great strides in the developing world, especially Africa where thousands of new Christian churches have been built. By 2050 Africa is expected to have 29% of the world's Christians, followed by Asia with 20%. Some Christian theologians refer to this trend as Christianity's "global center."

Christians are followers of the teachings of Jesus Christ, and they hold that He is the Son of God who will bring salvation and eternal life to all those who repent their sins and believe in Him. The message of Jesus, as detailed in the Four Gospels, is one of love and forgiveness. Christians are told to love God with all their heart, mind and soul, and strength, and to love their neighbor as they love themselves; to forgive the misdeeds of others; to help the poor, and above all to aim for the perfection displayed by God Himself. Christian faith is available to anyone who chooses to follow it irrespective of their social status, wealth, or ethnic origin. Members worship regularly, and partake in certain sacraments such as the Eucharist. It re-enacts Jesus' Last Supper with his disciples. By eating bread and drinking wine, it is said to represent the body and blood of Christ Himself. Baptism into the faith is another cornerstone of the religion.

GOD'S GRADUAL REVELATION OF DIVINE LAW:

Christians believe that God has revealed His divine law to man in seven major ways over the centuries, which are well worth mentioning. God first revealed his law to man by "writing it on nature" for all mankind to see (Psalm 19:1). He also revealed his law through man's conscience. In Romans 2:15, he says, "since they show that the requirements of the law are written on their hearts, their consciences also bearing witness, ..." God further reinforced his laws to man by "writing it on tablets of stone," which were given to Moses (Exodus 24:12). Later, God gave man his only begotten Son as a sacrifice for all man's sins. Jesus was the "Word became flesh" of God's laws for man (John 1:14). God also revealed his laws to man through the entire Holy Scriptures made available for all to read (Romans 15:4). In Hebrews 8:10, God says, "I will put my laws in their minds and write them on their hearts." Finally, we find God using Christians as "living Epistles," In II Corinthians 3:2, it says, "You yourselves are our letter, written on our hearts, known and read by everybody. You show that you are a letter from Christ, the result of our ministry, written not with ink but with the Spirit of the living God, not on tablets of stone but on tablets of human hearts." Romans 1:19 also goes on to say, "since what may be known about God is plain to them, because God has made it plain to them. For since the creation of the world God's invisible qualities – his eternal power and divine nature – have been clearly seen, being understood from what has been made, so that men are without excuse."

CHRISTIAN HISTORY:

In the long history of the church, it has diversified itself into many forms ranging in character from the Roman Catholic Church, with its hierarchical structure of pope, bishops, and priests, to the many Protestant churches that center attention on the Bible by allowing its followers to enjoy direct communion with God. These different Christian varieties have led to arguments about doctrine, but it has also become one of the faiths greatest strengths, and helps to explain why it has been able to set down its roots all over the world. This success demonstrates Christ's insistence that the faith should be open to everyone.

At first, the message of Jesus was directed towards the Jews to let them know their long awaited Messiah had finally arrived. But the Jews would not accept Jesus as God, and after a short, three-year ministry He was crucified on a cross, just as it had been prophesized, as a sacrifice for all mankind's sins (see Isaiah 53:4-5 a prophecy written about 700 years before Christ was born, and long before crucifixion was ever practiced). Three days later He was resurrected, and during the next 40 days He was seen by more than 500 witnesses. (1 Corinthians 15:6). After the crucifixion of Christ, His message was delivered to the Gentiles (non Jews) through Paul, who earlier, as a Jew himself, had persecuted many Christian followers. Paul was a Jewish scholar, who on a journey to persecute Christians in Damascus, was struck with temporary blindness before hearing the words of Jesus that caused him to convert to the Christian faith (Acts 9:1-6).The many Pauline epistles in the New Testament were written by Paul on his missionary journeys in taking Christ's message across the Middle East and Europe.

CORE BELIEFS:

The whole of Christianity is pivotal on a belief in, and the teachings of, the Lord Jesus Christ. You will find many of Jesus' teachings are in the form of parables, which are stories that often begin with the phrase: "The kingdom of God is like ..." In His teachings, Jesus makes it very clear His kingdom is not restricted to people of a particular race or class, but open to anyone who is receptive to His Word, such as the Good Samaritan who belonged to a race hated by the Jews, but nonetheless helped an injured man whom others had ignored. Even Jesus himself often associated with hated tax collectors, prostitutes, lepers, sinners, and was always the first to see the good in a person.

THE SERMON ON THE MOUNT:

The Sermon on the Mount was delivered by Jesus, as mentioned in the Gospel of Matthew (chapters 5, 6 and 7), which contain a summary of His teachings. It is the longest piece of teaching from Jesus in the New Testament, and is one of the most widely quoted elements of the Gospels. The sermon outlines Jesus' view on Jewish law, setting higher standards for His followers than those previously imposed by the law, and stressing that any follower of God should try to emulate God's perfection in order to enter His kingdom. Among other things, followers of Christianity should put God above all other things i.e. money, possessions, and never be overly critical or discriminatory. Christians should also pray with an open, sincere heart.

We find in the Sermon on the Mount, that Christ first communicates the eight progressive steps by which all men are able to reach a higher level of spiritual life. The eight steps begin with man developing humility (Matthew 5:3); Penitence (Matthew 5:4); Meekness (Matthew 5:5); Spiritual Hunger (Matthew 5:6); Mercifulness (Matthew 5:7); Inward Purity (Matthew 5:8);

Peacemaking (Matthew 5:9), and Sacrificial Suffering (Matthew 5:10-12). Jesus then clarifies the fundamental truth of the Kingdom of God.

THE BEATITUDES:

Matthew chapter 5:1-12 is often referred to as the Beatitudes. It points out that it is not always the pious who get into heaven. Belief in God should offer hope and consolation to those who are poor, deprived, humble, and oppressed, and believers should always welcome those who come in peace rather than those who use violence. Jesus expressed this point of view in a series of verses in the Beatitudes, which can also be found in Luke 6:20-22 that says" "Blessed are you who are poor, for yours is the kingdom of God." This shows that belief in God can bring rewards to those who have lived well, and compensation for those whose time on earth have been spent in poverty sufferings or other difficulties.

CHRISTIAN CONDUCT:

Jesus spent a lot of time teaching his followers how they should behave towards their fellow man, and His expectations were always high. Even though His many followers were familiar with the words: "Thou shalt not murder," they found that Jesus said this was not enough in that they should renounce hatred as well. They knew they should not commit adultery, but Jesus said they should not even entertain lustful thoughts. They should exercise forgiveness even when it is difficult. He told the story of the prodigal son, who had gone away and squandered his inheritance, but who was welcomed back by his father unconditionally. Also, rather than repaying a violent assault with violence, He advised His followers to "turn the other cheek." His teachings centered on the "Golden Rule," which was to do unto others as you would have them do unto you. He advocated Moses' Ten Commandments, but also said the two greatest commandments were to Love your God with all your heart, soul, mind and strength, and to love your neighbor as yourself. He said that the prophets and the other laws hang on these two commandments. Jesus Christ, the greatest man who ever lived, has changed practically every aspect of our lives, but do we have a true appreciation for the legacy He left behind?

WHAT IF JESUS HAD NEVER COME?:

Have you ever wondered what life would be like here on earth if Jesus had never been born a man? The affect that Jesus Christ has had on the people of this world is so great that no superlative could do it justice. In order to provide an insight into Jesus' contribution to our societies, I have devoted Chapter Eleven to cover this vitally interesting subject.

A SPIRITUAL WAGER:

Remember Blaise Pascal's wager back in chapter one? As the father of modern philosophy you may at this point wish to revisit his wager. Who in his right mind would argue with the intellect and pure logic of Pascal's position? Why take the chance of risking a potential great opportunity of enjoying an eternal existence through God's plan for your life, rather than choosing your own plan, and losing out on an eternal life with God? 60 to 80 years in this mortal existence is nothing compared to a life of eternity, so why listen to other men who may possess great degrees behind their names, but who know far less than God? Be emboldened by Psalm 118:8-9, which says: "It is better to take refuge in the Lord than to trust in man. It is better to take refuge in the Lord than to trust in princes." We can all let ourselves down; other men can let us down, but God never will.

CHAPTER SEVEN

INSIGHTS INTO ISLAM AND WORLD-WIDE ANIMISM

So far we have discussed eastern religions, and the western religions of Judaism and Christianity. Now we will discuss a world-wide religion, Islam that is somewhat a late comer to the party in that it did not evolve until the 7th century, much later than all the other religions that came before it. Afterwards we will discuss Animism, which is also a world-wide form of religion with hundreds of millions of followers.

ISLAM

Before I move forward with this section on Islam, I must mention that it is not my intent to turn this discussion into a polemic, but rather an attempt to create an open, honest discussion of a great faith based religious system by pointing out issues both pro and con. Unfortunately, Islam has incurred a great deal of controversy in recent years caused by a few Muslim extremists that have negatively impacted the many good, law abiding Muslims, who want nothing more than to raise their families in peace, with the hope of a better life for their children.

Islam claims to be the fastest growing major religion in the world, and the latest figure state they represent some 1.6 billion Muslims, or about 23% of the total world population. This religion is second only to Christianity in number of followers, but if the current trend continues, Islam will become the largest religion in the world over the next 30 years according to Pew Research. Today, Islam is on the minds of many people due to much violence and unrest in many countries where the Islamic faith is dominant. This violence, unfortunately, is being exported around the world, and is threatening civilization as a whole. We have witnessed a large increase in Muslim terrorist organizations such as ISIS/ISIL, al Qaeda, Boko Haram, Al Shabbab, Hamas, AQIM, Hezbollah, The Taliban, AQAP, MNLF, and the Sudanese Islamist Regime, to name a few. These groups appear to have hi-jacked the teachings of Islam by using the faith as a tool to justify their own despicable ideology on innocent victims.

Upon closer inspection you will also find that many Islamic countries are poorly managed by their leaders, resulting in high poverty levels, and poor educational systems. This results in limited opportunities for people to advance from their present conditions, and it creates a fertile environment to recruit young men and women to the cause of Jiihad (interpreted as" holy war" in the West). You will also find Islamic governments tend to be theocratic (no separation of church and state), and are controlled by despotic rulers who put their own interests above the people.

So, with the above introduction used as a back drop to the subject of Islam, let us now in good faith try to better understand the followers of this religion, that continues to make almost daily news around the world.

According to the religion of Islam (which means 'submission'), in about 610 AD (almost six hundred years after the resurrection of Christ), the Angel, Gabriel, is said to have appeared to a man named, Muhammad, in the city of Mecca, in modern day Saudi Arabia, who claimed God (whom Muslims refer to as Allah), had summoned him to become God's last prophet on earth. This revelation formed the 114 suras (like chapters in the Bible) that are contained in their holy book, the Qur'an (also known as the Koran).

Muhammad believed he was restoring and completing the original religion of humanity, and he stood in the line of biblical prophets whom he claimed he had been sent by God to call all people to submit to God. He did practice polygamy, having nine wives, including three Jews, and numerous concubines. He was also a strong military leader. There is also evidence that he committed murder. He recited many suras advocating violence, and although some of his sura's have been abrogated, the ones that mention violence are not among them. Nowhere does Muhammad preach, "love your enemies and pray for those who persecute you" (Matthew 5:44). He appears to cast Allah as a fearsome, impersonal, vengeful God, who exacts severe penalties for those who do not believe in him. Despite these documented facts, Muslims are very sensitive to anything that raises doubts about Muhammad. The type of questions any freshman in college would be expected to raise in a term paper on any historical person, may be taken as an intentional insult when raised about Muhammad.

ISLAM CONNECTION TO JUDAISM AND CHRISTIANITY:

Muslims share many of the same basic beliefs as Christians and Jews, while differing fundamentally in a number of important ways. Muslims, for instance, trace their ancestry back to Abraham, as do the Jews and Christians.

Other compatible points include: 1) they believe in a monotheistic God that created the world and all that is in it. 2) Their God established, in His revealed word, the principles by which we live, including concern for the poor. 3) One should not worship other gods, money power or self. 4) At the end of time God will judge all people, and if a person has fulfilled his divine command, he or she will go to heaven. Christians have no disagreement on these points. However, followers of Islam do not enjoy a loving God, but rather a fearful one; they do not believe that Jesus Christ is the Son of God, and they do not believe in the Christian Trinity, which states that God manifests himself to people in three personalities. To a Muslim this is *shirk* (a blasphemy against Allah), which can be punishable by death in some Islamic countries.

AFTER THE DEATH OF MUHAMMAD:

Upon Muhammad's death in 632 AD, there was a power struggle for possession and leadership of the faith, and it resulted in a schism in the religion that resulted in about 80% of today's Muslims classifying themselves as Sunni, about 15% as Shi'a, and the rest are made up of Sufis, Salafis, and other smaller groups. The two main groups differ on many issues, and so it is best to understand the Middle East today by reviewing the composite majority/minority break-down of the two sects. Most Muslim countries in this region have a majority Sunni population, with the exception of Iraq, Iran, Bahrain, and Azerbaijan, who have a majority of Shi'a. The largest Muslim populations, however, are outside of the Middle East, such as Indonesia (170 million), Pakistan (140 million), and Bangladesh (120 million). The so called Arab League has twenty two member countries, and they often vote in unity at all United Nations voting opportunities. Most of them take anti-Jewish voting positions when Israel comes up for discussion, which is another deep study within itself. This unity of voting provides the Arab League with a good amount of political pull, which, along with their rich oil resources, has been used quite effectively in pushing their pet causes. I should also point out that there are currently 48 majority Muslim countries, but it is also important to mention that not all Muslims are Arabs, and not all Arabs are Muslims. Many Arabs living in the United States, for instance, claim to be Christians.

FIVE PILLARS OF FAITH:

All faithful Muslims share a belief system that is referred to as the Five Pillars of Faith, which are: 1) To faithfully recite the "*Shahada*," the basic creed:"There is no God but Allah, and Muhammad is his Prophet." 2) To recite prayers (known as "*Salatt*") of praise for Allah five times each day while facing the city of Mecca. 3) Give money to the poor, known as "*Zakat*," which is 2.5% of all liquid assets and income producing property. A person's home is not counted. 4) To honor Ramadan by fasting for one month each year during daylight hours, and 5) making a once in a life-time pilgrimage to Mecca, where Allah revealed the Qur'an to Muhammad. This is known as the "Hajj."

ISLAM'S HOLY BOOK – THE QUR'AN:

World societies have evolved considerably over the past 1400 years, but Islam's holy book, the Qur'an, has not changed, nor will it ever change. It is considered by all true Muslims to be the infallible word of God, or Allah as they call him, and therefore perfect, and not subject to change (see Hadiths on next page). The name, Qur'an, means recitation, but the text is also known as *al-Furqan,* which means discrimination between the truth and falsehood. Muslims also use the term *Umm al-kitab,* which means the mother of all books. Because the Qur'an is made up of God's words, the reproduction of its text is done with great accuracy, and in the original Arabic. It is also often written in calligraphic form.

The majority of Muslims all view the Qur'an as literally and eternally true, including its sura's concerning violence. Liberalism and modernism have not penetrated the House of Islam in any significant way, nor have they had any general influence on the way the average Muslim reads the Qur'an.

Just as Christian fundamentalist live according to the teachings of Jesus Christ, which is a clear message of love and peace with your fellow neighbor, the fundamentalist Muslim lives his life according to the dictates of the Qur'an. Unfortunately, the Qur'an states many things that are quite controversial not only within Islam itself, but throughout the rest of the world. The average Muslim will look to muftis for guidance, but will also read the Qur'an on their own. On the subject of how to treat non-Muslims, the sacred book will tell them "Prophet, make war on the unbelievers and the hypocrites, and deal rigorously with them. Hell shall be their home: an evil fate (Sura 9:73). Also, in Sura 4:76 it says: "Those who believe, fight in the cause of Allah, and those who reject faith, fight in the cause of Evil: so you fight against the friends of Satan: feeble indeed is the cunning of Satan." We also need to keep in mind that muftis, who interpret the Qur'an, are fallible men like the rest of us. But when they issue a fatwa, it becomes the law (until possibly changed), and all faithful Muslims must abide by it.

You will also find that Islam is both religious and political with no central authority to appeal to other than their God (Allah). Islamic doctrine is interpreted by a (mufti) from a particular Islamic law school, who issues a fatwa, which may be contested by other muftis. Nonetheless, the Qur'an is the highest authority in Islam, and in the Muslim world the Qur'an far surpasses the authority of the Bible in the West. The Qur'an is written in Arabic, and the dominance of Arabic is one of the main features shared by all Muslims, regardless of their native tongue. It has been said that to read the Qur'an without reciting it in Arabic, is like trying to appreciate a song by only reading the score. Making translations from its original Arabic form is frowned upon within Islam.

The Qur'an contains laws and dogmas, and is the Muslim's fundamental guide to living. As previously mentioned, the Qur'an means" recitation," meaning to recite, proclaim or read out loud. In Sura 96:1-5, you find the Angel Gabriel telling Muhammad to "recite." He does not tell him to read or write anything, which was just as well considering Muhammad was illiterate. The verb, "say," appears more than 300 times in the text. Even today, beginning at about the age of seven, children begin to recite the Qur'an. Community contests are often held, and prizes are awarded to the child who can recite every word of the Qur'an. The child is then held in very high esteem in the community. This practice is not unlike the spelling bee contest for kids in America.

Muhammad did not have any of his scribes write down the Suras (Qur'an verses). Instead he had them orally recite them to others. A typical English translation would take up about 500 pages, which over a 22 year period (the time-line that the suras were cited), amounts to almost two-pages per month. If you take the full 6200 verses, it calculates to less than one verse per day. The Qur'an is about four-fifths the size of the Bible's New Testament, and contains 114 suras that appear to be organized by the number of words in the Sura, with some exceptions. It is written in a non-linear fashion, and as mentioned, it is recited mainly in Arabic even though that may not be the language of the reciter. This would tend to put the reciter in a position of knowing all the words in the Qur'an, but perhaps not being able to necessarily understand it.

Reading the Qur'an for a Westerner is difficult, as I have found, having read it several times. A famous English historian, Thomas Carlyle, once said: "The reading of the Koran is as toilsome reading as I ever undertook . . .nothing but a sense of duty could carry any European through the Koran." [1] What is interesting about Carlyle was that he was a noted sympathizer toward Muhammad and Islam in general. On the other hand, a famous English Muslim convert, Mohammad Marmaduke Pickthall, commented: "The Qur'an is an inimitable symphony, the very sound of which moves men to tears of ecstasy." [2] No doubt it reads and sounds better in Arabic than it does in English.

ISLAMIC TRADITION:

According to the Muslim tradition, there were at least four different versions of the Qur'an after Muhammad died, but they were all later compiled into what is referred to as the Uthamanic version, which is the one used to this day. The Qur'an also has some abrogated verses, where God revealed some verses and later annulled them. The Qur'an is also contradicted by many of the Hadiths (explained below), which further confuses many of their adherents. It is also fair to state that Islam has never experienced a Reformation similar to Christianity, which has always tended to be more theological than Islam.

SUNNAH AND HADITHS:

To allow for the development of a more sophisticated society, Muslim legal scholars have created the Sunnah (traditions) composed of Hadiths (narrative), and sirah (journey). There are thousands of Hadiths which have been written over the ensuing centuries that have helped to support the Qur'an itself, and there are now some nine volumes consisting of 93 books. Unfortunately, as mentioned above, they tend to sometimes contradict each other. A Hadith contains one or more of four main types of materials: 1) something Muhammad did, 2) something Muhammad said, 3) something that happened in Muhammad's presence, and 4) words of God to Muhammad that aren't in the Qur'an.

There have been numerous attempts over the years to review and consolidate the Hadiths, and several great Islamic scholars have grouped the ones that most Muslims accept today. To eliminate Hadiths not fundamentally sound, the scholars used the following purging process: 1) sound (sahih), these are ones that are almost certainly true, 2) good (hasan), very possibly true, and 3) weak (da'if), which are ones that cannot be considered true unless confirmed by other traditions. Nonetheless, contradictions between the Hadiths and the Qur'an still exist, and there are Hadiths that contradict both Sunni and Shi'a interpretations, which leads to even more confusion for the average Muslim. For instance, the Qur'an treats women equal to men, although Sura 4:34 allows a man to beat his wife. On the other hand, the Hadiths clearly cast the man as superior. The Qur'an itself also has some interesting issues that require further clarity. An example is found in Sura 4:3 that says a man may have up to four wives, but only if he treats them equally. Sura 4:129 says a man is unable to treat multiple wives equally, which contradicts Sura 4:3. Some Islamic scholars combine the two Suras together to justify that the Qur'an does not approve of polygamy. So to recap: A man can have more than one wife if he treats them equally, but no man can treat multiple wives equally, therefore, no man can have more than one wife!

SHARI'A LAW (ALLAH'S LAW):

Understanding Allah's law requires some explanation. From the earliest period of Islam, Muslims have attempted to live their lives according to Shari'a, which to them is God's Law (see Sura 5:48). In non-religious terms, Shari'a is the path to a watering hole. When applied to religion, however, Shari'a is the path to life, and the divinely revealed laws that define that path. To know what God's plan is, a Muslim is expected to first turn to the Qur'an. However, only about 500 to 600 verses out of a total of 6219 verses in the Qur'an contain legal materials upon which society can form its laws. Furthermore, you will also find the majority of these verses concern ritual and worship. Consequently, there are not enough laws contained in the Qur'an to provide society with legal guidance. In the early days of Islam, personal opinion and local custom dictated the law, but by the 10th century, muftis (highly trained legal scholars), were able to provide legal opinions (fatwas) on matters not covered by previous rulings or the Qur'an itself.

APPLICATION OF PENALTIES UNDER SHAR'IA LAW:

It is true that Islam has received much bad press in the West for some of its stricter penalties found in the Qur'an. Examples include execution for murder, cutting off a hand for theft, and public lashings for other acts. *Hudud* means statutes that have been mandated by the Qur'an. Tradition, however, states crimes that come under the *hudud* should be handled carefully, and strict penalties only exercised as a last resort. There are restrictions in executing *hudud* penalties. For instance, Sura 124 states a penalty of 100 lashes for adultery, but the Qur'an also requires that four witnesses must see the act of penetration in case of adultery, which isn't likely to be found. In some Islamic countries the penalty for adultery is public stoning. Sura 24:5 also adds, "Unless they repent," which can abrogate the penalty. In the case of theft, a judge must also valuate the items stolen to see if there are any extenuating circumstances. For instance, if a starving Muslim steals a loaf of bread to feed his hungry family, then a judge would take the position that the whole community is guilty in not assisting the man's family, and therefore the penalty would not be imposed.

TEMPORARY MARRIAGES:

You will also find under Shi'ite law (not Sunni law) temporary marriages are allowed to avoid a married man from fornicating while away from home. The Sunni and Shi'ite continue to dispute this idea, but Shi'ites like to refer to the Arabic version of the Qur'an, which reads differently than the English version I have read. According to Shi'ites, they like to translate Sura 4:24 as follows: "To women whom you choose in temporary and conditional marriage (*muwaqat* and *muta'a*), give their dowry as a duty." [3] Shi'ites defend the practice as a method to avoid fornication, which is considered a wise decision of the Prophet that creates a sexual outlet to avoid masturbation, which is morally inferior to their method.

In Iran, for instance, which is a majority Shi'ite population, many married men travel to holy cities like Qom, for periods of religious education. While there they can enter into a temporary marriage contract stating the terms of the relationship, which can be for as little time as one hour, or for a more extended period. Many of the women are young widows, and if they end up getting pregnant, they are not entitled to child support. It is interesting to question how temporary marriage is any different than prostitution, which happens to be illegal in Iran.

IJTIHAD:

By the end of the 10th century, legal scholars felt all major legal issues contained in the original Qur'an had been decided, and therefore the "door of interpretation" (*Ijtihad*) was closed, and from that day forward all Muslims would have to consult past decisions collected in the books of the various law schools (*taqlid*). Leaders from each country decide which rules of the major law schools apply in their respective country, but the people could decide which school rules apply in their daily lives. If a legal case is presented that is not addressed in older law, then a judge will generally ask for a legal opinion from a mufti who, after reviewing the case, will issue a Fatwa, which becomes the new law of the land.

GETTING AROUND THE LAW:

Within Sunni Islam, all Sunnis can choose any of the four Sunni law schools, known as *Madhad* for interpretation of Islamic law. The four schools are: Hanifite (by far the largest and most lenient of the Sunni schools, and found mostly in Middle Eastern countries); Malikite (dominant in West Africa, Sudan, Egypt, Bahrain and Kuwait); Shafi'ite (dominant in Egypt, Southern Arabia, East Africa, Indonesia, and Malaysia); Hanbalite (most conservative of the Sunni schools, which is dominant only in Saudi Arabia, Qatar and Oman).

Most Shi'ites follow the Ja'farite Law School, which clashes with Sunni interpretations on a number of issues. Within Sunni Islam, any of the four law schools constitute a valid body of law even when they disagree with one another. One school can be strict on an issue while another school might be more lenient. So, by picking and choosing among the different rulings of the four schools, a person or a government could gain considerable flexibility in resolving problems. The concept of patching (*talfiq*) goes further than the idea of selection. By combining part of a ruling from one school with part of a ruling from another school, a person or a government could come up with a new legal ruling.

A case in point would be a woman whose husband has disappeared, who must wait until the end of his expected life to remarry according to the Hanifite School. However, in the Malikite School of Law the waiting period is only four-years. By patching the four-year law with the present law, the woman would be free to marry after four-years of waiting. Another example is the prohibition of usury (charging interest on debt), which has been difficult for Islamic banks and businessmen to transact business like in the West. To get around this issue, clever Muslim lawyers have created complicated language in contracts that accomplish the purpose of charging interest without taking the form of interest.

MILITANT COMPONENT OF ISLAM:

Islam today is perceived as being the most violent of the major religions for reasons previously mentioned. Part of the problem appears attributable to the fact that Islam, unlike Christianity, has been unable to make progress as Muslims have evolved from a 7th century, barbaric society, to a more modern, and enlightened one. This has caused great friction within Muslim societies, but also for the world as well.

Upon closer inspection we find Islam has never really known about the separation of church and state, which, when it happened in Europe, helped to determine and shape the social and political evolution that transpired. Beginning in the 16th century, this church-state separation led Europe from absolutism, like the divine right of kings, to democracy, with a higher respect for civil rights, thanks to the Reformation movement and the Enlightenment periods. Europe also evolved over time from blind faith to rational reasoning. Islam, Judaism and Christianity are all revealed religions, but Islam with its holy book, the Qur'an, being their true words of God, makes it superior and perfect to all other holy texts in the minds of Muslims. This means it has no incentive to evolve like the other two religions.

Islam is now some 1400 years old, and so it may provide some perspective by asking what was the state of Christianity when it had evolved 1400 years from the crucifixion of Christ? It is sad to say that Christians were burning heretics in the fire. I believe, therefore, there is still hope that Islam will change, and embrace more scrutiny from objective scholars who can hold Islam up to the light and transparency that it sadly needs.

Today, the Islamic world is controlled by Islamic religious and secular rulers who have developed the reputation over a long period of time as being despotic. As a result, the rule of law is something to be negotiated. Everywhere I have travelled in the Middle East, which includes nine countries, you can't help but witness a military presence, with secret police operating somewhere in the background. Such an environment stifles and inhibits the creative energies of good Muslims who want a better life for themselves and their families. Sectarian violence between Sunni and Shi'ite is on the rise, as is violence with other religious and ethnic groups. As a consequence, there is a high level of unemployment, poverty and ignorance, and a severe lack of opportunity in many Muslim lands where large numbers of Muslims have no "skin in the game." If a young unemployed Muslim is asked to show up at Tahir Square in Cairo tomorrow night in order to demonstrate some cause, he will simply show up and throw rocks at the police until he gets tired and goes home. He has nothing to lose, but the incident is carried viral on CNN and Al Jazeera television all over the free world. What was achieved? If he was employed with a career path, courting marriage, or perhaps already married with kids, he would certainly think twice about showing up to throw rocks at the police.

Poverty and ignorance drive the social unrest in the Middle East, which is causing young men with no future prospects to become volatile and even dangerous. If some of these young men are asked to strap on a bomb and go kill some people, they earnestly believe they will be rewarded by Allah. Muslims all around the perimeters of the Islamic world are fighting their neighbors – pagan animists and Christians in Africa, Hindus in India, Communists and Buddhist Chinese in China and Southeast Asia, and Christians and Jews in scores of other countries.

According to Open Doors' World Watch Persecution Index (2012), of the top 50 countries that aggressively persecute Christians, 39 of them are Islamic. A lack of Islamic education results in ignorance, which stifles opportunity to advance, thus resulting in high unemployment rates. We also have to consider many of the Muslim leaders take attention away from themselves when they engage in wars with their neighbors. They believe that this sort of friction has the benefit of leading to further dominance of Islam around the world, which moves some of them closer to their goal of a world-wide caliphate that will eventually rule every country on earth.

ISLAMIC LEADERSHIP (?):

So who speaks for Islam regarding Muslim terror attacks and persecutions of people of other religions? It all depends on whom you ask. Many learned Muslims, for instance, are split on the issue of terrorism. This is due to the nature of authority in Islam. The religion has no central authority other than the Qur'an, which sometimes is at odds with itself on some issues, and is contradicted by Hadiths, the four Sunni law schools, and the Shi'ites. Yes, they also make decisions based on consensus (*ijma*) and reason (*ijtihad*), but it is easy to understand why there is so much confusion within the House of Islam. There is no supreme Islamic leader who can tell Muslims, and the world, what Islam is and what it isn't. This situation makes for a multiplicity of voices within Islam, all appealing to Qur'anic authority, various hadiths, or some mufti Fatwa, and they all claim to be speaking for true Islam. Here is just one example that furthers the point. When Iran's Ayatollah Khomeini was still alive, this is what he said:

"Islam makes it incumbent on all adult males, provided that they are not disabled or incapacitated, to prepare themselves for the conquest of other countries so that the writ of Islam is obeyed in every country in the world . . . But those who study Islamic Holy War will understand why Islam wants to conquer the whole world. Those who know nothing of Islam pretend that Islam counsels against war. Those who say this are witless. Islam says: Kill all the unbelievers just as they would kill you all! Does this mean that Muslims should just sit back until they are devoured by the unbelievers? Islam says: Kill them (the non-Muslims), put them to the sword and scatter (their armies). Does this mean sitting back until (non-Muslims) overcome us? Islam says: Kill in the service of Allah those who want to kill you! Does this mean that we should surrender to the enemy? Islam says: Whatever good there is exists thanks to the sword and in the shadow of the sword! The sword is the key to paradise, which can be opened only for the Holy Warriors! There are hundreds of other Qur'anic psalms and hadiths urging Muslims to value war and to fight. Does all this mean that Islam is a religion that prevents men from waging war? I spit upon those foolish souls who make such a claim."[4]

The Ayatollah Khomeini was considered at that time as being one of the highest and most exalted of all Islam's leaders, yet in the above passage there is absolutely no mention of love or forgiveness or an attempt to negotiate peace with his enemies. By June 1982, Khomeini's army had recaptured all Iranian land taken by Sadaam Hussein during the Iraqi-Iranian War. Yet, instead of brokering for peace, the war continued until August, 1988, resulting in between 300,000 and 900,000 Iranian military casualties. The war was fought somewhat like World War I in Europe, with long trench warfare, barbed wire fences, machine gun posts, bayonet charges, human wave attacks, (often using young boys), and the use of chemical weapons.

Khomeini also remarked, "What is the good of us (i.e., the mullahs) asking for the hand of a thief to be severed or an adulterer to be stoned to death when all we can do is recommend such punishments, having no power to implement them? [5] He was saying that democracy does not work, because the Qur'an presents an absolute law of Allah, which must be executed by the mullahs. This means that a government ruled by Islamic law has no place in it for representative government. In other words, you cannot interpret God's law by voting or public opinion.

Khomeini died in 1989, not long after the war ended, but not before issuing his famous fatwa to kill Salman Rushdie, the author who wrote, *The Satanic Verses.* This worldwide attempt to kill Rushdie without an opportunity to defend himself was unprecedented in Islamic Law. When Khomeini was pressed to answer what he would do if Rushdie repented, he answered: *"Even if Salman Rushdie repents and becomes the most pious man of all time, it is incumbent on every Muslim to employ everything he has got, his life and wealth, to send him to hell!"*[6]

The Ayatollah Khomeini is now dead, but I am glad to report that Rushdie still lives, even though two Japanese publishers were murdered for translating his book into Japanese. As a Muslim himself, Rushdie does have some regrets for the firestorm he created so many years ago, but his courage to speak out has been well noted by the world.

HOW TAQIYYA WORKS:

Further exacerbating the conflict between Islam and the West is the concept of *"taqiyya,"* which means: "Concealing, precaution, guarding." It is used to disguise a Muslim's beliefs, feelings, convictions, opinions or strategies. According to the Middle Eastern Quarterly (Winter 2010), the subject of *taqiyya* is permissible in Islam according to Shari'a law, which allows Muslims to lie and use deception on non-believers. At one time *taqiyya* was used to protect Muslims during times of persecution, but that is no longer the case. David Pryce-Jones states, "Lying and cheating in the Arab world is not really a moral matter but a method of safeguarding honor and status, avoiding shame, and at all times exploiting possibilities, for those with the wits for it, deftly and expeditiously to convert shame into honor on their own account and vice versa for their opponents. If honor so demands, lies and cheating may become absolute imperatives." [7] Pryce-Jones goes on to say, "No dishonor attaches to such primary transactions as selling short weight, deceiving anyone about quality, quantity or kinds of goods, cheating at gambling, and bearing false witness. The doer of these things is merely quicker off the mark than the next fellow; owing him nothing, he is not to be blamed for taking what he can." [8]

Muslims are allowed to lie to unbelievers (Christians and Jews) in order to defeat them. Using *Taqiyya* – saying something that is not true, and applying *kitman* – lying by omission, are two Muslim tools that have been used with great success. [9] Deceit among individuals in Islam is one thing, but how can we trust Islamic politicians when they are supposed to be negotiating in trust on a subject like nuclear bombs? Clearly the West needs to address this issue as part of an overall strategy when dealing with Middle Eastern governments. Even scarier is the thought that our government may not know about *taqiyya or kitman!*

FOOD INSECURITIES:

Meanwhile, Islamic countries have become food insecure, and have to import much of their wheat from other countries. Egypt, for instance, imports about 50% of its wheat, and a good percentage of its people's food calories come from abroad. In 2009, Egypt imported $55 billion worth of goods, but only exported $29 billion in goods. In that same year the trade gap was partially covered by $15 billion in tourist revenues and about $8 billion of remittances from Egyptians working abroad. Since the "Arab Spring," tourist revenues have nose-dived leaving the country in desperate financial shape. When families have to pay such a high percentage of their monthly family budget for food, you can easily see how a spike in worldwide finite food prices can have an exaggerated negative effect on Muslim households. Food price increases were the untold story behind the recent "Arab Spring," that resulted from increased standards of living in China and South East Asia, whose people could then afford to pay higher prices than the people in Muslim countries.

Many Islamic countries are ready to implode, being restricted by their ancient customs and beliefs. Most people are very poor, and food shortages abound. Educational standards are miserable compared to the West, and there is a clear lack of qualitative analytical skills in their approach to solving problems. Consequently there is a severe brain drain, and due to their customs regarding women, who represent half the population, they are not being utilized effectively for the common good. All these issues cause foreign investments to be minimal.

As a result, you will find places like Tunisia, Syria, Yemen, Bahrain, and a number of Islamic African countries such as Egypt, Libya, and Sudan, have become unstable, and present a real threat not only to the survival of their own people, but a threat to world civilization as a whole. Is it any wonder that 80% of the world's refugees are Muslims? Anything less than a complete paradigm shift will ever uproot the embedded culture of a people still seeking solutions to modern day problems from a 7th century holy book, and, supplemental Hadiths that are inconsistent and sometimes contradictory to the Qur'an itself. In the meantime, of course, we can only continue to pray for Muslims of good faith who only wish to live righteous lives and be good citizens. Unfortunately, if a Muslim does try to rescind his faith, he is committing apostasy according to the hadiths and all the Sunni and Shi'a law schools, which can yield the death penalty.

CAN ISLAM SURVIVE?:

At some point in the future, Islam is going to have to face facts and realize that there is something clearly wrong with their 7th century religious practices. When 50% of the population are enslaved by their spouses, not allowed to work or get an education, and the Qur'an clearly allows wife beating (Surah 4:34), the religion needs to take pause and do some reflecting. Traditional life in the Muslim world envelops the individual with relentless totality. The maintenance of traditional Muslim society requires the wiping out of female identity, effected by strong societal sanctions, up to and including the threat of violence.

While American society is based on the peoples "inalienable rights," derived from a God who grants such rights to every individual by eternal covenant, so no king, petty official, or family member can impair them, we find Islam's legal system is much closer to the pagan society of ancient Rome than perhaps people realize. In Islam a father is the "governor" of his own family, and appears to be able to do with his family what he wishes. He can love them, hate them, punish them, beat them, and in some cases even kill them to save the family honor. This societal attitude is pervasive here in the 21st century even though Islam's sacred law was written in a barbaric age so alien from modern society.

Islamic culture makes the father a miniature head of state in his own home. The relationship of citizen and sovereignty is reproduced at each level of society-state-tribe-clan-family. Ties of blood are much more important than individual rights.

In Amman, Jordan, I was once told by my Muslim guide: "Me against my brother; my brother and me against our cousin; my brother, cousin and me against our neighbor, and all of us against the stranger." While I was in Amman, a three judge Sharia tribunal had just ended. Three young men had been accused of "honor" killing their sisters for one reason or other. It had to do with shaming the family. Each was found not guilty and released. While we in the West live in a conscious based culture, in the Middle East they practice an honor/shame culture, and the family's reputation must be protected at all cost even if they know that a family member has done wrong.

We can now see more clearly why wife beating is so pervasive in the hyper-masculine Muslim world, and such practices are too embedded in sacred Sharia law to be easily changed. Unfortunately, the blessing of the Qur'an to beat your wife has other implications that go far beyond wife beating. Honor killings, female genital mutilation (in some Islamic countries as high as 90%),[10] consanguineous marriages (above 30% in most Islamic countries, and as high as 55% in Afghanistan), [11] slavery of women and Christians (common in Sudan, Mauritania, and Saudi Arabia), easy divorce for men, and men practicing polygamy with up to four wives or more. Even rape laws are clearly in favor of men in that it has to be physically observed by four witnesses. Add to this mix the temporary marriage contracts I mentioned earlier, and a strong case can be made for reform of women's rights in the Islamic world.

All of these cultural practices are completely different from Judaic and Christian practices, which were enacted some 600 plus years before Islam. The Jews and Christians have never sanctioned wife beating, and the Jewish Talmud mandates "unconditional respect for a wife's person." The notion that a man is an intermediate sovereign "governor" over his own family is inconceivable under Jewish law, as they believe there is only one sovereign, the King of Kings, God Himself. The powers of the earthly sovereign are derived from God, and are limited by God's laws. Every individual stands in a direct covenantal relationship with God.

Here is another interesting comment by David Pryce-Jones from his book, *The Closed Circle:*

"Arabs have been organizing their society for half a century or so of independence, and have made a wretched job of it. A whole range of one-man rulers, whether hereditary monarchs or presidents, have proved unable or unwilling to devise political regimes that allow their people to have any say in their destinies . . . Perhaps Islam and representative democracy are two beautiful but incompatible ideals. Arab states have not built the institutions that are indispensable for dealing with contemporary problems. In Islam, state authority and religious authority have always gone together. Nobody so far has been able to devise some way of separating them and thus laying the foundations of a civil society." [12] With 48 Muslim majority countries, including one struggling democracy, the facts speak for themselves.

Certain powerful groups within Islam have turned the religion into an aggressive force that is bent on creating a world-wide caliphate, and will use almost any means to achieve that end. Islamic leaders also wish to maintain the status quo, which is for them to live in luxury while the rest eke out a marginal living on the edge of survival. More is being spent on bullets than the needs of its citizens. This circumstance, I believe, must change for the good of so many innocent people. At this point in our history, only the power of global intercessory prayer will effect change.

MAIN DIFFERENCES IN THE THREE MONOTHEISTIC RELIGIONS

It is worth summarizing where Islam, Judaism and Christianity, agree, as well as where they disagree. All three religions agree on the following tenets:

- All three religions believe in one single, all powerful, all-knowing God, (whom the Muslims call, Allah,) who created everything in the universe, and beyond.
- They all believe in the Abrahamic faith, that God gave human beings free will to decide how they would live.
- These three Abrahamic religions believe God will eventually redeem the world from all its sins and imperfections, and then create an age of universal peace.
- These religions believe God has worked and continues to work through the events of history, and has commanded His people to do His will.

In order of age, the three sacred books are the Hebrew Bible for the Jews; the New Testament of the Bible for Christians (Christians also consider the Hebrew Old Testament Bible to be sacred, and it is included in the Christian Bible). The Muslims also refer to some of the Old Testament in their Qur'an.

Unfortunately, there are a number of areas where these three religions disagree, but I will only mention three:

- Christians believe in a Trinity whereby God expresses Himself to man in three distinct personalities: God the Father, God the Son (Jesus, who was also fully man), and the Holy Spirit. To the Jews this looks like Christians worship three different gods, and this increases the separation of the two religions. We also find Muslims have the same problem with the Trinity as the Jews do. They believe the Trinity tends to compromise Christianity's belief in only one God.
- To all Christians, Jesus is the Messiah, the Savior, but the Jews believe the Messiah was supposed to be a king who would bring world peace, and create a gathering of all exiled Jews. Because Jesus did not do this, it created another separation between Judaism and Christianity. Muslims believe Jesus was a great prophet similar to Abraham, Moses, and Muhammad.
- Christians believe Jesus is the Son of God, which differs from the Jewish and Islamic belief that God could never become a man. Muslims believe Jesus was a prophet, but not the Son of God.

In summary, as we continue to pray for Muslims all over the world, we can only hope that the guiding light of Jesus Christ will lead them to an acknowledgement of His true way.

ANIMISM

It has been estimated by Gaily Van Rheenen, an expert on animistic religions, that animism accounts for about 40% of the world population if you combine tribal religionists with other major religious groups that practice some form of animism.[13] This form of religion is more pervasive than most people think and it is not necessarily restricted to the developing world. New Agers practice forms of animism, and it has been stated there are more registered witches in France than Catholic priests! It can also be said all major religions have some followers who practice animistic rituals alongside formal activities. This may happen undercover when the formal religion forbids such activities, or it may be incorporated into the formal structure in a process called syncretism.

Animistic forms of religion are also called "folk religions," such as folk Chinese, folk Hindu or folk Islam. What makes them attractive is that they offer people a way to cope with everyday needs, such as finding a job, excelling in school, restoring a relationship, finding a mate, being healed of an illness, protection from evil spirits, or to gain guidance for the future.

ANIMISM EXPLAINED:

The term animism comes from a Latin word, anima, which means "soul" or breath." It is referring to what gives power or life to something. Animism sees the physical world as being controlled by spiritual forces, both personal and impersonal. In this way they perceive objects as having spiritual significance, and events have spiritual causes. As a consequence, if someone gets sick, or has an accident, they believe there is a spiritual cause behind the event that must be considered. Without studying this spiritual component, the cause of the sickness or accident cannot be fully understood and cured.

The spirit world of the animist can include spirits of both men and animals, especially the dead, as well as spirits of angels or demons influencing human activities or even natural phenomenon. As the world has been "flattened" providing us with more access to peoples around the world, we have learned that Animism is not only the religion of wild and savage tribes before contact with civilization, but the background of the religious philosophy of the Hindu, the Buddhist, the Shinto, Confucianism, and the Muslim. It is also at the bottom of all folklore before Christendom in Europe, as well as the mythology of Egypt, Babylonia, Assyria, Greece, Rome and Scandinavia. And in the Americas, before the conquest by Spain and Portugal, we find animism in a highly developed form as the religion of the Aztecs of Mexico and the Incas of Peru.

THE SHAMAN:

I have been introduced to Shamans in a number of places around the world, and I find them all to be fascinating people who can mesmerize locals into believing all types of strange occurrences through the use of concoctions, magic, and rituals. I have met them in Peru in the Sacred Valley; in a village close to Victoria Falls in Zimbabwe; in the Fiji Islands of the South Pacific; in the highlands of the Hmong in Laos; in the Aboriginal lands of northern Australia; in the Maori communities in New Zealand; and the native tribes of Kenya, and central Tanzania. Shamans all believe they are inspired by the gods, and are able to make spiritual journeys to heaven and hell, and to control incarnate spirits. They use their powers in various ways including healing, acting to protect a person from evil spirits, settling disputes, and helping to defeat enemies.

Shamans are thought of as doctors, priests, social workers, and mystics, and use various tools to solve issues including wearing masks as a way to attract a spirit, and sometimes to become the spirit, or to become possessed by it. In places like Siberia, and North and South America, the Shaman believe the cosmos are populated by many nature spirits who live inside such things as trees and animals, or they may be souls of human ancestors. The spirits also vary and can be good or evil, and many Shamans enjoy special relationships with certain spirits to whom they claim to be "married." Often they may use hallucinogenic substances such as magic mushrooms, which tribal people have used for centuries as a way to induce a trancelike state.

Van Rheenen continues: "Some Shamans claim their soul can leave their body and travel to other parts of the cosmos either upwards or downwards to the lowest depths of the earth. They have been around for thousands of years, and claim they have been chosen by spirits, taught by them to enter into a trance, and to fly with one's soul to other worlds in the sky or clamber through dangerous crevasses into the terror of subterranean worlds, being stripped of one's flesh, reduced to a skeleton, and then reassembled and reborn, gaining the power to combat spirits and heal their victims, to kill enemies and save one's own people from disease and starvation." [14] These are features of Shamanic religions that occur in many parts of the world.

Tools used by the Shaman often include using a variety of special rituals and techniques to reach spiritually heightened or inspired states. Ceremonies often include music, with the drum, their most popular instrument for awakening the spirits. The facial mask is often used to attract a spirit and in some cultures enables the Shaman to "become" the spirit, or to become possessed by it.

CONTEMPORARY SHAMANISM:

Today you will find Shamanic ideas generally form only one strand among the doctrines and authority structures of other religious ideologies or practices. In the distant past there were pure Shamanic communities, but today they are scattered, and there is no Shamanic church or priests. In fact there is no order and structure. The Shaman often isolates himself from the other villagers, but in Zimbabwe I found the Shaman was also the king of his village, and he primarily acted as healer, and was busily working on a cure for AIDS, which was rampant in his community. In the highlands of Laos I found the Shaman was also the head of a village tribe of Hmong, and he explained how he was negotiating with the Communist government on how much rice and poultry his village had to supply to pay their taxes. He had two wives, and often cured his villagers in exchange for a pig or a goat as payment. The Shaman appeared to have an endless supply of various concoctions to cure the many health issues of his villagers.

FINDING COMMON GROUND:

Upon further investigation it is found Christianity and Animism have a number of elements in common, that can create an opportunity for finding common ground in the way the two groups connect with each other. First, both animists and Christians believe in the existence and influence of the supernatural, and they would agree that they stand in opposition to naturalistic thinking that says only matter exists. Both agree that while man may plant the seeds and cultivate the soil, there is a supernatural process which causes the growth of the seed. Both religions also believe in consequences for offending the supernatural. To the animist they would include sickness, accidents, or financial ruin, whereas a Christian's conscience would believe he has put distance between himself and God until the sin is rectified. You will also find the two groups have hope that there is a way by which they can escape the consequences of their transgressions, and finally animists also believe in some type of Supreme Being who stands above the spirits and their powers.

Animism is a practical form of religion that concerns itself with solving real everyday problems people face, whereas major religions concern themselves with ultimate issues of sin and salvation. Animism is not a religion that concerns itself with sin, but rather is more concerned in offending local spirits. As a result Animists live in constant fear that the spirits will exact some type of revenge in the form of illness, calamity, or strife in their lives. This is clearly a religion of darkness and superstition, and many animists live lives today where they expect something of a negative nature to happen to them at any time. This mental burden can weigh heavily on their lives, and can cause much sorrow and sadness in their darkness, as opposed to the joy and happiness experienced in the light of the Christian walk.

CHAPTER EIGHT

MAN'S WAR AGAINST GOD

In previous chapters we discussed man's search for meaning and spiritual fulfillment going back to the dawn of history. Man has devolved from having a loving, personal relationship with God, the creator of all things, as mentioned in the First book of the Bible, to a distancing of that relationship as man defied God and went his own way. Man has not been seeking God as much as God has been seeking man. Modern archeologists now admit that religions in every case have degenerated from primitive monotheism into pantheism, polytheism, and from there to either animism or occultism or even atheism, and our examination of other religions has demonstrated that fact. Evolutionist, whom we will discuss in a moment, believe just the opposite happened.

THREE CHANCES WASTED:

God had already given man three chances to get his life right with God. First, God provided Adam, the first man, a wonderful opportunity to live in a sinless world where the lion lay down with the lamb. Unfortunately, Adam disobeyed God, and sin entered the world (Genesis 1 – 3). Later, man decayed into debauchery with sin becoming pervasive, and God decided to create a great flood and destroy all of mankind (Genesis 6: 9-22). God said, "My spirit will not contend with man forever, for he is mortal, his days will be a hundred and twenty years." (Genesis 6:3). Meanwhile, God instructed a righteous man, Noah, to build a great ark, and supply it with two of every kind of animals. However, when it was time to set sail, only he, his family, and the animals, were on board, and the rest of mankind perished in the flood. Later God instructed Moses to climb Mount Sinai and bring down two tablets containing the Ten Commandments instructing the people how to live a righteous life (Exodus 20:1-17). The people later violated these commandments, thus causing the wrath of God. In many other parts of the Old Testament you will find it replete with stories of how man disobeyed God, and consequently paid the penalty.

Then, about 2,000 years ago, God gave everyone who has lived and died since, the invitation to accept the Lord Jesus Christ as Lord and Savior. God did this to lay the foundation and the correct way that man should live his life in order to earn eternal salvation. So, if you are a non-believer, this is <u>Your Last Chance to Get it Right!</u> Since then numerous people have accepted this divine opportunity, but many others have not. Jesus was born a Jew, and the Bible tells us some 2,000 years before Jesus arrived on earth, Abraham, the founder of the Jewish people, entered into a special covenant with God (Genesis 15), and Jews have been God's chosen people ever since. The Jews, up until the coming of Jesus, were the only people on earth who worshipped a monotheistic God. All the rest worshipped multiple gods or none at all.

Thanks to the teachings of Jesus, billions of people have accepted Him as their Lord and Savior over these many years since his resurrection, and have been promised an eternal life with Him after they leave this mortal existence. You will find more than two billion Christians populate the earth today, but unfortunately billions of others have traveled down a different road leading to a spiritual disconnect from the one true God. Man's search for meaning and spiritual fulfillment has created thousands of religions across the world today, and the large competing religions to Christianity such as Islam, Hindu, Buddhism Taoism etc., have created mass confusion leading to darkness instead of the light of Christ.

The battle for men's souls has continued down through the centuries, but it reached a high note after the age of reason and enlightenment periods. The invention of the scientific method, and the acceleration of knowledge over the last 400 years, caused man to think he now had all the answers, and God played only a minor role in his life.

DEADLY IDEAS:

Victor Hugo once said, "One resists the invasion of armies. One does not resist the invasion of ideas." And it was Josef Stalin who once said: "Ideas are more powerful than guns. We would not let our enemies have guns, why should we let them have ideas?" The hubris and ego of man knows no bounds, and the power of just one man's thinking can change the world, often for the worse. Men like Darwin, Marx, Neitchze, are all complicit in the changing of man's thinking that led to the blood bath in Europe and other places in the 20th century. Evil men, such as: Talaat Pasha, Enver Pasha, and Djmel Pasha (Turkey), Lenin and Stalin (Russia), Hitler (Germany), Mao Zedong and Chiang Kai-shek (China), Tojo Hideki (Japan),

Pol Pot (Cambodia), Yahya Khan (Pakistan), and Josip Tito (Yugoslavia), were responsible for mega murders that included either democide (death by government), genocide, or both. Other genocides of a lesser scale committed in the 20th century included: Mexico (1900 – 1920), North Korea (1948 -), Vietnam (1945 – 1987), Poland (1945-1948), Bosnia (1993), and a plane crash that killed both the president of Rwanda and the president of Burundi, helped to set off the machete slaying genocide in Rwanda between the Hutsi and Tutsi resulting in over a million violent deaths (1994).

The above events were caused by evil leaders who were either communists or fascists, acting in ways contrary to God's plan for mankind. Some of these men are responsible for the deaths of millions of people, and in hindsight you have to ask yourself for what? Did they accomplish anything in their zest for power and fame? The evidence is damning, they did not, yet they changed forever countless millions of lives either through death or through the dislocation of families. These men were disconnected from their own spiritual natures. According to John Liffiton, an English professor at Arizona State University, some 50 smaller genocides have been committed since the end of World War II, and we have every reason to believe, based on historical evidence, genocide will happened again in the future.

It is easy to discuss these terrible events in the abstract, but when you get into the mind of just one person who actually lived the experience, only then is it possible to comprehend the true horror of what millions of people experienced. I actually had such an opportunity when I listened to a talk in Krakow, Poland, where a 92 year old survivor of Auschwitz told us a horrifying, eye-witness account of what it was like during the four-years he was incarcerated by the Nazis. The torture, medical experimentations, and systematic killing of millions of humans went on seven-days a week with rarely an interruption, as the godless Nazi regime went about exterminating anyone considered inferior to themselves. Those considered "inferior" included gypsies, homosexuals, Slavs, and particularly Jewish men, women and their children. A quote, generally attributed to Josef Stalin stated: "One man's death is a tragedy, but the death of a million is just a statistic."

In his book, *Death by Government,* author, R.J. Rummel has a lot to say about democide, a phrase he coined to mean the killing of people by government; similar to the domestic crime of murder by individuals, using the word *murder* as an appropriate label for those regimes that commit democide. He said, "20th century mega murderers, those killings in cold blood, aside from warfare, one million or more men, women and children, have wiped out 151 million people, almost four times the approximate 38,500,000 battle dead from all this century's international and civil wars up to 1987. The fifteen top mega murderers include: USSR, China (includes: PRC, KMT and Mao Soviets period), Germany, Japan, Cambodia, Turkey, Vietnam, Poland, Pakistan, Yugoslavia (Tito), North Korea, Mexico, and Russia (1900 – 1917). The most absolute powers, namely, communist USSR, China, and preceding Mao guerillas, the Khmer Rouge, Cambodia, Vietnam, Yugoslavia, and fascist Germany, account for 128 million of them, or 84%."
[1] Rummel goes on to provide a list of the centuries bloodiest megamurderers:

Dictator	Ideology	Country	Years	Murdered (000)a
Joseph Stalin	C	USSR	1929-53	42,672[b]
Mao Tse-tung	C	China	1923-76	37,828[c]
Adolf Hitler	F	Germany	1933-45	20,946
Chiang Kai-shek	M/F	China	1921-48	10,214[d]
Vladimir Lenin	C	USSR	1917-24	4,017[e]
Tojo Hideki	M/F	Japan	1941-45	3,990[f]
Pol Pot	C	Cambodia	1968-87	2,397[c]
Yahya Khan	M	Pakistan	1971	1,500
Josip Broz Tito	C	Yugoslavia	1941-87	1,172[c]

Key: C = Communist; F = Fascist; M/F = Militarist/Fascist; M= Militarist

a These are the most probable estimates from a low to a high range. Estimates are from or based on Rummel 1990, 1991, 1992 and Statistics of Democide

b Citizens only Includes his guerilla period

c Includes his warlord period

d Includes one-third the democide for the NEP period 1923- 1928

e Estimated as one-half the 1937-45 democide in China plus the World War II democide

Rummel further points out that in total during the first 80 years of the 20th century, almost 170 million men, women, and children have been shot, beaten, tortured, knifed, burned, starved, frozen, crushed, or worked to deaf; buried alive, drowned, hung, bombed, or killed in a myriad of ways governments have inflicted death on unarmed, helpless citizens and foreigners. The dead could conceivably be 360 million people. It is as though our species has been devastated by a modern Black Plague. And indeed it has, but a plague of Power, not germs.

Why does man continue to attempt to enslave his fellow man? Is total power over the common man a worthwhile endeavor? Two great men put power into perspective when they said:

Power gradually extirpates for the mind every humane and gentle virtue – Edmund Burke

Power tends to corrupt; absolute power corrupts absolutely – Lord Acton

Even today, according to Freedomhouse.org, only 40% of the world's people can call themselves free, notwithstanding the horrors brought about during the 20th century by atheists who had disavowed God. Here are their figures:

40% Free - 2,826,850,000
25% Partly Free - 1,822,000,000*
35% Not Free - 2,467,900,000

*Partly free means states that have many of the characteristics of a free state, but also have many damaging elements, such as political corruption and discrimination against minorities. Military and /or foreign elements often influence the political system, and there may not be an independent judiciary. Partly free states have some degree of protection for civil liberties, but some liberties are restricted.

Today, we are still living with the legacies of men who have since passed away, with their many layers of errors built on the faulty foundation of Evolutionism. Humanism is the natural result, and it is also true that atheism is the twin brother of humanism. The average man on the street knows or cares very little about the errors of evolutionary theory, and yet it constantly influences his life. Adultery, divorce, pornography, homosexuality and the destruction of the nuclear family are all weeds grown from Satan's big lie about the universe. Today we are adopting animalism in human practice, promiscuity, vandalism, and hedonism. Even the Holocaust is being explained by evolutionary theory. Hitler's extermination of the Jews grew out of his desire to speed up the evolutionary process, and many now claim the Holocaust never happened! Dietrich Bonhoeffer, the great German pastor who was executed by Hitler, once said: "Silence in the face of evil is itself evil. God will not hold us guiltless. Not to speak is to speak. Not to act is to act."

When we look carefully at the destruction and carnage of the evolutionary dogma, it is unfathomable how its influence has pervaded the thinking of mankind. Many wonder as to how Darwinism became so widespread and anti-Christian when it was developed by an apostate divinity student (Darwin), a lawyer (Lyell), an agriculturist (Hutton), a journalist (Chambers), and a group of other non-scientists. But as we will see later, the idea of evolution did not begin with Darwin as it has been basic in ancient and modern ethnic religions, and in all forms of pantheism.

THE PIVOTAL MOMENT:

Although an anti-God evolutionary theory has been around for centuries, in modern times evolutionary theory came to the forefront of man's thinking when Charles Darwin, an Englishman, wrote and published his book, *The Origin of Species,* in 1859. His hypothesis was that the origin and development of all things came about by natural properties and processes in a closed universe, one with no involvement by any external supernatural creator, i.e. God. In other words, life came about gradually by evolutionary changes over billions of years by chance mutations, and natural selection, and Almighty God had nothing to do with it. This view of the creator of life itself is diametrically opposite to the Christian world-view that the whole universe, and everything in it, including man, was created by God.

The impact of evolutionary thinking, interestingly enough, has been felt more in the social sciences and humanities based on a belief that evolutionary theory has been "proven" by the natural sciences. The facts, however, are much different. Natural sciences are often thought of in an evolutionary framework although no one has ever observed real evolution taking place, not even in the life sciences, let alone earth or physical sciences. We all know, thanks to the invention of the Scientific Method in the 17th century that true science has to be observable, measurable, and repeatable. Even if evolutionary theory were true, it is far too slow for man to observe and measure. It is therefore outside the scope of genuine science, and evolutionary theory has certainly never been "proved" by science. Nonetheless, men like Huxley, Dobzhansky and Mayr have been able to dominate evolutionary thought through at least beyond the mid 20th century, and although they have all passed into history, their neo-Darwinism thoughts remain pervasive.

Many scientists assume evolutionary theory, and try very hard to interpret their data from an evolutionary point of view, which is especially true in the biological sciences. Since Darwin, the mantra has been argued that, "Nothing in biology makes sense except in the light of evolution." How many times over the years have we heard: "We know evolution is true, even though we don't know how it works, and have never seen it happen."

SOCIAL DARWINISM:

No sooner had Darwin published his *Origin of Species,* history tells us industrialists in England, and later in America, used the principles in the book to great effect. Men like John D. Rockefeller and Andrew Carnegie began using the concept and terms of "struggle for existence," followed by "natural selection" and "survival of the fittest," to justify their laissez-faire form of capitalism, which heartlessly exploited labor, and created monopolistic practices to gain all the profits, power and glory they could lay their hands on legally. This system became known as "social Darwinism," and it became significant in the business, industrial and political practices in both Europe and America for almost a century.

Although these trade practices proved to be an embarrassment to evolutionists in that day, they claimed in response that evolutionism was being misunderstood. If this is true, then the leading evolutionists of the day also misunderstood evolution. In some ways Darwinism was developed to justify the socio-economic military beliefs and practices prevalent at that time, and it happened in an age of expansion and technological progress in the western nations. Darwin was deeply committed to the theories of Thomas Malthus (he was the man in Chapter

One who worried about population increases outstripping the available food supply). He argued any proposed measures to improve the lot of the laboring classes would only encourage them to reproduce more and thus make the struggle for existence more severe than ever. Since populations always seem to grow faster than the food supply, there would always be too many people unless growth could somehow be discouraged. This thinking fit right into Darwin's "struggle for existence" in nature, with animals reproducing faster than the food supply, which resulted in the reign of tooth and claw, and only the strongest surviving.

All of this thinking, of course, was diametrically opposite to what God told man when he commanded him to go forth and multiply. John D. Rockefeller is famous for stating: "This is not an evil tendency in business. It is merely the working out of a law of nature and a law of God." [2]

Even Andrew Carnegie, a Scottish immigrant, who went on to become one of the richest men in America, and who was ruthless and heartless towards labor in his own day, later became a great philanthropist, stated:

"I remember that light came in like a flood and all was clear. Not only had I got rid of theology and the supernatural, but I had found the truth of evolution."[3]

THE BITTER FRUITS OF SOCIAL DARWINISM:

This idea that a loving, wise and powerful God would use evolution with its "struggle for existence" and "survival of the fittest," as His method of creation is not only absurd, but goes against the principles of American democracy as expressed in the Declaration of Independence and the Bill of Rights, and is directly in conflict with biblical Christianity.

Evolution is the cruelest and most wasteful method of creation that could ever be devised, not to mention it is scientifically invalid, and calls God Almighty a liar! The idea of billions of animals suffering and dying in the evolutionist quest for "progress" from an amoeba to man is a direct assault on God himself who most certainly had the capability of creating each organ complete with its own perfectly designed structure, for its own unique purpose right from the very beginning of creation.

Is it any wonder, therefore, in view of the excesses of the past, this old form of social Darwinism has been replaced by evolutionism from the left (socialism, communism), instead of freedom and rights of the individual?

RACISM:

We know that racism started long before Darwin was born, but in his lifetime he gave racism a form of scientific respectability, which somehow justified the prevailing attitudes of his day. In Darwin's later book, *The Descent of Man,* he wrote:

"At some future period, not very distant as measured by centuries, the civilized races of man will almost certainly exterminate and replace throughout the world the savage races. At the same time the anthropomorphous apes . . . will no doubt be exterminated. The break between man and his nearest allies will then be wider, for it will intervene between man in a more civilized state, as we may hope, than the Caucasian, and some ape as low as a baboon, instead of as at present between the Negro or Australian Aborigine, and the gorilla."

In his theory, Darwin stated that the variety of races of man were at different evolutionary distances from the apes, and his charts showed the Negroes at the bottom, and the Caucasians at the top. This concept was prevalent among evolutionary scientists of his day, causing one to think that they were all racists!

With racism gaining emphasis in the growing human sciences, it is understandable in retrospect in explaining how the concept of Aryan supremacy would come to the forefront of German thinking. This led to a form of institutional racism in Germany in the 1930s, and later it would take up its roots in South Africa with apartheid, that lasted until 1994. Irrespective of the source of these beliefs, it was certainly not the Bible, which clearly states that God, "From one man made every nation of men, that they should inhabit the whole earth." (Acts 17:26). Also, in Malachi 2:10, it says, "Have we not all one Father?"

Over the years, evolutionists have deliberately tried to distort biblical passages to serve their purpose, by attempting to make the Bible racist. One example is the Hamitic curse, which has been used to justify racism even though the biblical text does not curse Ham, and makes no mention of the color of one's skin. In fact, it is clearly opposed to any form of racism. Neither the concept of "race" nor the word itself is ever found in the Bible. Interestingly, it should be pointed out that modern day evolutionists now agree with the biblical doctrine of one race for all mankind, although they still do not agree with the biblical doctrine of creation.

THE WHITE MAN'S BURDEN:

Over the last 150 years or so, we have witnessed social Darwinism in action in the business practice struggles between the individual man and big business. Due to improvements in transportation, this struggle was easily transferred abroad becoming a form of militaristic nationalism. We have determined that when racism is spread beyond national boundaries, it can easily become imperialism, as we read of the European global expansion. Each of these concepts: racism, militarism and imperialism have been around for a very long time, but it was the 19th century evolutionists that provided their idea of a scientific explanation, and a blind justification, for their actions.

In her 1959 book, Gertrude Himmelfarb states:

"Social Darwinism has often been misunderstood in this sense: as a philosophy, exalting competition, power and violence over convention, ethics and religion. Thus it has become a portmanteau of nationalism, imperialism, militarism, and dictatorship, of the cults of the hero, the superman, and the master race."[4]

Support for imperialism and social Darwinism, was given a strong boost when Otto Von Bismarck, the first chancellor of Germany, defeated France in 1870. Evolutionary thinking also contributed to the "white man's burden," when it was fueled by the British thinking that the Anglo Saxon was superior to all other races. This led to the expansion of the British Empire.

The popularity of Darwin's books led to many other language translations, and unduly influenced the last 40 plus years leading up to the First World War when homicidal leaders were thirsting for blood. Consequently, when we dig deeper into the details, we find that in every European country during this time period, there were various political parties and powerful people making great demands to alter the status quo. Some wanted a free hand in controlling peoples in Africa and Central America; others demanded ruthless competition, and yet others called for huge financial outlays in arms build-up. The racist attitudes of the time also called for the ousting of aliens, which led later to the Turkish genocide of the Armenians. Yes, Darwin's theories were on full display!

After the Franco-Prussian War, we find Darwinism being applied consistently in Germany, leading up to World War I. This is when Friedrich Nietzsche comes into the picture. A brilliant German philosopher, Nietzsche, is well remembered for his *"God is Dead"* statement, based on his belief that Darwin had it right, but had disagreed with Darwin on how it would be achieved through "random selection." Rather, Nietzsche thought it could be achieved faster and more efficiently through warfare and eugenics, with merciless extinction of inferior peoples and races! Although Nietzsche later went insane, his beliefs had a powerful impact on German leaders, and his writing made a significant contribution towards German militarism and the myth of Teutonic racial supremacy.

In Germany, Ernest Haeckel provided a major advancement to German thinking on the subject of evolutionary theory by introducing his famous sketches that showed the embryos of all mammals, including man, were basically the same for sometime after conception. He later had to admit that he had fabricated his sketches, but by then much damage had been done that provided further legitimacy to social Darwinism.

Many historians have since come to realize that the works of Darwin, Nietzsche and Haeckel, have provided the impetus for the great arms build-up that led to the First World War of the 20th century.

WORLD WAR I:

There is no need to catalogue the horrors here of the history of World War I, which resulted in more than 22 million casualties,[5] as they can readily be found in many good textbooks on the subject. My interest here is pointing out that racist attitudes and ethnic superiority based on an anti-God form of social Darwinism, played a leading part in causing the militaristic and aggressive attitudes of the European leaders that created the war. Numerous countries, not only in Europe, but many others around the world, were dragged into this blood-bath, and God was quietly taken off the radar screen.

2OTH CENTURY'S FIRST GENOCIDE:

Traveling around Turkey and seeing some of the battle sites of World War I, I came to realize there is one side note of the war, which does not get much attention these days. It was the witnessing of the first act of genocide in the 20th century. The premeditated calculation to destroy a whole ethnic group of people based on a combination of racial, ethnic and religious differences overwhelms the senses. It happened when the Young Turks, who had taken over the government of the Ottomans in Turkey, wanted a "pure" ethnically cleansed country based on the laws of Islam, and where a pan-Turkish movement would reunite all Turkish people.

In Turkey at that time there were a significant number of large minority groups, including Bulgarians, Greeks, and Armenians. Due to the fact the Turks had lost the war in the Balkans against

Bulgaria, most Bulgarians in Turkey found themselves safe as Bulgarians. The Greeks living in Turkey were also relatively safe because the Turks did not want to create a war with Greece. The Armenians, on the other hand, were not safe, and very vulnerable because they had "no big brother" to protect their interests. To this day, the Turkish government has still not apologized for the rape, torture and extermination of about one and a half million Armenian men, women and children. Here are the words of the Minister of the Interior of Turkey, Talaat, as discovered in a telegram by British forces:

"It has previously been communicated that the government by the order of the Assembly (Jemiet), has decided to exterminate entirely all the Armenians living in Turkey. Those who oppose this order can no longer function as part of the government. Without regard to women, children and invalids, however tragic may be the means of transportation, an end must be put to their existence."[6]

The government orders were carried out with impunity, and whether an Armenian was a patriotic Turkish front-line soldier or a pregnant woman, a famous professor or high priest, important business person or an ardent patriot, it made no difference. All one and a half million were killed, along with many Christians, Greeks, and other ethnic groups creating a blood bath that remains in the minds and hearts of the descendents of these persecuted peoples to this very day.

How did the Turkish government justify this horrendous act? The Turks had massacred large numbers of Armenians in the past, as in the case of Sultan Abdul Hamid, who had some 300,000 Armenians killed between 1894 and 1896. But there was nothing in history to explain how men like Talaat Pasha,

Enver Pasha, and Djemal Pasha, could justify their actions to systematically kill, without conscience, such a huge number of human beings. The answer to why, is linked to the fact that they were all atheists, who had taken over the government of Turkey, and were obsessed with the idea of "cleansing" all other ethnic minority groups from the country. They used the Islamic faith as a tool to incite the masses against the non-believing minority groups based on recreating the glory days of the Ottoman Empire. They considered the Turk superior to all others, and yearned for a return of the Golden Age of the classic Turk, strong, proud, nationalistic, with all ethnic Turks living in one great nation. They glorified Turkism much like the Nazi would later glorify the Aryan race. They glorified themselves rather than God, and all three of them were killed or assassinated by no later than 1922, just four years after the tragic world war came to an end.

Of interest is the fact that successive Turkish governments, including the current one, continue to deny the Armenian holocaust ever took place. Turkey is aided by the silence of many nations whose archives clearly document the genocide event, yet they do nothing to rectify the wrong. One of those nations is the United States, who did make an attempt to bring the issue to light, which caused the Turkish ambassador in Washington to vacate his office. Nothing transpired.

THE NAZI REIGN OF TERROR:

It is unimaginable to think that less than 20 years after the end of World War I there would be another great European war that resulted in an incredible number of deaths and injuries estimated at well over 80 million.[7] Those figures do not take into consideration the ruination and displacement of millions of other families. Even in the abstract it is hard for any sane person to understand such carnage. It is so incomprehensible, yet in reality it actually happened.

History is filled with the horrors of the concentration death camps I mentioned earlier. However, the six million Jewish death figures generally ignore the vast number of others killed by Nazi extermination. Taking into consideration the well documented Nazi genocide of Jews, Slavs, Serbs, Czechs, Ukrainians, Frenchmen, Italians, Gypsies, homosexuals, and others, we also have to account for the killing of hostages, deaths by forced labor, starvation, euthanasia, exposure, medical experiments, terror bombings, religious reasons, and reprisal raids that made the death figures much higher. Totals range between 15 million to over 31 million deaths, with a figure of 21 million being a good consensus. It has also been estimated more than a million children under the age of eighteen were also exterminated. [8]

All the documentation of this horrible war demonstrate the Nazis were racists of the worst kind, not because they thought about such matters, but because they acted on them with impunity. They believed absolutely in the supremacy of the Aryan race, and they were at the top of racial evolution. To reinforce this point, here is an extract from the SS main office communiqué that was distributed to all SS units:

"The sub-human, this apparently fully equal creation of nature, when seen from the biological viewpoint, with hands, feet and a sort of brain, with eyes and a mouth, nevertheless is quite a different, a dreadful creature, is only an imitation of man with man-resembling features, but inferior to any other animal as regards intellect and soul. In its interior, this being is a cruel chaos of wild, unrestricted passions, with a nameless will to destruction, with a most primitive lust, and of unmasked depravity. For not everything is alike that has a human face."[9]

Among the fog and blood of war, it appears the Nazi thought all inferior races were like a cancerous body part that must be removed to save the body. All the Nazi doctors agreed to this policy despite their pledge to the Hippocratic Oath, and this is how they justified the horrors committed on so many "inferior" beings.

At the top of the Nazi pinnacle of power stood one man, Adolf Hitler, who was a known racist, anti-Semite, and a lover of the occult. Although he remained a formal member of the Catholic Church, his biographer, Albert Speers, opined: "He had no real attachment to it." The *Encyclopedia Britannica* states, "Hitler believed Christianity and Nazism were incompatible, and he intended to replace Christianity with a form of warrior paganism after the war."

Alan Bullock, the Hitler biographer who wrote, *Hitler, a Study in Tyranny,* also stated that Hitler: "was a rationalist and a materialist, who saw Christianity as a religion 'fit for slaves,' and against the natural law of selection and survival of the fittest. He was a Social Darwinist through and through. Although Hitler showed some respect for the Catholic Church, he later became hostile to its teachings."

Hitler was not a well educated man, but did possess effective oratory and leadership skills. He put these skills to good use to climb to the top of the government ladder. During his days in power, he placed his country on a war footing that would not end until he committed suicide in a Berlin bunker at the age of 56. All the intellectual and cultural heritage of the German people, was for one brief moment in time, subjected to the lowest form of barbarianism. I believe that the people lost touch with God Almighty, and placed their trust in one ordinary man instead. This should be a lesson for us all. Jesus once said, "Give unto Caesar what is Caesar's, and give unto God what is God's." One way to interpret this, is that whenever there is a conflict between man's laws and God's laws, then we must follow God's law even if it means imprisonment. Man's laws may say that it is OK to kill a fetus in its mother's womb, but God says this is wrong: Psalm 139: 13-16.

THE COMMUNIST INFECTION:

Another pernicious idea stemming from the evolutionary principles of Social Darwinism that has had a terrible destructive effect on the lives of millions of people, is the system of Communism devised by Karl Marx. Marx was a German who believed in the idea of a worker's paradise where everyone would contribute to the common good, and be treated equally with all other men. There would be no place for God in this new system for man, and his two famous books, *The Communist Manifesto,* and *Das Kapital,* played well to the ranks of the oppressed and downtrodden. Marx was a contemporary of Charles Darwin, and was very impressed with Darwin's work. He even asked Darwin to provide a foreword for his book, which Darwin declined to do. Marx was an atheist who spent most of his life pursuing his dream of dramatically changing society. Meanwhile, his wife and children often went without food, and died at an early age.

In 1917, the first major effect of communist principles was brought to the forefront of modern thinking when the Bolsheviks overran the 300 year reign of the Romanovs in Russia, and installed an atheistic, communist government under the leadership of Lenin. To give you an idea of Lenin's thinking I simply mention the Russian famine on the Volga in 1891-92. Lenin opposed sending food aid arguing famine would radicalize the masses. He is quoted as saying:

"Psychologically, this talk of feeding the starving is nothing but an expression of the saccharine-sweet sentimentality so characteristic of our intelligentsia." [10]

Lenin suddenly died in 1924, and one of the worst despots of the 20th century, Josef Stalin, took command of the Russian Empire. His cruelty towards his own people knew no bounds, and it has been estimated some 61 million people were murdered in the Soviet Gulag State up until his death in 1953.

According to Ronald Higley's book, *Joseph Stalin, Man and Legend*, Stalin killed virtually everyone who had furthered his rise to power. Among his victims were his contemporary Soviet biographers, murdered as part of a campaign to destroy the truth and to substitute a glossy pseudo-biography, *The Stalin Legend.* He attempted to be worshipped like a god, and had the ability to even exploit his own colossal blunders. He established a murder by quota system where his generals were ordered to kill a certain number of people in a given area. Solzhenitsyn makes this comment about the quotas during the Great Terror of 1936 -1938:

"The real law underlying the arrests of those years was the assignment of quotas, the norms set, and the planned allocations of an established number of murders. Every city, every district, every military unit was assigned a specific quota of arrests to be carried out by a stipulated time. From then on, everything else depended on the ingenuity of the Security operations personnel. [11] Finding "enemies of the people," however, was an acute problem for the local NKVD (The People's Commissariat for Internal Affairs), and so they had to kill people at random for committing no crimes at all in order to fill their quotas.

In a famous interview in 1931, Lady Astor met Stalin and asked him point blank: "How long will you keep killing people?" Stalin answered: "The process will continue on as long as is necessary to establish a communist society." Ronald Higley went on to say Stalin made no distinction between enemy combatants and enemies of the state, versus ordinary civilians. Of the 61 million people who lost their lives under his leadership, about 54 million were civilians: old and young, healthy and sick; men, women and little children; landowners and peasants alike; Kulaks, Kalmyks, Volga Germans, and anyone from a political faction that defied him. Neither Stalin's evil nor his achievements can be buried with his bones.

From 1917 until 1991, the Russian government outlawed God, and tried to turn the Union of Soviet Socialist Republics into a man-made worker's paradise. Their "guns and butter" economy, and their attempt to spread communism around the world during the Cold War, was finally exposed for what it was, a great lie! Soon the government crumbled, and the Russian people gained back much of their lost freedom, including the right to worship God in a church of their choice.

The results of living 75 years without God has taken a tremendous toll on the psyche of the Russian people, and high alcoholism rates, coupled with high abortion and divorce rates, have left many Russians with little hope for the future. The population is not re-producing itself, and has been reduced to less than 140 million (this is also partly due to the result of the break-up of the U.S.S.R. in 1991). This is a serious problem considering it is by far the largest country in the world by landmass. A people without Almighty God in their daily lives to keep them connected to their own consciences, to guide them based on the Golden Rule in doing what is right by their fellow man, is doomed to a bad ending.

This hopeless state of affairs was made abundantly clear to me as I traveled throughout Russia on two occasions, where I observed the general despondency of the people in sharp contrast to the upbeat attitudes of the average American. We can only pray future Russian leadership will foster an atmosphere of open, transparent government, based on principles of freedom, with encouragement for the people to get back to church, and make Christ the center of their lives.

MAO AND THE CHINESE CATASTROPHE:

The largest population on earth was infected with communism under the leadership of Mao Zedong, who, until his death in 1976, caused the deaths of millions of his own people. Starting with the Long March, where one in ten of his people actually survived, he began the *Great Leap Forward* in 1959 to transfer China into a modern economy by concentrating on the production of steel with less emphasis on food production. In 1959 grain production dropped 15%, with another 10% drop in 1960, and flat thereafter. Consequently, some 45 million Chinese died of starvation according to professor Frank Dikotter. In his book he quotes Mao from a 1959 meeting in a Shanghai hotel when Mao said: "When there is not enough food to eat, people starve to death. It is better to let half the people die so that the other half can eat their fill." [12] Again, during the Cultural Revolution (1966 – 1976), another 40 to 70 million people died of starvation, forced labor or executions.

Dikotter also mentions another insightful quote from his book when Mao is talking about nuclear war:

"Let us imagine how people would die if war broke out. There are 2.7 billion people in the world, and a third could be lost. If it is a little higher, it could be half. I say that if the worst came to the worst and one-half dies, there will still be one-half left, but imperialism will be razed to the ground, and the whole world would become socialist. Within a few years there would be 2.7 billion again."

As I visited the Mausoleum of Mao Zedong at Tiananmen Square in Beijing, I could not help but notice the long lines of people purchasing flowers to venerate Mao. It soon became obvious that criticism of Mao within China is severely restricted, but it is not the case outside the country. The legacy of Mao and his atheistic leaders is not a good one. While they might be credited with lifting China out of a feudal backwater into one of the most powerful countries in the world, they did so at the cost of tremendous suffering and loss of human life. It is interesting to note that Mao is still venerated within China, but in a much freer society like modern day Germany, you must not speak Hitler's name above a whisper.

THE METASTASIZING OF COMMUNIST THOUGHT:

The communistic teachings of Karl Marx had a horrific impact on Russian and Chinese societies, and it lives on today in brutal regimes such as North Korea. It further demonstrates how one bad idea, thought up by an atheist, can have such a world-wide influence on the lives of so many people who never get to hear about God's teachings of His Son, Jesus Christ as their only savior. A ship needs a good rudder to steer it in the right direction, and man is like a ship cast out on the high seas of life, bobbing and weaving in the waves because he has either ignored God or never knew Him. Consequently, man tries to navigate his own way through life instead of allowing God to direct him through the troubled waters. As a result, he drowns in his own sins.

LESSONS LEARNED FROM CAMBODIA

Another case in point is the atrocities committed on Cambodians by the atheist, Pol Pot, the leader of the communist Khmer Rouge, who had the distinction in four short years (1975 – 1979) of torturing and killing almost two million of his own countrymen. What makes this horror even more significant is there were only seven million people living in the country at that time! Proportionally speaking, this is the highest rate of democide committed in the 20th century when expressed as a percentage of the population.

Travelling around Cambodia with my expert guide, I was shown the infamous "Killing Fields," where thousands of men, women and children were subjected to daily harassment, and tortured and murdered for the least infraction. There were no doctors to take care of a foot blister or a tooth ache, and women had babies with no doctor to help. People were treated like animals by their teenage captors who had no problem killing anyone for any reason. In many places there were mass graves, and I saw piles of skulls stacked like pyramids inside a large, glass stupa. I also visited the infamous murder and torture chamber known as S21 in the capitol, Phnom Phem, where some 20,000 captives were taken to be tortured and murdered based on false charges of being connected with the CIA, or some other foreign government. Only six survived the ordeal, and the trial against some of their perpetrators was still ongoing when I was there in 2009. Slow are the wheels of justice when one is rich and powerful, and has the right connections.

Interestingly, Pol Pot, an anti-God humanist – communist, who presided over this four-year reign of madness, had the opportunity to march into the capitol, Phnom Penh, in 1975 and declare peace as the victor, and unify the Cambodian people. Instead, within days, he chose to evacuate the two million residents by clearing out prisons, hospitals and insane asylums, and to force everyone to march into the fields to create a rice economy. The hardship on the people was horrendous, and they died like flies, with as much as half the population suffering from malaria. Pol Pot treated people like animals, and his anger and rage knew no bounds. He trained young teenagers to become vicious killers, and he continued with this legacy until the end. Although he was never captured, and reputedly died of old age, it proves that justice does not always occur in this mortal life. On the other side of the veil, however, I believe a different kind of torment awaits Pol Pot and his henchmen.

As these stories demonstrate, there has been a long war against God that continues right up to the present time, and we all need to learn the lessons of what happens to man when he loses God in his life. Limited space forces me not to document many other horrific leaders from around the world, past and present, that were and are repressing and subjugating their people in terrible ways due to their ignorance of God. We in America, with our basic freedoms enshrined in the Constitution, sometimes take for granted what we have until we step onto the soil of foreign lands. Then, we soon realize how great America is, and why she continues to be a light for the world.

So the message here is simple: we don't have a lot of time here on earth to get it right. We are blessed with exposure to more knowledge than any other time in man's history, but the span of our lives has been compressed into only a few short years compared to the age of the world itself. Therefore, we need to get with the program, and start digging into the treasures that God offers so that we can enjoy a rich, spiritual life that also provides a bonus of an even better life after this one.

CHAPTER NINE

EXCELLING IN EVIL

The dictionary defines Evil as profound immorality, wickedness and depravity – a supernatural force. Sin is defined as an immoral act considered a transgression against divine law, i.e. against God Himself. In previous chapters I have stressed the age old battle between the friends of God and His enemies; those who choose light and those who choose darkness. Another term often used is to say it is a battle between good and evil. In this chapter we will discuss the concepts of evil, and why man commits sin.

SCIENCE CLAIMS THAT EVIL DOES NOT EXIST (?)

I will start this important subject by calling your attention to a recent scientific paper written by neuroscientists that claim evil is over, and science has driven a stake through its dark heart. These scientists state that the concept of referring to evil as a metaphysical force is now antiquated, and does more harm than good to judge it in that way. They claim the 'evil' concept needs to be replaced with physical explanations, such as malfunctions or malformations of the brain. They go on to state that although people still commit bad actions, the idea that people make conscious decisions to hurt or harm someone is no longer sustainable. They claim, for instance, there is no such thing as free-will, which decides to commit evil, claiming this concept, along with the old evil concept, is antiquated as well. Autonomous, conscious decision making itself may well be an illusion, thus making intentional evil impossible.[1] If this were true, I believe a case could be made that moral agency and personal responsibility no longer apply as well.

These neuroscientists go on to say that perhaps those who commit acts of cruelty, murder and torture, are just victims themselves of a faulty part in their head that falls under the category of a factory warranty, similar to a factory warranty for a car that malfunctions, causing it to be fixed at no charge to the person who bought it. Under this notion, Adolf Hitler could be excused for the atrocities he caused during World War II.

Have MRIs, that create illuminated etchings of the skull, succeeded where religion has failed?

Have they pinpointed the hidden anomalies in the amygdale, dysfunctions in the prefrontal lobes, and the electronic source of impulses that led Jared Loughner, and James Holmes, to commit the atrocities they did? I personally think not.

INTELLECTUAL FOOLS:

It appears men of great intellect continue to pooh-pooh the idea that genuine evil exists in the world, even though a good reading of the Bible attests to the power of evil almost from the beginning of man's existence on this planet. Nonetheless, some very powerful people continue to push an agenda of evil upon American society, just like they have done in most of Europe. As a result of their efforts, Americans have come to tolerate, embrace, and even support things that would have shocked previous generations.

In one generation we have torn down the Ten Commandments, allowed homosexuals to legally marry; allowed pornography to invade computer screens in our homes for our teenagers to watch; blithely sat by while all traces of religion and prayer in our public schools were washed away, and elected our political representatives to pass laws that make us cringe at the very thought of them. Does this mean the current generation of Americans is more degenerate than other generations? The answer is a resounding NO! Rather they have been manipulated by evil people practicing professional marketing techniques which tap into American's deep sense of values of fairness, generosity, and tolerance. These despicable people have successfully created a new society tolerating and accepting evil. Here are some examples:

- How is man on man sex with hundreds of different partners justified?
- How does exterminating a healthy baby in its mother's womb become acceptable?
- How does child molestation become man-boy love?
- How does quoting the Bible become hate speech?
- How is evil made into good, and good made into evil?
- How can an openly gay, ex-alcoholic Episcopalian Bishop state that Jesus led an alternative lifestyle, intimating what we know not to be true?

How can same sex marriages be allowed when it can obviously set a possible legal precedent for other deviant relationships, such as multiple partners in a marriage, a man marrying his dog, or a father marrying his son to save inheritance taxes! The Bible clearly says that marriage is between one man and one woman. The two elements in that statement are "gender" and "number." Now that the US Supreme Court has eliminated the gender part, how long will it be before they delete the number part moving us closer to lowering Dobson's DD standard bar even lower?

Our ship is losing its moorings. How can we abandon the old notions of right and wrong, and replace it with consensual reasoning, meaning people can do whatever they wish, no matter how deviant, as long as they believe no one is harmed? It has been said that evil is 'live' spelled backwards, thus making evil go against life, and even attempt to destroy it.

It is hard for me to believe social mores can change so rapidly in a fifty-year period, and the new "normal" seamlessly becoming part of our everyday lives. With this thought in mind, let us look closer at some of the evil promoted during this time period, and look into the details of how this happened.

ACCEPTING HOMOSEXUALITY AS NORMAL BEHAVIOR:

Homosexuality was widespread in the times of the Greek and Roman Empires, and we have seen what happened to their great societies as they were destroyed from within. But then Christ came, and the Christian Church was founded, causing homosexuality to fade into the background. For hundreds of years homosexuals worried about being exposed for fear of being tortured and killed. During the sexual revolution of the 1960's, homosexuals began to be heard. The seminal event took place in the summer of 1969, when a crowd of homosexuals rioted at the Stonegate Pub in New York City. Groups were galvanized with funding to push their cause, and soon the American Psychiatric Association removed homosexuality from their official list of mental disorders. Then came AIDS, and ACT-UP (AIDS Coalition to Unleash Power) who became very militant, and even overran members of New York City's St. Patrick Cathedral in 1989 while services were in session. Celebrities like Rock Hudson, Max Robinson, and Rudolf Nureyev, died of AIDS. So did young Kimberley Bergalis, who contracted AIDS from her homosexual dentist, David Acer. Also, 18 year old Ryan White, a hemophiliac, died from a tainted AIDS blood transfusion. The public was rightly outraged by these events.

In 1988 a large group of homosexuals met with the goal of forcing acceptance of homosexual culture in the mainstream, to silence opposition, and eventually convert American society to the acceptance of homosexuality as "normal" behavior. We know in public relations warfare that he who frames the terms of the debate almost always wins in the end. To accomplish this, some of the leaders of the homosexual community recommended that the homosexual image needed to be changed, if only for a short time while they made progress with their plans. They did this by asking the fringe element of the movement, the so called trans-genders, cross dressers, and sadomasochists etc., to go underground for a while in order to present a more positive image to the general public. Later, once a more "palatable" image had been sold through very clever marketing techniques, the fringe could then come back onto the radar screen. They began their constant "in our face" strategy that eventually worked so effectively it wore down public resistance, and even resulted in homosexuality being taught to our kids in public schools across the country.

DESENTISIZING AMERICA FOR GAY ACCEPTANCE:

The whole idea was to desensitize the public by introducing a flood of continuous "gay" (yes, they changed homosexuals to "gays" to make them more acceptable) related advertising that presented gays in the most positive light. TV ads showing gays and straights having a beer together like it was normal, and there was no difference between them. I remember many years ago building a swing set in my back yard in Los Angeles for my daughter, when on the radio Doctor James Dobson, the great Christian leader, commented on DD up and DD down. He wanted the audience to imagine in their mind's eye a horizontal line that represented normal, acceptable behavior. DD up meant defining deviancy upwards above the normal limits, and DD down meant defining deviancy as far down below normal as possible. In this way, the gays were trying to lower the "bar", or standard, in order to get Main Street America to eventually accept this lower bar. Once you get straights to think that homosexuality is just another social issue, meriting no more importance than any other social issue, the battle is won.

GAY TECHNIQUES TO FURTHER THEIR GOALS:

Homosexual leaders went further with their campaign by silencing radio and TV personalities, and Christian leaders they perceived as the enemy. They accomplished this through various methods of intimidation including constantly bombarding the "target," and openly lying about facts until the white flag of surrender went up. Lying and insinuations became common place, and anyone in public life with a scandal in their background was exposed if it served the cause. Even famous historical figures were marketed to be homosexuals without a shred of evidence to back up the claims. This all out frontal attack on anyone who does not agree with the homosexual position will continue until anyone with an objection to their lifestyle is either shut up, discredited or converted to their way of thinking. Who are the real losers of this campaign of evil? Everyone! Our impressionable kids are questioning their own gender identity; the general public has been "beaten" down to the point that they seem no longer to care, and the homosexuals themselves have won all of the battles, but have they won the war? Somewhere hidden in all the "noise" is a simple forgotten fact, which is that homosexuality is abhorrent in the sight of God. Homosexual behavior goes against all the vestiges of civil societies going back six thousand years of man's recorded history. It serves no purpose to accept or embrace it. It is simply wrong, period.

THE COMPLICITY OF THE PRESS AND MEDIA:

The National Lesbian and Gay Journalists Association (NLGJA), which has grown into a powerful force in promoting the homosexual agenda, has successfully used their megaphone to blast the virtues of homosexuality all over America. As a result, they have been tremendously successful in shaping the mind of the American public. Today, all of the various news agencies support homosexual rights, and have been used and manipulated successfully as a catalyst for bringing homosexual rights into the mainstream of public life.

One example that proves the success of the homosexual agenda is the magazine for teenagers called, *Seventeen*. A poll was conducted in the 1990's in which 17% of its young readers approved of homosexuality. Another poll was completed ten-years later, and it found that 54% approved of homosexuality.[2] This stunning gain for gays is now reflected in all areas of our society, whether it be government, entertainment, business, education, news distribution, and even in some churches. Do you remember the Episcopalian Church promoting an openly gay man to the position of Bishop who later had to retract his statement that Jesus was homosexual?

A REALITY CHECK:

While we have been living in a type of fantasy world created by gay organizations and the media, we must not forget the reality of the subject we are discussing. The homosexual marketing blitz has caused us to forget there is something very wrong with homosexual behavior. Such behavior is unnatural and self-destructive, just as the West has long understood it. The physical and spiritual damage done to gays is incalculable, and we are aware that sexually abused males are up to seven times more likely to self-identify as gay or bisexual than those who have not been abused.[3] When gays claim they were born gay, we now know better.

ATTITUDES OF YESTERDAY AND TODAY:

In the past we were taught to believe that homosexuality was clearly wrong by any standard of morality. We believed that homosexuals were not born into their lifestyle, and that their gender identity had somehow been disturbed during early childhood. Poor parenting may have been to blame causing kids to develop confusion with their own identity In those days we were more aware of our Judeo-Christian heritage, and there was more of an effort to please God, who was clearly against homosexuality - See Leviticus 18:22; Leviticus 20:13; I Kings 14:24; Romans 1:24, 26, 27. Later, however, many Americans were beguiled in believing that God was no longer a potent force in their lives, and if their actions did not harm someone else, then it was OK to do whatever they wanted. The moral code was breaking down, and even pedophiles could justify sexual acts with children on the grounds that they were just loving them, and not subjecting them to physical harm! In this new environment it is now easier to look back and see how homosexuals were so successful in moving into the mainstream of American life. They were not hurting anyone as long as it was done behind closed doors. The proven facts are much different, however, in that someone always gets hurt. Isaiah 5:20-21 says: "Woe to those who call evil good and good evil, who put darkness for light and light for darkness, who put bitter for sweet and sweet for bitter. Woe to those who are wise in their own eyes and clever in their own sight."

Please also take note that the phenomenon I have just described is not just happening in the United States. In fact, many hate crime laws in other countries, such as Canada, Europe, and Australia and New Zealand, have already been updated to make it a criminal offense to criticize homosexuals in print or from the pulpit of the local church.

What are Christians to do? We must continue to love the homosexual but despise what they do. This classical Christian response has more power than we perhaps give it credit for, because homosexuals have consciences too! They know they are doing wrong, and the old adage: a problem well stated is a problem half solved, fits very nicely here because they have already stated the problem correctly in their own minds. We must encourage them to seek spiritual counsel, and if you have a family member or close friend who is homosexual, as a Christian you have a unique opportunity to bring him or her to God. Homosexuals should enjoy all the privileges that all citizens are given, but to promote homosexuality, or give homosexuals special rights based on their sexual orientation is wrong, and that's where society should draw the line. As a society, we cannot keep going down this "slippery road" without facing serious moral issues for our children and grandchildren, and society as a whole.

Remember, homosexuality goes against the laws of God, but we also know that God wants none of His creation to be lost. Therefore, we should love all homosexuals, but let them clearly know that their conduct is not acceptable. God has a big "house" that is large enough to take care of all of us no matter how much sin we have committed, as long as we accept Jesus as our Lord and Savior. So don't miss out on the great opportunity to help a homosexual who needs help. All of us can play a part.

ABORTING THE RIGHT TO LIFE

They say what goes around comes around, and the subject of abortion is no different in that after having been classified as illegal for hundreds of years, it is now back in full force in modern America. Has man not learned anything from the history of ancient Rome and Greece? God's Laws have not changed, the Bible has not changed, and man has not changed. He is still a slave to his own ego, pride, lust, envy, ambition and greed. Despite all the education and large body of knowledge at his disposal, he is still capable of going against God. How else can we explain the horrible moral conditions of our society today?

Thanks to Jesus Christ and the Christian faith, the all powerful church successfully condemned and prohibited abortion and infanticide in general, for the promotion of good public morals right up through the late 20th century, when the church began to lose its influence due to the chaotic disorder of the 1960s. In the midst of the Vietnam War, American values were shaken, and our society witnessed various liberation movements taking place almost simultaneously. Soon we were inundated with Black liberation, sexual liberation, gay liberation, women's liberation, multicultural liberation, and others, which all led to gross infidelity, divorce, family breakdown, riots, increases in drug use, and a diminishing respect for society as a whole. James Dobson's "bar" was clearly being pushed downwards.

Out of this environment sprung a small, disciplined group of dedicated activists who decided to change America's abortion laws in all 50 states, causing America to step back nearly 2,000 years in time to the barbarity of the ancients, all under the guise of protecting a woman's rights.

DEATH BY LYING:

Abortion activists intended to accomplish their goal by any means necessary. They even lied to, and deceived both the media and the general public, by persuading public opinion through the press. Their effective campaign of lies was so successful that by 1973 their goal was achieved with the announcement by the US Supreme Court making abortion legal (the infamous Roe vs. Wade case). Interestingly, the plaintiff in the above case was a woman named, Norma McCorvey, who claimed she was raped, which was used by her two female attorneys to justify a case for abortion of the child. Later we find the rape allegation turned out not to be true, and she gave birth while waiting for the trial result. So the test case for abortion that changed the laws on abortion in all 50 states was an abortion that never happened. Norma later worked in a number of abortion clinics before coming to the realization that what she was doing was wrong, and she converted to Christianity. She has since spent her life speaking out against abortion across the country, and my heart goes out to her for doing the right thing.

Since 1973, we have aborted more than 57 million babies through April, 2014, and on a worldwide scale the number exceeds 1.3 billion according to USAbortionclock.org. China alone has aborted 336 million babies since 1971, averaging about 13 million per year, or 1500 per hour. During that time the government has also sterilized about 196 million men and women. [4] Chinese couples are using ultrasound with a vengeance to determine the sex of their unborn child in deciding whether to keep the child or abort it. Meanwhile, the government's One Child Policy continues, and as a result it has been estimated there are more than fifty million more males than females in the country. Obviously, many men will never enjoy the experience of marriage and procreation of a child.

Abortion has become so pervasive that America has exported abortion practices around the world by adding it as a condition to receiving our foreign aid. We also now have sonograms that allow a couple to determine the sex of their child, and amniocentesis methods to determine if the child is abnormal. Both methods have led to an increase in abortions in the USA and around the world. Girls are aborted far more often than boys in most countries. A majority of Americans are pro-life, and would like to see Roe vs. Wade overturned. Unfortunately, it is the same old story in public relations wars where those that shape the terms of the debate usually win. These clever marketers of evil are still at it, and will continue to do so despite the evidence we are destroying real life in the mother's womb.

ONE DOCTOR'S STORY:

The history of how America was seduced and manipulated into allowing abortion rights to become legal in all states is a very compelling story full of lies, deception, and outright evil based on a false debate of a woman's right to choose what she does with her own body, rather than a discussion of the real issue of what really happens to the unborn child, and the devastating psychological results visited upon the mother. Killing an innocent baby was no longer the issue, but who <u>decides</u> became the mantra of the day, and still is.

We can gain no better insight into the twisted logic that caused this holocaust in America over the past fifty plus years, than to look into the life of Doctor Bernard Nathanson who was one of the founding members of NARAL (National Association for the Repeal of Abortion Laws). Through his own admitted lying and deception, he and his cohorts were not only successful in overturning New York State's Right to Life Law, but were most instrumental in engineering the Roe vs. Wade decision.

The good doctor stated: "Knowing that if a true poll were taken, we would be soundly defeated, we simply fabricated the results of fictional polls. We claimed that our polls said 60% of Americans were in favor of abortion, which ended up becoming a self-fulfilling lie. We aroused enough sympathy by telling the public that the number of illegal abortions in the U.S. was a million per year, when in actual fact it was about 100,000. Repeating the big lie often enough eventually convinced the public. The number of women dying from illegal abortions was around 200 -250 per year, but we constantly fed the media a figure of 10,000. These false figures took root in the consciousness of the public and convinced many that we needed to overturn the abortion law." [5] Nathanson went on to say: "Another myth we fed to the public was that legalizing abortion would only mean that the abortions taking place illegally would be done legally. Of course, abortion is now being used as a primary method of birth control in the U.S. and the annual number of abortions has increased by 1500% since legalization."[6]

Nathanson, went on to become the director of C.R.A.S.H (Center for Reproductive and Sexual Health), in Manhattan, where some 75,000 abortions were completed under his guidance before he later resigned. He also claimed to have performed an abortion on a woman he had impregnated.

Nathanson, like so many others, ended up experiencing an epiphany that changed his life forever. New medical technologies were becoming available that allowed doctors to see a "window into the womb," such as: real time utrasound, fetoscopy, electrical fetal heart monitoring, and Cordocentesis, among others. Now, for the first time, doctors were able to see what was really taking place inside a woman whose fetus was about to be removed. Doctor Nathanson concluded: "As a result of this technology – looking at this baby, examining it, investigating it, watching its metabolic functions, watching it urinate, swallow, move and sleep, watching it dream, which you could see by its rapid eye movements via ultrasound, treating it, operating on it – I finally came to the conviction that this was my patient. This was a person! I was a physician, pledged to save my patient's lives, not to destroy them. So I changed my mind on the subject of abortion."[7]

In all fairness to Nathanson, instead of quietly moving into a profitable retirement, he decided to join the pro-lifers, and do everything he could to reverse Roe vs. Wade. Like Norma McCorvey, he tried to reverse the horrible damage that had been done. Unfortunately, it was too little too late. As a self-proclaimed Jewish-atheist he converted to Catholicism at age 69, and died in 2011 at age 84. When asked why he converted to Christianity he replied: "No religion matches the special role of forgiveness that is afforded by the Catholic Church." [8]

Nathanson created the vector theory for life, which states from the moment of conception there exists a self-directed life force, if not interrupted, that will lead to the birth of a human being. To interrupt this natural progressive flow of life by aborting a child goes against the will of God,

who creates all things. If any of the readers of this book wish to know more about the abhorrent details involved in aborting a child, they need to look no further than YouTube, where they can witness all the sordidness of the operation by watching two films Nathanson created. The first one, *Silent Scream,* demonstrates what happens to a fetus aborted at twelve weeks, and the other film, *Eclipse of Reason,* shows the viewer what happens to an aborted fetus in the third trimester of life. Please be forewarned to expect graphic detail, as it is not for the faint of heart.

Abortion is big business in America, with about a million performed each year with an average cost of $500.00 or more depending on the number of elapsed weeks. That translates into about a half trillion dollars, mainly cash, into the hands of abortionist doctors. When looking at a fetus, abortion doctors don't see what the average person would see. Even though the fetus is perfectly formed as a human being, abortionists only see a non-human disposable lump of matter. Their eyes have been blinded by the "blood" money that can make them rich. These doctors, unlike Nathanson, who did not have the benefit of new medical technology to really see what he was doing to a fetus, are without excuse, and we should all pray for their souls.

EVIL INCORPORATED

By all accounts, America is still a powerful country with a gross domestic product in excess of 18 trillion dollars a year, which is greater than China's economy with a population about four times larger. With only five-percent of the world's population, and only six-percent of the world's land-mass, America has military arms expenditures greater than the top ten other countries arms expenses combined. Our international assets, and political influence are still very strong, but we are slipping towards lesser status as the 21st century continues.

Unfortunately, we are rotting from within, and America is up for sale to the highest bidders. We now have more than 30,000 paid Washington lobbyists who do everything in their power to corrupt our political leaders with bribes, large campaign contributions, and assurances they will support their re-election hopes. In this kind of carnival atmosphere anything goes, and much of the legislation enacted makes no sense to the average person. When we see government blessing same sex marriages, supporting homosexuality, exporting our abortion laws abroad as a condition to developing countries receiving foreign aid, we shake our heads in shame.

Our government has run up more than 19 trillion dollars in sovereign debt as of this writing, and it has been reckoned that unfunded liabilities at both federal and state levels now exceed 100 trillion dollars. There has been an orgy of spending, and greed has become a god in our culture. A mathematician pointed out if we wrote a check for $1,000,000.00 every hour of every day, of every year going back two thousand years to the birth of Christ, we would not be able to spend all the 19 trillion dollars we owe! In fact, we would still be writing checks into the B.C. era!

Our debts are unfathomable, and angst and fear pervade the minds of many Americans. Our educational system is in decline, and God has been banned from American classrooms. Evil has its tentacles in the deepest parts of our government's heart, and it is that government that we look to for leadership, moral guidance, justice and fairness.

Unfortunately, our hard earned tax dollars today are not giving us a fair return on our money; in fact our taxes are being used to support all types of evil that would cause our grandparents to roll over in their graves. We elect our politicians in good faith in the hope they will change Washington, but somehow they end up changing once they are exposed to the cesspool within the beltway of our capitol. Evil and sin are winning, and we have to look to God for the answers if we are ever to turn our great country around and make it the place that it once was, a beacon of life, hope, and freedom, for people from all around the world. Sadly, America today is driven by greed, and the lust for profits, and any rules that get in the way are to be discarded.

SINS OF CORPORATE AMERICA

Before turning our attention to American corporations, let me quote a reference made by an unknown university business professor in the early part of the 20th century:

"Man is created individually by God; the corporation is an individual created by man. Like a man, the corporation has a body. It has arms and legs; it has not four but thousands of members. It has a mind and purpose. It has eyes and ears and a kind of brain; it thinks and plans and remembers. And it can grow to be huge and strong. But it has no conscience! Thus the corporation never suffers from a sense of guilt. It can kill and be killed; it can do evil and it can do good; it can be sick, and it can die. But, on the other hand, it has no pity and, no matter what suffering or damage it causes, it suffers no remorse."

The above statement made about 100 years ago, is as true today as when it was made. Corporations do not have a conscience, and only laws prevent them from running rough shod over our economy. Although it is true that corporations who do wrong in modern society have a price to pay for their sins, we often find the cost is dwarfed by the profits gained, which creates an incentive to keep doing the same thing. From experience we have found that corporate evil is often covert, and the public never hears about it until a scandal breaks out later in the press.

American corporations have developed the habit of tying their whole management compensation packages to increasing the bottom line for the shareholders in the current fiscal year, and this often leads to management decisions that are short-term, without concern for the long-term ramification of their decisions, or the effect their decisions have on society, especially our young. Profit is their only god!

Corporations are treating our kids like lab rats where their every move is carefully watched in order to fine tune and target products and services to meet their needs, whatever those needs are. Instead of corporations shaping kids minds in a positive way by taking a leadership role, they lower their standards (Dobson's DD down) to the level of kids and teenagers, thus allowing young minds to shape and define deviancy. This is like the tail wagging the dog, and it would not be believable if the facts did not support it.

Musical lyrics that promote sex and violence, even cop killings, are pervading kids' minds. Then we have pornography (now the seventh largest industry and most profitable) invading any home in America where people, including teenagers wish to watch it. Today we are living in an American culture that is awash in personal freedoms to do whatever we like as long as it doesn't hurt anyone else. And corporate America is only too glad to oblige. How much longer can this insanity continue?

SO WHAT EVER HAPPENED TO SIN IN OUR SOCIETY?

History teaches us that President Eisenhower was the last president to use the word "sin" in a speech to the nation (1953). When Eisenhower used the word "sin" he borrowed the words for his proclamation from a call issued in 1863 by Abraham Lincoln, who said:

"It is the duty of nations as well as of men to owe their dependence upon the overruling power of God, to confess their sins and transgressions in humble sorrow, yet with assured hope that the genuine repentance will lead to mercy and pardon."

DEFINING SIN:

The word "sin" was once a proud word; it was a strong word, and a word to be taken seriously. Goethe's *Faust,* and Nathaniel Hawthorne's, *The Scarlett Letter,* can provide the reader with a good view of how serious sin was in former times. Penalties for sin were very severe: The public stocks, tongue-splitting, cheek branding, and the wearing of a scarlet "A" on a person for committing adultery created great shame. But now it is a word that is rarely used in everyday life. Why is this? Doesn't anyone sin anymore? Do people no longer believe in sin? Psychologists and other mental therapists have stopped using the word "sin" in their patient sessions because of its strong reproachful quality. It appears that as a nation we stopped sinning about sixty years ago, although we instinctively know it is not true. The only place left in our society where the word "sin" is used is on a Sunday morning during church services.

Earlier I defined sin from the dictionary as: "An immoral act considered to be a transgression against divine moral code or the individual conscience or both." Like a cancer, sin eats away at the soul until the act of repentance is complete. People of great wealth can lead miserable lives if they have committed sin that scorches their conscience, causes them worry, and leaves them with a restless spirit. Christian therapists will tell you sin is still with us, by us, and in us somewhere, and it will not go away until confronted with a humble, contrite heart.

Some people are made uneasy by their conscience and try to blame others, or ascribe responsibility to a group, or look for a scapegoat. The word "conscience" means "with knowing" so we are all without excuse. God has given all men, irrespective of their education, or life circumstance, the knowledge they need in order to do the right thing. Rudolf Hoss, mentioned earlier, knew exactly what he was doing, but after committing the first murder, it became easier for him to justify it in his own mind. In the Bible, it tells us how this seduction process works, whereby we ignore our conscience so that we can gain some advantage, but unfortunately it leads to spiritual blindness. In the Book of Acts 28: 26-27, it says: "You will be ever hearing but never understanding; you will be ever seeing but never perceiving. For this people's hearts have become calloused; they hardly hear with their ears, and they have closed their eyes. Otherwise they may see with their eyes, hear with their ears, understand with their hearts and turn, and I would heal them."

It has also been stated that sin is a willful, defiant, or disloyal quality, and implies the willful disregard or sacrifice of the welfare of others for the welfare and satisfaction of the self. St.

Augustine describes it as a "turning" away from the universal whole to the individual part . . ." He goes on to say: "There is nothing greater than the whole. Hence, when man desires to be greater he grows smaller."

Making sin disappear requires a shift in allocation of responsibility for evil. But there it remains until properly addressed. I believe the above definition of sin is broad enough to satisfy both believers and non-believers, because sin traditionally implies guilt, responsibility, and demands an answer. For many people this implies making confession, showing contrition, repairing the wrong, repentance, forgiveness, and atonement. This definition can certainly be challenged by some, but I am convinced there is a lot of social value in retaining such tenets. Just because the word "sin" is only used on Sundays doesn't mean it goes away during the week.

THE TRANSFERRING OF SIN:

The transferring of authority for major social offences from the home and church, to the Crown or state, began during the reign of Henry VIII who wanted a divorce, but the Catholic Church would not allow it. Henry decided to break from the Catholic Church and set up the Church of England so he could have his own way. Soon, a litany of specific transgressions became defined as laws, and the appropriate punishments were codified in the law. This shifted a lot of the responsibility from the church and home to the government. Sin was now not only immoral, but it was also becoming illegal. We then found attempting to legislate morality to coerce virtue by law became the standard. Making sins into crimes rendered sin increasingly pointless from a practical point of view, and it came about that only the seven cardinal sins remained as part of the domain of the church. Sin as sin became a personal matter, an offence contrary to conscience or moral standard. Dealing with it became the task of the pulpit, the confessional, and the individual's conscience. So let's take a further look at the seven "cardinal" sins:

THE SEVEN CARDINAL SINS:

The traditional list include: pride, envy, anger, sloth, avarice, gluttony and lust. Johannes Cassianus (360 – 435AD) added fornication, dejection and vainglory (instead of pride), but dropped envy. Gregory the Great, the Pope from 590-604AD put pride at the head of the list and considered it the source of all the others. His list still remains in vogue to this day. Interestingly, dishonesty, vindictiveness, cruelty, bigotry nor infidelity is mentioned.

PRIDE: Synonyms for pride are vanity, egocentricity, hubris, arrogance, self-adoration, selfishness, self-love, and narcissism, all subject to modern condemnation. They may not be considered crimes or diseases, but they are not liked by most people. The sin of pride appears most conspicuously in group pride – tribalism, nationalism, jingoism, and racism, as well as individual pride. Remember the "I" in pride – it's the letter in the center! A Christian needs to put God first rather than himself, and this is done by humbling to Christ so Christ becomes larger and the Christian becomes smaller.

LUST: The sins of sensuality include not only lust, but also, fornication, adultery, and pornography. We have literally gone through a revolution during the last 60 years whereby many forms of sexual activity, which for centuries were considered immoral, and sinful, are now talked and written about, and displayed on both stage and screen without as much as a second thought with regards to the effect on our young. The word "lust" in English implies a kind of ruthless, evil and sinful indulgence of the sexual drive. During the 16th and 19th centuries, sex was for procreation purposes and nothing more, therefore, all sexual pleasure was considered sinful. Even to this day, in many parts of the world, you will find that little girls are reported to be mutilated (clitorectomy) by their parents in order to prevent them from being lustful, sensuous, and tempted to passionate indulgence. This is particularly prevalent in Islam.

GLUTTONY: The consuming of far more food and drink than one needs, despite the threat of complications from obesity, diabetes, nephritis, heart problems, gastro-intestinal issues, and many other ailments is often seen in people who claim helplessness in the throes of the craving. This can be a disease as well as a sin. Gluttony in all its forms is a form of sin, and can include: alcohol, cocaine, morphine, heroin, hashish, barbituric acid salts, tobacco, and marijuana, which are all potentially harmful when used in excess. They create a form of self-love, which is potentially destructive causing a shortening of life. Shakespeare once said: "Temperance in all things," and how right he was.

ANGER: Our society strives in large part to find ways to reduce anger, violence and aggression in its purest forms by offering alternatives to physical violence, which was once man's chief defensive resource. With each new generation we find violence receding in our society due to public awareness and better education, notwithstanding the fact the world in general is becoming a more dangerous place. We are learning anger leads to hurtful words, or acts, and can be a personal individual transgression that needs to be controlled in its outward expression before it dictates destructive behavior.

SLOTH: This is a good old Anglo-Saxon word meaning the temptation to "goof off." It is described as laziness, avoidance of exertion, idling, or an inclination to take it easy. There is certainly a sin in not doing, or not finding out what one must do – in short of just not caring, because it hurts other people beside the lazy person.

GREED: The sins of greed, envy, avarice and affluence have led to people coveting what belongs to someone else, and taking steps to gain it for themselves. Envy is a sister of greed, and the half sister of stealing. Greediness in adults arouses disgust in observers, and the vulgarity of this residual infantile behavior is precisely what education in self-control and social concerns is supposed to avert. Greed is the crucial issue that has split off various economic systems such as Socialism and Communism, which were supposed to correct greed in society. But just as Freud said so many years ago: "The Communist is still a human being with the same instincts as a capitalist, the same lust for power, the same greed and yearning for acquisition, and the same impulses to fight and to be self-destructive."

ENVY: "You shall not covet," is part of the Old Testament Ten Commandments, and over time it is a word that has changed to "envy." We find envy is the yearning to possess something belonging to someone else. Envy is a failure to be satisfied with what you have. Therefore, it is important to accept the reality of your existence, and then try to improve your position by exercising the old Judeo-Christian work ethic that has made so many millions of people successful in their own right. Accepting personal responsibility for your life, the one that God has given you, should cause you to be thrilled to live your life free to pursue your dreams, and earn your way forward by the sweat of your own brow. There is hardly anything more self-fulfilling than achieving success on your own, because then there will be no place in your life for envy of others.

Sin has become so pervasive in our society, yet it has taken on a subtlety that many people do not recognize it as such, because it has become the accepted norm. Therefore, being able to recognize sin for what it is, and then live a life where you become sensitive to it, is the best way to keep it from entering your life. This chapter, if anything, should give you a better understanding of the tricks of our enemies, who are clearly working against God. To be forewarned, is to be forearmed. The lesson to be taken from this chapter, is to look to God for your answers, and not to mankind.

CHAPTER TEN

IS AMERICA GOING THE WAY OF EUROPE?

It is a well known fact that modern Europe has moved far from God, and become a secular continent. Atheistic-humanism continues to gain ground, and many young Europeans are eager to find some type of hope for their future. They know something is very wrong, but they have been denied a spiritual upbringing, and are therefore disconnected from the qualities that once made Europe great. Political answers alone cannot account for the moral decay of European societies, and why its people are committing demographic suicide (see more below). Europe's problems, which are becoming America's problems, are best understood in moral and cultural terms. So the pending question before us is very clear and straightforward. Is America going the same way as Europe? When we look at Europe today, are we looking at America tomorrow?

It is not an easy task to discuss why European leaders, the architects of public mores, have shaped their citizens to think in anti-Christian ways. These leaders have progressed down a twisted road of godless thinking, self-centeredness, and a type of bravado that makes them think they have all the best answers, when social performance clearly demonstrates otherwise. With these thoughts in mind, let us now delve into this fascinating state of affairs in Europe by taking a brief journey into European history. This is the only way I know of that can provide us the insight into the heart of European problems today.

EUROPE'S DEVASTATING 20TH CENTURY

Two major wars in the 20th century, within 20 years of each other, should likely have destroyed Europe. This experience has caused its leaders to believe future security threats can and should be met, not by traditional "hard power" military application, but rather by using "soft power" methods, by the furthering of international legal and political tools for conflict resolution. By using these "soft power" approaches, European leaders see themselves using the philosophy of Immanuel Kant's vision of perpetual peace laid out back in 1795, shortly after the French Revolution.

By Europe rejecting power politics, and systematically reducing the size of its military forces, it has become too dependent on American military forces to apply the "hard" power necessary to maintain peace. Is it too simplistic to think that American military power has caused Europeans to think "hard" power was no longer important. This has resulted in Europeans having neither the will nor the ability to guard their own sacred turf, and keep it from being overrun both spiritually and physically, by a world that does not seem to play by the same rules of moral consciousness.

Rather than invest in their own independent protection, Europeans have minimized their military budgets, used the savings to increase social programs (which have resulted in huge debts that may never be repaid), and have become overly dependent on America's willingness to use its military might to deter or defeat those around the world who still believe in "hard" power politics. Rather than look to God for answers, and take initiatives to protect themselves, they have invested in man, i.e. Americans, for their security, which is a very poor second choice.

The German commentator, Josef Joffe, helps us to get closer to some answers when he asks us to focus on Europe's mid-twentieth century trauma, the years when Europe lost its moorings:

"Much of Western Europe has drawn its post-Holocaust identity from the rejection of the darkest part of the continent's proud history. The battle cry of post-war Europe is 'Never Again.' Europeans say 'no' to fuehrers, duces, caudillos, to colonialism, conquest, and discrimination against others. To regain moral stature, Europeans have turned antifascism into a doctrine of worldly transcendence, with a secular Decalogue that reads in part: thou shalt not practice power politics; thus halt or relinquish sovereignty and rejoice in cooperation." [1] All the collective guilt that has built up in Europe since the 16th century religious wars, the French Revolution, World War I, the Spanish Civil War, the Ukraine terror famine, and the Holocaust during World War II, just to mention a few, appears to be an attempt at vindication of those sins. Attempts at redemption take many forms.

THE UNANSWERED WHYS OF EUROPEAN POLICIES:

I mentioned earlier, original man made progress by asking the simple question, why? He did so because he did not have the answers. Today in Europe the *whys* are still being asked, though in this case Europeans do have the answers, but refuse to face the implications of those answers! Instead, they apply all types of policies and nonsense that defy facts and hard evidence. Here are some examples:

- Why do they believe Tehran will not use nuclear energy for military purposes when they have been proved to be untrustworthy? Surely they understand the concept of Taqiyya and Kitman, which allows Tehran to use deceptive practices to gain advantage.
- During the Cold War, why did they not condemn Russian Communism as being evil?
- Why did they believe that China and India (two of the biggest polluters in the world) would actually comply with the Kyoto Treaty, and other carbon reducing agreements, when they have been on record as stating that jobs at home are more important to them than clean air?
- Why do they use anti-Jewish policies against Israel (the only democracy in the Middle East) by believing for years the hateful propaganda from the Arab League nations?
- Also, why do they to this day, side with Arabs against Jews on nearly every resolution that comes before the United Nations?
- Why do they place so much faith in the United Nations, a totally biased, anti-Semitic, and corrupt organization of kleptocracies, theocracies, and despotic states, as the solution for all the world's problems?
- Why do they believe all conflicts of interest should be settled by consultation, conciliation, and the intervention

by international agencies? Try selling that idea to the Russians, the Chinese, or North Koreans for that matter! Why do they continue to defend nonsense on so many others issues, when their positions do not square with reality?

The European approach of leading from behind on so many issues, when they clearly have both the answers and resources to correct the problems, is baffling to say the least. This inability to take corrective action based on proven evidence is also having a major effect on all types of social issues as well. For instance:

- Why are European leaders anti-Christian by agreeing to wipe out Christianity's contribution to their civilization, which is not mentioned in their constitution? More on this later.
- Why is the birth rate across most of Europe well below normal standards?
- Why is European productivity dwindling, while their capital markets sink in huge debts?

Perhaps the most important question of all is to ask why are Europeans committing demographic suicide? According to the CIA World Fact Book (2010), there are 24 European countries that have a crude death rate higher than their crude birth rate.

Why do so many Europeans deny these demographics, which are without parallel in human history, absent wars, plagues or natural disasters? Low birth rates have become the defining reality in Europe, and do not bode well as we progress deeper into the 21st century.

As if Europe does not have enough problems of its own, its courts seek to expand their international jurisdiction, which defies the democratically agreed arrangements made by other free people. When I was in Kenya recently, there was a furor among the people due to the ICC (Europe's International Criminal Court) attempting to place the country's president and vice-president on trial in Europe for alleged crimes brought against them from their political opponents. Never mind that the people freely elected both men into office!

There are other cases that come to mind such as the Israeli opposition leader threatened with arrest if she stepped off a plane in London. Why? Because the Israelis were accused of being heavy handed in the way they defended themselves from missile attacks from the Gaza Strip. Never mind that Hamas started the ruckus. I wonder how a European nation would feel if their next door neighbor lobbed rockets onto their turf, thus killing innocent people and damaging property?

Why are Europeans so quick to try to solve other countries problems when they can't even fix their own? The more institutionalized atheistic humanism becomes on the European continent, the further apart from God the continent gets.

The European 20th century started off well, with a high level of confidence in the future as great accomplishments were being achieved, and a high sense that man could achieve anything. But the play book turned out much differently with major wars, totalitarian governments, horrific episodes of murder and mayhem, and the shame of the Holocaust. Could it be that God had been forgotten?

AMERICA HAS PLENTY OF HER OWN PROBLEMS TOO:

In order to be fair, there is plenty to be concerned about in the United States, where we have a government that does more to protect animals and fish than it does to protect an unborn child. Americans disagree on capital punishment, abortion, illegal immigration, border control, same sex marriage, gun control, and a host of other subjects. We find ourselves exposed to many moral polluting outlets such as Internet pornography (40,000 websites for world-wide distribution) making us the largest exporter of moral filth.

Our government is constantly experiencing an inability for both parties to agree on meaningful legislation, and consequently critical programs such as Social Security, Medicare, Medicaid, and government pension plans are tremendously underfunded. We are mired in a myriad of spiraling debt that becomes worse each year. Worse is the fact that there is no political will to tackle it.

We experience high divorce rates and sky-rocketing out of wed-lock births; we seem to be unable to effectively debate issues like ethics on embryo research, or even the meaning of marriage itself, and these issues go against the beliefs of many Christians. We are now living in a society where political correctness continues to gain ground, and this limits free speech and the lack of any serious arguments in our higher places of learning. As if these problems were not enough, we also have courts that continually override our elected officials and grass root referendums approved by the people. This "hi-jacking" of the Constitution by our judiciary is creating even more secularism in both public and private life.

It defies simple common sense for a population of some 320 million Americans electing 535 representatives to enact laws of the land, that are then later overturned by nine men and women in black gowns, with questionable approaches to interpreting the Constitution! Who has the power? Year after year these nine men and women amend the Constitution by simply voting on what they consider what the Constitution means, rather than what our founding fathers meant. The future of American values is clearly within the province of these nine powerful people.

Yes, there is plenty to criticize about America, but it cannot yet be accused of an anti-Christian sentiment like the one placing a dark cloud over Europe, although trends tell us that we are moving in that direction. Charitable giving and volunteerism in America are still very strong, and America has a much higher rate of church goers than Europe. When it comes to race issues, America is more egalitarian that most other nations, due to the hard struggle for civil rights for everyone, that took many years to create. Also, America's birth replacement numbers are much higher than in Europe, and therefore the population base is not losing ground.

It may seem like an oversimplification in explaining why Americans see the world so differently than Europeans, when I wonder if it is the church experience of Americans that makes the difference. Loving God and loving your fellow man, are the number one and two commandments of God that take precedence over all else. Those commandments are still respected and continue to be honored by many Americans, and let's hope it continues.

Many in America still believe Christian principles are worth fighting for and defending. Man has to believe in ideals greater than himself, and be willing to die for those principles. If there is nothing worth dying for, then there is nothing worth living for either. That helps to explain why so many Americans have died in foreign lands to rescue people they don't even know, in order to save them from oppression and bondage, and give them the freedom they deserve."Greater love has no one than this, that he lay down his life for his friend." John 15:13.

A man who is spiritually nourished knows this life is temporary, and is generally not afraid of death. So why not live life with honor, integrity and truthfulness, instead of living in fear and worry? Jesus wants us all to be happy and enjoy our temporary mortal existence. The question then becomes, do Europeans believe in fighting for anything? Today that is an open question.

A SMALL LIGHT IN EUROPE:

One bright spot in Europe is the Slav's continued commitment to their Lord and Savior, Jesus Christ. The Slavic nation of Poland is an excellent example, and I was most impressed with the Pole's commitment to God when I visited some of their churches, which are usually packed on Sundays. Some services last for three-hours, sometimes without seating! Having lost their country for more than 100 years, they regained their independence in 1918, only to lose it again to the Russians for another 50 years. Then, in 1989 they once again became an independent nation. How did the Poles survive? Further study reveals that Polish culture is very strong resulting in a deep psychological bond among the people that formed the basis for common ideals of honor, worship, and values that were worth fighting and dying for. They also enjoyed a strong traditional literature based on a distinctive language. Most importantly, they never forgot their Christian faith. As a result, the Pole, despite tremendous hardship, persevered and survived.

Poles have a classical sense of history that actually traces its roots way back to the works of St. Augustine in the fourth century, and the concepts in his famous book, *The City of God.* So a case can be made that it is the Slavs who have preserved the Christian underpinnings of European societies, which are prevalent to this day. It appears that while the Slavs held on to their strong Christian heritage, the rest of Europe did not. Here are the telling words of one great Slav, Aleksandra Solzhenitsyn, who lived through the brutal experience of a Russian slave camp. He summed up the horrors of the 20th century by saying:

"The failings of human consciousness, deprived of its divine dimension, have been a determining factor in all major crimes of the 20th century. The first of these was World War I, and much of our present predicament can be traced back to it. That war took place when Europe, bursting with health and abundance, fell into a rage of self-mutilation that could not but sap its strength for a century or more, and perhaps forever. The only possible explanation for this is a mental eclipse among the leaders of Europe due to their lost awareness of a Supreme Power above them. Only the loss of that higher institution from God could have allowed the West to accept calmly after World War I, the protracted agony of Russia as she was being torn apart by a handful of cannibals. The West did not perceive that this was in fact the beginning of a lengthy process that spells disaster for the whole world." [2]

Yes, we are now well into the 21st century, and so far a nuclear holocaust has been avoided. This does not discount the important points Solzhenitsyn raised, however, that 1914 marked the beginning of a civilization crisis for Europe, where the after effects are much on display to this day. Solzhenitsyn believed this phenomenon represents the expression of a profound, long standing crisis of civilization morale. It can also be said that World War II can be brought closer into focus when we look at it from the point it began in 1914, and did not actually end until August, 1991.This is when the Soviet Union collapsed under western pressure; the weight of its own falsehoods, and the demands of the peoples of the Soviet Empire for national freedom. World War I, known as the Great War, set the 20th century on a distinctive course. It all happened, according to Solzhenitsyn, because man had forgotten God!

INSIGHTS OF HENRI DE LUBEC:

Henri de Lubec (1896 – 1991), lived a life that mirrored much of the 20th century turmoil that took place in Europe. He is considered one of the last century's most honored Catholic theologians, who also happened to be a good friend of Pope John Paul II, who later made de Lubec a cardinal. He witnessed much of the horror that took place, and spent much of his life questioning what happened, and why it happened. Any reader can gain great insight into why the carnage of World War II had to happen, by reading extracts from two of his writings, *Christian Resistance to Anti-Semitism: Memories from 1940 – 1944 (1945),* and *The Drama of Atheistic Humanism (1983).* Let us take a look at some of the comments that this great man made.

De Lubec claimed in his writings that the crisis Europe found itself in during World War II was the product of what he called atheistic humanism – the deliberate rejection of the God of the Bible, the God of Abraham, Isaac, Jacob and Jesus, all in the name of authentic human liberation. He went on to say that what biblical man once perceived as liberation, the proponents of atheistic humanism perceived as bondage. The atheistic humanists claimed human freedom could not coexist with the God of Jews and Christians. Human greatness required rejecting the biblical God, according to their "new" faith. This, according to de Lubec, was something new, something different from past history. This was not the type of atheism for idle chatter at cocktail parties, or something to shock or impress without follow through. This was a new form of atheistic humanism with a strong ideology designed to shake up and re-design the world.

As a man of many good ideas, de Lubec knew that ideas have consequences, and that bad ideas can create very ugly results. He found inside the pit of evil and darkness was wrapped the despotic megalomania of Fascism, Communism, and Nazism. He made important connections tying together the negative effects of the relationship between the new modern technology, and the new ability of atheists to change the culture of how man should live. He said, "It is not true, as it is sometimes said, that man cannot organize the world without God. What is true is, without God he can only organize it against man. That is what the tyrannies of the mid 20th century had proven – ultra mundane humanism is inevitably inhuman humanism. And inhuman humanism cannot sustain, nor nurture, nor defend the democratic project. It can only undermine it or attack it."

De Lubec concluded that Fascism, Communism and Nazism, were manifestations of an atheistic humanism that was built on the shoulders of men like August Comte, the man who once implied it was empirical science that was man's answer to what ails him; Karl Marx who alluded to the spiritual world as a fanciful idea, a false doctrine. Also included are men like Nietzsche whose radical ideas of the will to use power were the hallmark of human greatness, and, of course, Charles Darwin himself, whose whole theory of evolution started the whole process. Unfortunately, the full weight of the material affects of this atheistic humanistic thinking was later turned into a reality in the human slaughter houses of German concentration camps, where human killing and destruction reached a level unheard of in the annals of man's history.

Later, de Lubec developed the thought that man had forgotten God due to the result of an incorrect approach to human freedom, which included living a secular life in order to be free. This explains why pushing God out of society became so complete during this phase of man's history. In attempting to read this history through a theological lens, de Lubec's essay of the drama of atheistic humanism provided insight into Solzhenitsyn's identification of 1914 – 1918 as the moment when European civilization went into crisis.

It has been said that the institutional philosophy of atheistic humanism as expressed in Fascism, Communism and Nazism was eliminated in World War II. However, there remained a pollution of intellectual, spiritual, and moral poison that carried over into the Cold War period that lasted until 1991. European man has since that time convinced himself that in order to be free, he must be humanistic, secular, and even radical.

This way of thinking has had dire consequences for the entire European continent, and has become pervasive in public life and in the culture of the people.

Europe today is now the benefactor of this form of radical thinking, and it cuts deep into the soul of their moral crisis. We are now getting closer to explaining why Europeans are becoming more disinterested in the political process. Instead of looking to God for answers, they prefer the illusion of security provided by the United Nations and the Americans. Consequently, they are forfeiting their own future.

CREATING THE EUROPEAN CONSTITUTION:

It is interesting to note that after ten new members were accepted into the European Union on May 1st, 2004, it began the heavy task of creating the (EU) European Union's very first constitutional treaty. As with the creation of the American one worked out back in 1787, this constitution also experienced a lot of bitter in-fighting, deal-making, and backroom negotiations as the older members tried to find ways for EU decision making to be made in such a way that it protected the rights of smaller members, while at the same time acknowledging the many contributions of the larger members.

During negotiations the EU struggled with a very important issue, which was whether or not to mention a reference to "Christianity" in its preamble as the source of Europe's distinct civilization. After many rounds of bitter negotiations, the final treaty ended up stating the roots of modern European civilization and its commitments to democracy, human rights, and the rule of law, were identified as the continent's classical heritage of the Enlightenment.

In one single day we find that 1500 years of Christian influence on the formation of what is now Europe vanished from European history. Although it is true that some countries fought hard for the principles of Christianity to be boldly placed in the preamble, they were all denied. For the record, those countries included: Italy, Poland, Czech Republic, Malta, Lithuania, and Portugal. Obviously, they were "out gunned" by France, Germany, Spain and Great Britain, among others.

The new constitution was enacted in June, 2004, and it contained some 70,000 words without mentioning Christianity or God, which is a challenge in itself considering that the foundation of Europe was established on the shoulders of great Christians right up to the attempt to form the first European Union after World War II. In providing a simple comparison, we find that the American Constitution, with about ten-percent of the words of the European version, is based on biblical principles of a creator. It is therefore quite understandable why Pope John Paul II registered grave concerns against the language used, and was grieved because he had fought hard to bring Poland into the European Union. (Note: by November of that year, the Pope had gained more than one million signatures from Europeans who wanted the European Parliament to recognize Europe's Christian heritage). See Article 1-52 below.

The secular leader of France, President Jacques Chirac, summed up the debate as follows: "France is a lay state, and as such she does not have a habit of calling for insertions of a religious nature into constitutional texts." Chirac concluded, "The lay character of French public institutions, would not allow a religious reference in the new Euro-constitution."[3]

Socialist leaning members of the French Chamber of Deputies, along with support from some British members of parliament, endorsed Chirac by going on to state that any mention of God or Christianity in a European Constitution would be absurd, because doing so would also exclude Muslims, other non-Christians, and atheists from the political community of the new Europe. It is perhaps worth recycling the words of former French President, Val'ery Giscard d'Estaing, who officially presided over the convention when he said, "Europeans live in a purely secular political system, where religion does not play an important role."[4] What was so striking about this comment was his words went against more than half of the individual member countries' own constitutions that supported established churches, or formally acknowledged God in their constitutions. Article I-52 was later added to respect the legal personalities and juridical status of churches and other "religious associations" under existing national laws. Still, the preamble was weak, and it has caused much divisiveness among the European population.

When I read about the debates over the EU Constitution, I found it interesting as to why the debate against placing Christian principles into the EU Constitution was so controversial. One cannot help but wonder why the humanist lobbying groups were so aggressive in their demands to keep those principles out all together. To exclude Christian contributions to European civilization in order to appease Jews, Muslims, homosexuals and non-believers, is mystifying when one considers the constitutional words of some of the individual European countries such as Poland where a compromise was successfully worked out between Christians and other believers. In the case of the European Constitution, the secular humanists were inflexible.

When we take a closer look at the EU preamble, it leads to the obvious conclusion that as far as Europeans are concerned, Christianity is not only negligible in modern European life, but it is also a stumbling block to a Europe that wants peace at almost any price; a Europe that wants to be a champion for human rights, and a continent that wants to govern itself democratically.

We can now see more clearly that by destroying Europe's Christian heritage as a necessary condition, European leaders are attempting to achieve a continent wide unity of purpose without the help of God. Also, by adopting a neutral world-view, their leaders are able to achieve the only form of democracy that they can imagine.

In summary, the argument over acknowledging any Christian contribution to the democratic civilization of the 21st century in Europe, speaks volumes about the understanding of "democracy" and "human rights," which were both developed from Christian principles. We can now see more clearly in hindsight that the European Constitution was hurriedly ratified, for whatever reasons, and as a result some very important conditions were not properly thought out. Unfortunately, the race-to-record mentality of the secular humanistic community ended up winning the day. They won, Christians lost.

DEFENDING THE FAITH AGAINST THE CONSTITUTION:

The European Constitution has since been challenged a number of times along legal, philosophical, and political grounds, and the fight continues. The case has been made that the Constitution has deliberately ignored Europe's Christian roots, and therefore it is illegitimate. Most country's constitutions are designed to be responsible for organizing state functions, identifying the responsibilities of the legislature, and to also define the relationship between citizens and the state. This last point has apparently been ignored, and has thus created the legal challenges to correct it.

We find it most interesting that the Polish Constitution does not appear to have a problem in creating a set of words that satisfies all its citizens, and one wonders why the European Constitution was unable to do the same. Here are some words from the Polish Constitution:

"Taking care for the existence and the future of our Fatherland, which recovered the possibility of a sovereign and democratic determination of its own destiny in 1989, we, the Polish nation, all the citizens of the Republic – both those who believe in God as the font of truth, justice, and beauty, and those who do not share this faith but respect these universal values as they derive from different fonts – equal in rights and responsibilities with regard to the common good – Poland . . ."

When we look back, it is hard to believe that Europe was constitutionally put together without a word being mentioned regarding its Christian heritage. No individual country has ever done that, but collectively there are now 28 countries that are in compliance with it. What makes the whole issue so sad is the fact that the founding fathers of today's European Union were all serious Christians who looked at European integration as evolving from Christian civilization. So in now stating that the origins of today's Europe were secularists and humanistic is totally false and misleading. The complexity of the matter becomes more so when a simple question is asked: How can a united Europe delight in a shared moral community, and have a shared commitment to their future, when their shared history has been erased of its Christian heritage? Imagine a man who has lost his memory trying to teach his son about their family history.

WAS EUROPE DEVELOPED ON JUDEO-CHRISTIAN ETHICS?:

Can we take Christianity out of Europe and make the case that Christianity had nothing to do with the creation of modern Europe, and Europe is better off without Christianity? Let's take a look at some European history to see if the facts support such a claim.

What remained of Roman civilization was preserved by monks during the so called Dark Ages. These monks later travelled from their home environment to convert the barbarian hordes of Europe. Their greatest success was with the Franks, who subsequently produced Charlemagne, whose Carolingian Empire preserved the achievements of Roman civilization, and set forth the foundations for what we now call Europe. The high point of the story comes on Christmas Day in 800 AD, when Charlemagne was crowned Holy Roman Emperor by Pope Leo III. In Charlemagne and Pope Leo III, Rome and the barbarians became friends, and by extension Jerusalem and Athens. As a result, the civilization we call Europe was developed from its embryonic state into enjoying its great time in history, the Middle Ages. It was the strength of the Christian faith that made it pliable in shaping the European historical forces that led to the High Middle Ages, several hundred years later. Scholars down through the centuries have thus come to the belief that there could be no understanding of Europe without an understanding of Christianity.

CHRISTIAN ROOTS OF DEMOCRACY

We find as we review history, Anglo-Americans are taught that the roots of modern democracy can be found in the Glorious Revolution of 1688, which secured parliamentary supremacy against the unmitigated right of royal absolutism in what would later become Great Britain. Europeans, on the other hand, are taught that democracy began with the French Revolution in 1789. Both of these positions are reasonable until we take into consideration the many examples of European history, when the Christian civilization of the Middle Ages resolved numerous problems between the Church and State. As a result, Europe learned many valuable lessons that would later be used in the defense of human rights.

Church history also tells us that during the Investiture Controversy, which had to do with whether the church or the emperor would choose new bishops of the church, the church won out. This was a very important event that proved the state would not have complete control over religious matters. As a result, the idea of a limited state in a free society was created by the results of the Investiture Controversy, and the principles of Christian thought. Europe thus learned that a consistent order of justice from one generation to the next acted as a counter weight to public authority and its avaricious power. It also resulted in the people having a say in deciding what is right and wrong, and not just the people in power. Here we see the rule of law replacing the divine right of kings, which came about directly as a result of the ideas, and moral clarity brought about by European Christian thinking.

We have discovered that democracy is not just a set of procedures and systems, but rather is based on a set of ideas and values that developed during the Middle Ages. It was the influence of Christianity that gave the individual respect, and a new emphasis on the rights of the individual. European men now came to realize how their own lives played a part in the creation and redemption story, which allowed them to live according to their God given destiny in worshipping God.

The Church in Europe now had the responsibility to take the teachings from its Jewish parents, and Christianize the world. People now better understood their role of being in this world, but not of this world, and as a result we find that Christianity taught Europeans that they had a responsibility to spread the Christian message to the rest of the world. These Christian principles, grounded in God's natural law, created the cultural background for the development of modern scientific principles.

ANOTHER GREAT EUROPEAN MAN SPEAKS OUT:

Besides Henri de Lubec, if there was ever another great man who could speak with authority regarding the chaotic 20th century history of Europe, it had to be Pope John Paul II. He was much more than an observer of his time, and Mikhail Gorbachev once stated the Pope was most instrumental in creating the revolution of consciousness that stirred his own Polish countrymen into action. His support caused his people to march peacefully for freedom against a brutal, communistic regime who were well known to crush previous protestors, as in Hungary in 1956. This is a man who spoke eleven different languages: Polish, Latin, Slovak, Russian, Ukranian, Italian, French, Spanish, Portuguese, German, and English, and was adamantly qualified to "bridge" the gap between East and West. He lived through much of the bloody conflict of World War II, and is therefore well worth listening to in what he said about the future direction of Europe.

Here are some extracts from Pope John Paul II, when he wrote his *Ecclesia in Europa* (The Church in Europe) in 2003. He proposed, "That the Church of the 21st century must once again proclaim a message of hope to a Europe that seems to have lost sight of it." He went on to say "The Church was very much aware of the grave uncertainties at the levels of culture, anthropology, ethics, and spirituality." Instead of experiencing a new hope after more than 70 years of violence and bloodshed, Europe instead was experiencing a type of vagueness causing a loss of trust in the future. He further stated "That the most urgent matter Europe faces, in both East and West, is a growing need for hope, a hope which will enable us to give meaning to life and history, and to continue on our way together."

The Pope, and many European Christian leaders, were gravely concerned with the rising religious indifference that was creeping into European culture. As Europeans disconnected themselves from their religious roots, they were demonstrating less hope in their future. This form of soul emptiness was manifesting itself in the weakening of family structure, and a growing selfishness that creates a fractionalized society where individuals are interested in only their own needs as opposed to the greater good of society. This selfishness is also showing up in a diminishing number of births. In his *Ecclesia Europa*, the Pope went on to say,

"That one of the roots of hopelessness assailing many today, is their inability to see themselves as sinners and to allow themselves to be forgiven. They have an inability, often resulting from the isolation of those who, by living as if God did not exist, have no one from whom they can seek forgiveness."

Pope John Paul II was suggesting if Europe was experiencing hopelessness, as his conclusions had led him to believe, and if one of those symptoms was demographic suicide, then Europe was dying from an erroneous story, and the true story had to be told. He firmly believed that telling the real story of the development of Europe based on the foundation of Christianity must be told, and would be the cure for the soul sickness that prevails throughout Europe. Winston Churchill once said, "The truth is incontrovertible. Malice may attack it, ignorance may deride it, but in the end, there it is!" The Pope went further by saying, "Human effort will be of no avail unless it is accompanied by divine assistance: for 'unless the Lord builds the house, those who build it labor in vain'" – Psalm 27:1. He concluded, "For Europe to build on a solid foundation, there is a need to call upon authentic values grounded in the universal moral law written on the heart of every man and woman."

So a strong case can be made that the democratic form of government did not develop out of the Glorious Revolution of 1688 in Great Britain, or the French Revolution of 1789, but rather it came from European universities, who in turn gained their wisdom from Christian monks who had preserved Christian doctrine through the Dark Ages. These great Christian principles that had nurtured the ideas of self-governance, and moral clarity, were completely overlooked in the writing of the European Constitution. This is a tragedy of immense importance for the future.

Pope John Paul II made a convincing argument, I believe, that Europeans, and in many ways, Americans, need to reach back to their Judeo-Christian heritage and learn to re-connect with God. I offer some moral clarity by asking the reader to imagine studying American history without mention of the Constitution. This is what is being asked of Europeans today.

EUROPEAN CULTURAL SUICIDE:

One of the symptoms of hopelessness that Pope Paul II referred to earlier is manifesting itself in a population decline in developed countries. The birth rate of the whole developed world is well below replacement, and some parts of the decline have passed the point of no return. Considering it takes 2.1 babies per married couple just to maintain the population base, it is shocking to come to the realization most countries in Europe are producing well below that rate. With birth rates well below the numbers needed to maintain population levels, we are finding the nationals in many European countries will be reduced in size putting enormous pressure on pension plans, Social Security, the sick and the disabled. Only immigrants are preventing the population slide from being even worse.

TFRs (Total Fertility Rates) in Europe are at the lowest in their history averaging 1.59 as of 2009.[5] Here are some of the results: Germany (1.4), Holland (1.8), Belgium (1.8), Italy (1.4), France (1.6), Sweden (1.9), United Kingdom (1.9).[6] Life expectancy rates are also increasing, which places a greater future burden on workers to support an aging population in retirement.

SPIRITUAL DECLINE VS. LOWER FERTILITY RATES:

In the previous section, demographers gave us explanations as to why young people in Europe (a population zone of over 700 million people) are not having children at the same rate as their parents. However they failed to mention the relationship between fertility rates and spiritual commitments, which is now well proven. In 2011, a survey by the Pew Institute determined more than 50% of Americans said that religion was important to them. Compare this to Spain (22%), Germany (21%), Britain (17%), and France (13%).[7] A separate poll of French men determined that 47% claimed to be agnostic.[8] A Gallup poll also inquired into how many people in European countries attend church on a regular basis. Here are the results: Denmark (3%), Finland (5%), Sweden (5%), France (10%), Germany (10%), United Kingdom (10-15%).[9] Finally, Europeans were asked about their personal values. Twelve values were chosen, and the top three were: Peace (52%), Respect for Human Life (43%), and 41% for human rights. Rated at the bottom was religion at 7%.[10]

As we look at American fertility rates a little closer, we find Americans of faith are more likely to have larger families than secular Americans. Every year the GSS (General Social Survey), at the University of Chicago, interviews thousands of Americans about their religious thinking, and then compiles the results. Among other things the researchers attempt to compare demographic variables, such as the number of children per individual, with religious attitudes. What they have discovered is half of the families that never take part in religious activities have no children. We are also told that those families attending church services weekly show a fertility rate 27% higher than the national average.

Our young men and women are being taught that children are a cost rather than an asset. In America, for instance, it costs a family $245,000 to raise a child through age 18 in 2014. [11] It therefore becomes obvious, parents need to identify with something beyond their own needs in order to bring a child into the world. We call it altruism, and to put it plainly, the world cannot continue to exist without altruism. This explains why people of faith are having more children than non-religious people. People of faith believe that God created them out of love, and by bringing more people into the world they are imitating God's love, and playing the proper role in His creation.

So today we have two forces or cultures competing with each other for the viability of future generations. Secular families are having fewer children, and religious families who place their trust in God are having a greater number of children. This fact explains why America, with a far larger percentage of its citizens practicing their religious faith, are producing enough children to sustain their population, whereas Europeans, who place a far lower priority on religious faith, are in a death spiral that can only get worse.

AMERICA'S FUTURE?:

This brings us to the question that I raised at the beginning of this chapter – is America going the way of Europe? Are Americans doomed to witness a future secular society that ignores God, and allows atheistic humanism to dominate the landscape of our great country?

In business they say that the trend is your friend. However, when we look at the current trends in statistics regarding the state of religion in America the trend is not so good:

20% of Americans now claim to be non-religious
33% of adults under age 30 consider themselves non-religious
66% of adults say religion is losing its influence in American life [12]

When you combine the atheists, agnostics and non-religious together it represents about 20% of the population. This is a big increase from 30 years ago, and according to some sources it will only get larger in the future, unless Christians can turn it around. Although these numbers are high, they are not as high as Western Europe, and in the Far East atheists represent the majority of the population.

AMERICAN NON-RELIGIOUS ON THE RISE:

With the non-religious portion of the American population on the rise, this would have made the late Julian Huxley, one of the original founders of The American Humanist Association, inaugurated in 1933, very happy because the trend away from God appears to be increasing at the sacrifice of lower church attendance in general. Humanism, as the name suggests, is grounded as the apex of evolution and as the measure of all meaning, rejecting God as the creator of all things. In the Humanist journal dated Sept/October, 1987, Lloyd Morain defines humanists as follows:

"Humanism does not include the idea of God, and as such is considered a philosophy rather than a religion. In a way, it is an alternative to all religions . . . Those caught up by its religious aspects know that it provides a vibrant, satisfying faith. Those who think of it as a philosophy find it both reasonable and adequate."

The former president of the American Humanist Association, Dr. Isaac Asimov (1920-1992), readily accepted humanism as the same as atheism, and he went on to say:

"I am an atheist out and out. It took me a long time to say it. I've been an atheist for years and years, but somehow I felt it was intellectually unrespectable to say one was an atheist, because it assumed knowledge that one didn't have. Somehow it was better to say one was a humanist or an agnostic. I finally decided I'm a creature of emotion as well as of reason. Emotionally, I am an atheist. I don't have the evidence to prove God doesn't exist, but I strongly suspect he doesn't, that I don't want to waste my time."[13]

Asimov was one of the most prolific and popular writers on the subject of science in the entire world, who had written more than 300 books, yet with all his intellect and knowledge he could not acknowledge the existence of God as the creator of all things. Asimov admitted that he had no evidence to support his position there is no God, yet he embraced humanism because that is what he wanted to believe. One cannot wonder if Asimov, with all his wide reading, had ever taken the trouble to read Psalm 53:12, "The fool says in his heart, there is no God." America was founded on Judeo-Christian ethics, but unfortunately we are straying further from those roots in a similar fashion to Europe today.

In summary, this chapter had to be told, due to the importance of understanding that if we do continue to move in the future direction we are going in, then we will end up like Europe with all its dysfunctional ways of thinking that are anti-Christian, and where more and more of their citizens believe there is no room for God in their lives. Europeans were given ample opportunity to observe the godless societies of Russia and China for many years, yet did not heed the lessons, and the warnings received deaf ears. Why? America not only has the benefit of that same history, but Europe itself is a Petri dish of experimentation that has gone very wrong, and it is clear for every American to observe and learn from. Will we learn the lessons that will save our country? I strongly hope so, for America is the world's last great hope. We represent the last beacon of light in a very dark world. However, with the freedoms we still enjoy under our Constitution that allows us to speak out on the issues, we must begin to act to save the soul of our country for all future generations. So use your voting privilege to vote for men and women that place God before their own needs. We need men and women that have a grasp of the 'big picture' and not just the immediate concerns that cause politicians to put expediency and self survival above doing what is right for future generations. If our military men and women are willing to sacrifice their lives for America, then politicians should be willing to sacrifice their own self-interest for the good of all Americans, both present and future. Can we ask for anything less?

CHAPTER ELEVEN

IMAGINE A WORLD WITHOUT JESUS

In the introduction I mentioned there are two great forces dogging man almost from his inception on this planet. They are the forces of God versus Satan, the light versus the dark forces of this world. Our loving God offers man a transparent, open light of truth, whereas Satan offers man an opaque darkness that hides his motivations for destroying mankind. As I mentioned previously, Satan can destroy but he cannot create, and millions of people have experienced the results of Satan's wrath in their lives. Despite the higher education level of the average person today compared with ages past, they appear to be less educated about the true power of Satan. Consequently, people in the modern age are more likely to fall into the power of darkness without realizing they could have taken appropriate action to protect themselves. So please listen up!

There is a reason why Satan is mentioned more than 50 times in the Bible. He represents a powerful force for evil and sin in the lives of men. He is the father of lies. To identify him better I have provided a partial list of the names he goes by, their meaning, and the Bible citation:

NAME	MEANING	BIBLE CITATION
Satan	Adversary	Matthew 4:10
Devil	Slanderer	Matthew 4:1
Evil One	Intrinsically Evil	John 17:15
Great red dragon	Destructive creature	Revelation 12:3; 7, 9
Ancient serpent	Deceiver in Eden	Revelation 12:9
Abaddon	Destruction	Revelation 9:11
Apollyon	Destroyer	Revelation 9:11
Roaring lion	Opponent	1 Peter 5:8
Beelzebub	Lord of the flies	Matthew 12:26-27
Belial	Worthless	2 Corinthians 6:15
God of this Age	Controls philosophy of this world	2 Corinthians 4:4
Prince of this World	Rules world system	John 12:31
Ruler of the kingdom of the air	Control of unbelievers	Ephesians 2:2
Enemy	Opponent	Matthew 13:28
Tempter	Entices people to sin	Matthew 4:3
Murderer	Solicits people to eternal death	John 8:44
Liar	Perverts the truth	John 8:44
Accuser	Accuses believers before God	Revelation 12:10

The Bible tells us Satan was cast out of heaven by God along with a third of all the angels for demonstrating pride in wanting to be like God himself. Since that time Satan and his fallen angels have created havoc on earth, and he is doing everything in his power to win men away from God. Satan has achieved much success over the years, and consequently millions of lost souls have ended up in hell. Unfortunately, this is not taught in the public schools anymore, and many people today are ignorant of his ways and how he can potentially destroy any chance a man or woman will have of going to heaven after this life is completed.

We shall learn what ultimately happens to Satan in the end, and we will also learn about what God's overall plan is for mankind. The main point to be made here is to simply state that Satan has been at the root cause of man falling away from God since Adam in the Garden of Eden. Clearly, if Jesus Christ had never come to earth both as a man and God some 2000 year ago, to show man the true way of salvation of his soul, it is axiomatic Satan would have had a field day without any competition from Jesus for the hearts of men.

In this chapter, I intend to make a strong case for loving and accepting Jesus rather than listening to the lies of Satan. I will do this by demonstrating what life for mankind was like prior to Jesus arriving on earth as a man, and what happened to mankind after absorbing the teachings and principles for living, laid down by Jesus. There is no question in my mind our earthly experience would be far worse than all the sin and corruption we witness today, if Jesus had not walked among men to act as an example for all. Through His teachings He showed man a better way, the right way to live while our spirits are temporarily trapped in our earthly bodies.

OUR WORLD BEFORE JESUS CAME:

Whether mankind knows it or not, when Jesus Christ came to earth both as all man and all God, He changed the world in many profound ways. Most people to this day do not realize the tremendous impact He has had on millions of lives down through the centuries. Even time itself was changed from B.C. (Before Christ) to A.D. (Anno Domini, meaning the year of our Lord), or the beginning of the Christian era.

Prior to Jesus, we find man living in pagan societies, worshipping idols, deities, and practicing polytheism and animism. Men sacrificed children to their gods, and slavery was rampant. Life was of little value, and greed and avarice prevailed. Into this satanic darkness stepped Jesus, who poured light upon man's soul. He showed man a much better way to live his life through loving God and loving his fellow man. Man was given the opportunity of choosing Jesus or choosing a life of continual depravity. Through parables and examples, this sinless man became an emblem of the proper way to live life for all ages to follow. God had already given man at least three chances to alter his wicked ways, and each time man reverted back to his iniquities. Now, God was giving man a last chance, by allowing His only begotten Son to enter earth as a man in order to show men the evil of their ways. So we will begin by sharing below just some of the many ways that Jesus' life has impacted the life of mankind.

INCREASING RIGHTS FOR WOMEN:

Unlike Islam, which has now evolved some 1400 years and still suppresses the rights of women, we find that from the very start, the Christian movement aspired to treat all women as equal to men. As we delve into the history books of ancient man, we find much evidence to support the fact that women were treated in terrible ways by their men, and society in general. The ancient empires of Greece and Rome, and recorded history from India and China, tell us that women were thought of as inferior to men, and not capable of independence.

Even our very wise Aristotle (384 B.C. – 322 B.C.) once stated women were somewhere between a free man and a slave. Later, Plato (428 B.C. – 348 B.C.) is on record stating if a man is a coward in this life, he would come back as a woman in the next. Evidence that women were treated inferior to men was exemplified by the fact that little girls were abandoned in much greater numbers than boys, which later caused shortages of young, eligible women for marriage, resulting in them getting married at very early ages. Aristotle and Plato, were extremely well educated and enlightened men, having made a tremendous contribution to the advancement of world knowledge. Yet both of these great men were hostile towards the rights of women.

On the other hand, there are countless examples where Christians have improved the rights of women, but I will simply site the great English Christian missionary to India, William Carey (1761 – 1834). Prior to Carey arriving in India, it was the practice of some Indians to burn wives on the funeral pyres of their deceased husbands. This ritual was known as Suttee, and was part of the Sati system that had been around for hundreds of years. Thanks to the aggressive action taken by Carey, as he campaigned doggedly against great opposition from the Indians themselves, he finally succeeded, and it was abolished in 1829. *Christianity Today* states that during the time it took for Carey to carry out his campaign, some 300 wives were burned to death in Calcutta, and perhaps 10,000 across the sub-continent (Christianitytoday.com – 12/9/2009). Carey was also instrumental in banning the burning of lepers, the banning of infanticide, and helped eradicate the custom of child widows who were raised to grow up as temple prostitutes. Christians were behind all the positive forces causing these changes, and women especially benefited.

PROTECTING CHILDREN:

Pagan life before Jesus arrived was cheap, expendable, and not long lasting. We have discovered children being sacrificed to the gods, Baal and his wife, Ashtoreth, as a common occurrence. We are also aware that abortion was pandemic. In ancient Rome and Greece, most babies born with deformities were abandoned in the wilderness where they were devoured by wild animals. Any children who managed to outlive infancy became an exclusive asset of their father, who could do with them as he wished, which could include extreme cruelty, murder, or selling them off as slaves, all with the full approval of the state.

It is claimed only half the children lived beyond eight years of age during the time of ancient Rome and Greece. [1] Infanticide was not only legal then, it was actually promoted as a good thing. When Jesus came to earth these evil acts began to disappear as man learned the true ways of God. Christians since then have cherished life as sacred, including the unborn. Abortion disappeared in the early church period, along with infanticide and abandonment. It is so sad to see all the great progress made by Christians down through the centuries being turned upside down since 1973, when Roe vs. Wade legalized abortion in America, causing our society to once again practice pagan ways, en masse. Not only do we kill our children in their mother's womb, our government actually promotes abortion abroad by attaching abortion conditions to our foreign aid program. We are now witnessing wholesale abortion across the globe.

DIGNITY AND PROTECTION OF THE ELDERLY:

When we delve into history we find that killing of the elderly after they became non-productive, was an expedient way to eliminate suffering. This practice was common, and went on for hundreds of years in pagan societies. Christian missionaries are the ones who began to build homes for the elderly to allow them to spend their last years in peace and dignity, and this trend has strengthened over the last 100 years. Also bear in mind, however, that people did not live as long as we do today. In fact, up to the 19th century, only about one person in 100 lived to the age of 65, and the average life-span of a man in America as late as 1900 was only 46.

ELIMINATION OF CANNIBALISM:

Before the introduction of Christianity, cannibalism was common, and people ate each other under the mistaken belief they would triumph over their enemies, and convert the strength of their enemies into themselves. In ancient times we also have evidence of large pots that were set outside the walls of ancient cities containing the remains of the dead who had been cooked and consumed by the poorest of the population. Later, through the teachings of Christ, we have seen a gradual elimination of cannibalism, and finally ending it around the world in the early part of the 20th century.

I have visited some of the human sacrifice sites of the Aztec and Maya, in Mesoamerica, as well as Inca sites in South America, where thousands of people were ceremonially killed to please the Sun god. Much is heralded about their ritual of human sacrificing, but less has been said about their compulsion for cannibalism, which was rampant throughout many parts of Central and South America prior to the arrival of the conquistadors.

In some parts of the world, such as the Fiji Islands, where I had the distinct experience of meeting with a village chief, I discovered cannibalism was finally eliminated by the ethics of Christianity civilizing the tribes, and leading them to the one true God. While in Fiji I became acquainted with the missionary accomplishments of men like H.L. Hastings, who stated in his memoirs when he visited the country in 1844, that it was possible to buy a man for about $7.00, which was less than the cost of a cow. He returned many years later to discover men could not be purchased at any price due to the building of hundreds of Christian churches where the gospel of Jesus Christ was being preached.

While in the French Society Islands, I visited sites where the English sea captain, James Cook, had opened the "gates" allowing Christian missionaries to preach the powerful message of Jesus to the natives, which contributed greatly to the elimination of cannibalism. Cook was later killed by the natives in Hawaii, but they revere him to this day for the Christian work he accomplished. Yes, the overpowering message of Jesus won the day, and the sacredness of life in those parts prevailed.

FREEDOM FROM SLAVERY:

Slavery today is still practiced in a few countries, even though banned by the United Nations, and by all governments of good conscience. In the ancient world, however, slavery was pandemic, and even people of the same race enslaved each other. History tells us that half the population of the Roman Empire were slaves, and about 75% of the people in ancient Athens were slaves. In Greece, the citizens of the ancient city of Sparta systematically terrorized their slaves, and treated them almost like animals. Yet after Christ came we see a steady decline in man's slavery of other men. History tells us that down through the centuries, Christian households have led by example by demonstrating that all people are made in the image of God, and should be loved and treated equally. This attitude is irrespective of a person's social standing, color of their skin, or any other characteristics distinguishing one person from another.

One man among many, who should be singled out for the great work he did to end slavery, was the Christian, William Wilberforce (1759 –1833), a member of parliament from Yorkshire, England. He took up the abolition of slavery in 1787 to ban slavery in Great Britain. It took him 20 years before the Slave Trade Act of 1807 was formally passed. Not satisfied with that achievement, he continued to push for the elimination of slavery throughout the British Empire, which finally came in 1833, and some 700,000 slaves were finally freed. Wilberforce died three days after receiving the news.

William Wilberforce set an example that was later followed by Abraham Lincoln, and the Christian Abolitionists some 30 years later in America. It took a very long time for Christian principles of living to take hold in our evil and corrupt world, but the evil of slavery was finally eliminated from the developed nations as a result of Christianity. In countries where Christianity is banned due to local religious and secular laws, you will find evidence of slavery to this day. The Sudan and Mauritania are such examples.

GREATER COMPASSION FOR THE COMMON MAN:

Jesus once said the poor will always be with us, and that statement is as true today as it was 2,000 years ago. Throughout history we find the Church of Jesus Christ has done more to help eliminate poverty than any other institution in the world. This Christian example has been duplicated and copied by thousands of other faith based poverty relief organizations around the world, such as the Salvation Army, Mother Theresa's Sisters of Charity, The Red Cross, Food for the Hungry, World Vision, Samaritans Purse, and many more too numerous to count. Jesus taught us, and simply asked us to imitate Him. Unfortunately, many governments in modern times have taken over providing for the poor, which has proved disastrous.

I mentioned earlier that a former American president declared war on poverty, and although the tax payers have spent trillions of dollars to stamp out poverty, it is still with us. Can we conclude, therefore, that the government is not the answer to reducing poverty? After spending such tremendously large sums of money (more than $20 trillion), to attack poverty without success, that perhaps our government should heed the words of St. Paul.

We need to allow more room for faith based giving organizations to have a larger seat at the table, just like they once did. Churches, synagogues, mosques, charitable organizations, and man's application of the Golden Rule, common to all religions, is and always has been the most effective way to fight poverty. For the first 150 years of America's existence we find the government providing very little assistance to its citizens. As late as 1929, federal assistance was only $90 million dollars, about $800 million in today's value. Americans, not the federal government, made a total of $335 billion in charitable giving in 2013. Here is the breakdown (all numbers rounded):

Individuals	$241 billion
Foundations	$ 50 billion
Bequests	$ 27 billion
Corporations	$ 17 billion [3]

The same source states that 95% of American households give to charity, and those same households average $2,974.00 per year. All this giving was outside the largesse provided by American tax payers through forced payroll deductions, which are spent nowhere near as efficiently as private giving. Faith based giving, which Americans are renowned for all around the world, is still by far the best and most efficient way to combat poverty, and to help the disabled, the widows and the orphans in our society.

For instance, in the United States, you will find that churches are classified as 501-C non-profit corporations, and do not pay property taxes on their land and buildings, and individuals do not have to pay income tax on the amount of their income that they donate to churches or other charities (in fact the government provides a tax deduction for such giving). In the first amendment to the Constitution we find that "Government shall make no law respecting an establishment of religion." This means that our government does not support any one particular religion, but allows all religions to express themselves. This is in sharp contrast to other countries like the United Kingdom, where the Church of England is still the state church. You will also find in Scandinavian countries such as Sweden and Norway, the Lutheran Church is the state church. Many countries with high Catholic populations, such as Spain, support the Catholic Church as their state church. Interestingly, you will find that in Germany the government taxes Catholics, Protestants, and Jewish wage-earners, up to 9% of their total income. The government then disburses these funds to the churches to be used for social services.

In such an environment, you can readily see why direct support of churches by the government actually weakens church influence on society, as is noticed when we study the very low turn-out rate for Sunday services. The Christian faith is weakened, and Christians become Christians in name only, and their "fruits" are not evident.

In addressing poverty and demonstrating compassion for our fellow man in distress, we have to be careful not to aid and abet the circumstance, thus making the person more dependent rather than seeking a way out of his situation. There is a big difference between a "hand-out" versus a "hand-up." Someone once said if you give once, you elicit appreciation; if you give twice, you create anticipation; if you give three times, you create expectation; if you give four times, it becomes an entitlement, and if you give five times, you establish dependency! Today we are quickly reaching the point where about as many people receive a check from the government each month without working, as compared with those who actually do work. In other words, we are creating a society where more and more people depend on the government and are inclined to vote their pocket-book (i.e. vote for politicians who keep sending the free money), and they will soon outvote those who do actually work and pay taxes. This situation is causing many workers in America today to be resentful of forced payroll deductions that help pay for those people who are capable of working, but simply don't want to do it.

St. Paul, one of our greatest Christian leaders once said, "For even when we were with you we gave you this rule: If a man will not work he shall not eat." (II Thessalonians 3:10). Too many people in America today think they can live off the hard work of others, which challenges the true teachings of Christianity. This must change. We need to be compassionate towards the truly needy: the widows, orphans, disabled etc; but we also need to be smart in how we spend finite funds, while also tackling the huge social debt burden that has accumulated for many years due to governmental approaches that have not proved successful.

The world before Christ was a place where charitable giving was almost non-existent. Scholars have researched historical documents from antiquity and concluded there is no record of any type of organized giving. After Christ, we find giving and benevolence began to flourish. In his book, *Caesar and Christ,* Will Durant, while writing about ancient Rome, which was at the highest point in world civilizations at that time, said: "Charity found little scope in this frugal life. Hospitality survived as a mutual convenience at a time when Inns were poor and far between; but the sympathetic Polybius reports that 'in Rome no one ever gives away anything to anyone if he can help it' – doubtless an exaggeration.'"

It was Jesus who set the example for caring for the poor and the down and out, and one of His best parables is about the Good Samaritan (Luke 10:25-37), who stopped to help the stranger even when a priest and a Levite would not. This was despite the fact that Jews did not associate with Samaritans at the time (John 4:9). This parable had a profound effect on later Christian living. We also have the parable of the sheep and the goats (Mt. 25:31-46), where Jesus separated those who fed the hungry and quenched their thirst, from those who did not, but asked Jesus, "When did we see you hungry or thirsty . . .?" Jesus then replies, "I tell you the truth, whatever you did not do for one of the least of these brothers of mine, you did not do for me." Jesus made the case that there are people all around us that have unmet needs, but many are blind to them, because they are totally absorbed in their own lives. These parables had significant impact on Western civilization, because Jesus encouraged generosity towards the poor. The concept of being "Christ poor," is like treating the poor as though it was Jesus Himself.

Throughout the ages some have been called to give all they had to the poor. St. Francis of Assisi is a good example, and Mother Theresa yet another. Yale historian Dr. Kenneth Scott Latourette (1884 – 1968) in his two-volume book, *History of Christianity,* wrote:

"The Christian community stressed the support of its widows, orphans, sick, and disabled, and of those who, because of their faith, were thrown out of employment or were imprisoned. It ransomed men who were put to servile labor for their faith. It entertained travelers. One church would send aid to another church whose members were suffering from famine or persecution. In theory, and to no small degree in practice, the Christian community was a brotherhood, bound together in love, in which reciprocal material help was the rule."

THE FLATTENING OF EDUCATION FOR ALL:

Prior to Jesus coming to earth we find education was only for the elite of society. There were no public school systems, and the vast majority of the world's peoples were illiterate. When people are illiterate they tend towards superstition, which leads to the worship of idols and other deviant forms of behavior. Pagan societies abounded with people who spent their whole lives living in ignorance. Jews were somewhat of an exception to this trend, because they have always emphasized the importance of education. From those Jewish roots, Christianity placed great importance on teaching their followers the words and ways of God, and it became a teaching religion.

Christianity is the most theological of all the religions in the world, and Christians often spend their whole lives in a quest for knowledge in knowing God more intimately through His teachings in the Bible. It was this emphasis on learning that led to the concept of education for everyone, to the establishment of monasteries during the Dark Ages, which preserved Christian education. It finally led to the establishment of Christian universities at Oxford, Paris and Bologna, which were created in the 13th century. This movement created other universities across the continent, and Christian theology was the primary emphasis in the curricula.

The idea of developing a system of education for everyone did not take root until the Reformation period (1517 – 1648), even though attempts had been made prior to the 16th century.

A good example would be Emperor Charlemagne in France in the early part of the 8th century. He attempted to provide as much education for his subjects as he could during his reign over the Holy Roman Empire. Unfortunately, after his death his educational successes died with him.

During the Reformation period, a man of enormous faith and accomplishments, John Calvin, created an educational system that has had far reaching ramifications for Western education since. After Martin Luther's Protestant movement later split from the Roman Catholic Church, reformers like Calvin realized the only way to perpetuate the advancement of Protestantism was by educating its followers at all levels of society, and that meant making them all literate Bible readers. Thus began the real impetus for a thrust towards educating the masses.

Calvin, who was given the title of "Father of Modern Education," promoted the idea that the purpose of education was for people to know God and glorify Him, so that in both our personal and public lives we would walk in the way of God. Calvin promoted the odd idea that education should be the responsibility of the parents and not the state, which was a great idea, but now anathema to our public school officials today.

A student of Calvin, John Knox (1514 – 1572), who was an English priest exiled in Geneva, learned a great deal from Calvin regarding reform theology. He later became the founder of the Presbyterian Church in Scotland, and commented that his experience in Geneva made him realize that Calvin had created the greatest church of Christ over the last 2,000 years. He noticed that everything in life was conducted according to Scripture, and it was this legacy that was carried forward by the

Puritans and Pilgrims when they escaped religious persecution by fleeing to America.

Just like Calvin, the Pilgrims and Puritans placed great emphasis on creating a Christian education for everyone, and later in 1642, education became a legal requirement in their colonies. We find when we trace the history of education in America from 1620, when the Pilgrims landed, until 1837, all education in America was both private and Christian. We also find during this time period, Americans were generally far more literate than their counter-parts in England due to a greater emphasis on basic education skills.

In America we find, thanks to New England Puritans, well over 100 of the first universities established were founded on Christian principles. Once again it is sad to note these same campuses of higher learning are now secular in their philosophy, and have cut their umbilical cord with Christianity many years ago. Christianity may very well have been "air-brushed" from the campus curricula of modern American universities, but any study of history will provide volumes of facts to support the thesis that Christianity provided the back-bone of education that has made America the greatest country in the world. How could contemporary, intelligent, educated people of today be so ignorant of these facts available for all to see?

The legacy left to us by our Christian fathers has traveled down through the annals of history, so that by the time the Christian pilgrims landed at Plymouth Rock in 1620, they brought with them a very strong Christian faith, which unfortunately has been depleted considerably since that time. To provide you with some idea of the belief system of Americans during the 17th century, I will simply bring your attention to two documents from both a notable university, and from the New Hampshire Constitution, that demonstrate the great emphasis placed on a sound, biblical education.

In the 1636 Harvard University student handbook, it reads:

"Let every student be plainly instructed and earnestly pressed to consider well: the main end of his life as a student is to know God, and Jesus Christ, which is eternal life (John 17:3); and therefore to lay Christ in the bottom, as the only foundation of all sound knowledge and learning. And seeing the Lord only giveth wisdom, let everyone seriously set himself by prayer in secret to seek it of Him." (Proverbs 2:2-3).

You will also find in the preamble to the 1784 New Hampshire Constitution:

"Every individual has a natural and unalienable right to worship God according to the dictates of his own conscience, and reason . . . as morality and piety, rightly grounded in evangelical principles, will give the best and greatest security to government, and will lay in the hearts of men the strongest obligations to due subjection; and as the knowledge of these is most likely to be propagated through a society by the institution of the public worship of the Deity."

Interestingly, the first 100 plus American colleges and universities devoted their educational system so Americans could take their teachings of the Bible seriously, and they believed in training their children in the way of the Lord. They believed civil law, without a moral basis grounded in Biblical scripture, was no law at all. How far removed we have gotten today from this guiding principle. We know so much more today about our world and the universe in which we are a part. Our scientific breakthroughs since 1620 are astounding. We have access to more knowledge and evidence to substantiate the authenticity of Christ, thanks to the ground-breaking efforts by so many men and women who have devoted their entire lives in pursuit of the truth of Jesus, than at any other time in the history of man. Yet where is our spiritual progress?

If you have not already done so, you may find it interesting to walk around Washington D.C. Here, if you take the effort to look, you will find multiple, repeated evidence of the Bible, Jesus Christ, and Christianity in general. Visit some of the famous sites and witness of what I speak – The Washington Monument has a capstone with the Latin phrase, Laus Deo, which means "Praise God." You will also find engraved scriptures saying: "HOLY TO THE LORD" (Zechariah 14:20); "Search the Scriptures" (John 5:39), and Proverbs 10:7 stating: "The memory of the just is blessed." These are just a few examples of the many references to our Christian heritage that still remain there for all to see. Even our currency says: "In God we Trust." Psalms 33:12 says: "Blessed is the nation whose God is the Lord, the people He chose for His inheritance."

DEMOCRATIC FORMS OF GOVERNMENT:

In the 17th century, men fled with their families to America to escape the despotic rule of European rulers and their state forced forms of religion. It became obvious this new country needed to be founded on the basic principles of free men, and great minds were tasked to achieve the goal. By this time in history, man had several thousands of years of history to learn from, and thus the great American experience began upon the shoulders of great men who wanted a government unlike any other in the past.

Upon further reflection and study, these great early Americans found that the Anglo Saxons at one time considered themselves to be a commonwealth of free men causing all major decisions made by the elders to be executed with the consent of the people. Anglo Saxon rules were based on natural law (i.e. God's Laws). In practicality it meant the responsibility for solving problems was the sole province of the man of the household. If the problem could not be resolved then he was to turn it over to the leader of 10 families, then 50, then 100, then 1,000, and finally, if necessary, to the top leaders for final resolution.

Individual Anglo Saxon rights were considered sacred, and could not be broken without divine retribution upon the perpetrator. Out of all the many laws and customs held by these ancient people, only four were considered capital crimes: murder, treason, cowardice, and homosexuality. All other crimes were settled through reparation to the satisfaction of the bereaved party.

As we dig deeper into history, our founding fathers came to the realization that the ancient Jews under the leadership of Moses, experienced a similar social system to the Anglo Saxons. The individual was responsible for his own actions and those of his family, and irresolvable issues were elevated as high as the Council of 70. In the Book of Leviticus 25:10, we read: "Proclaim liberty throughout all the land unto all the inhabitants therefore."

Other resources the framers of our Constitution had available were the writings of the great Roman orator and writer, Cicero, who made the case that in order to create a government based on natural law, all that was necessary was to identify the right and proper personal conduct to ensure they coincided with

God's Law. In one of his writings, *Republic and the Laws,* Cicero made the case that God had given man adequate reasoning power, which when fully matured is called wisdom. Although Cicero lived in the B.C. era in a Roman pagan society, he nonetheless had the intellect and good sense to understand the creation of a society built on a foundation of love, both for God and man. They were, he thought, the pillars and support system that could create a long lasting moral society in harmony with God's attitude as to how man should live.

If all of man's laws were to be measured against God's Laws, the inevitable result would be a transparency that would easily identify differences, which could then be easily corrected. To provide some sense of where our founding fathers were coming from, when they included natural law in the Federalist Papers, The Constitution, and the Bill of Rights, we find below a number of people's rights, based on Natural Law, or God's Law, that have served America well over the years:

- Right to self government
- Right to free speech and freedom of the press
- Right to a free conscience allowing the free practice of religion.
- Right to enjoy the fruits of one's own labor
- Right to privacy
- Right to own property
- Right to defend family and property
- Right to determine a profession or trade
- Right to a fair contract
- Right to a fair trial, and be innocent until proven guilty
- Right to representation regarding taxes

The above freedoms are all based on natural law later written into the spirit of our Constitution and Bill of Rights.

Christian principles for the governance of men came from wise men like John Locke (1632 – 1704), who wrote the famous essay, *Essay Concerning Human Understanding,* that later proved to be of tremendous help in creating the framework for our Constitution based on Natural Laws. Locke maintained that all men have individual value, dignity, and are worthy of attention. Locke's aim was to seek ways to cultivate the power of the individual, not destroy it. He dismissed the belief that everything in our conscious mind came from unforeseen circumstances. Rather, he espoused the idea that it was not the forces of nature that invented a clock, or even the complications of the human body. The Creator of all things was involved - God. Locke went on to say that all men can know God, because man is made in the image of God as a creative, reasoning being, and therefore man should be able to follow God's plan for governance based on Natural Laws. Man is also aware that God demonstrates love and compassion, which He installed in mankind.

The American founders agreed with Locke's works, and it caused them to consider the existence of God as the most fundamental premise that underpinned all other thoughts in the creation of the Constitution. So we find in our Constitution that all self-evident truths proclaimed by our founding fathers are rooted in the belief of a divine Creator. By now it should also be self-evident that, without Christianity, America may never have come into existence. We have Jesus, and only Jesus, to thank for this great miracle country!

CHRISTIANS AND CAPITALISM:

Who would have thought capitalism and free enterprise came from principles of the Christian faith? In his book, John Chamberlain points out, "Christianity tends to create a capitalistic mode of life whenever siege conditions do not prevail."[4] Who can disagree that the principles of Capitalism have raised the standard of living for millions of people across the globe, and all from a strong bedrock of Christian thinking. We also find that before Jesus came to earth, we see the history of man despising manual labor, and forcing slaves to do it for him. As capitalism spread, and men were able to benefit directly from their own toil and sweat, it resulted in millions of people being removed from lives of poverty into a much more enriching lifestyle.

Christian Financial Concepts[5] points out that some 700 references are made about money in the Bible. More than two-thirds of the parables of Jesus discuss the managing of money. By applying the Law of Proportion, this fact alone should indicate how much importance is placed on the subject of money and economics in general. The right to private property ownership is clearly stated in Exodus 20:15, and 20:17, where it states, "Thou shalt not steal," and "thou shalt not covet thy neighbor's house," indicating you should not try to take what belongs to someone else.

John Locke, mentioned earlier, mentions our right to life, liberty, and property as being necessary to sustain life, and the importance of a free family unit enjoying a long life in the land of the Lord. Another great contribution to capitalism was the invention of the double-entry bookkeeping system created by an Italian Franciscan monk during the Renaissance period. Today in America, some 500 years later, we find every certified public accountant, along with countless corporate controllers, use the capitalistic idea of the double-entry method of accounting to keep the books and records of American businesses balanced. The only exception is our own federal government.

Protestant reformer, John Calvin, is often credited with being the father of capitalism, and in, *Religion and the Rise of Capitalism,* by R.H. Tawney, says of Calvin:

"He assumes credit for normal and inevitable incidents in the life of society. He therefore dismisses the oft-quoted passage from the Old Testament and the Fathers as irrelevant, because they were designed for conditions which no longer exist, and argues the payment of interest for capital is as reasonable as the payment of rent for land, and throws on the conscience of the individual the obligation of seeing it does not exceed the amount dictated by natural justice and the golden rule."[6] Christian history is replete with many examples promoting capitalism, which has proved such a positive force for mankind.

CHRISTIAN CONTRIBUTIONS TO THE ADVANCEMENT OF SCIENCE:

We discussed earlier the development of the great religions of the world, Hinduism, Buddhism, Daoism, Judaism, Christianity and Islam. Of these religions, only Christianity is based on reason. The beliefs of Jews and Moslems are founded on laws from a Creator who issues laws for the conduct of man and nature. The laws applying to Jews are for their people only. Everyone else is excluded. For Moslems, they believe their laws apply to everyone in the world. In either case, the laws are divinely revealed and must be strictly complied with.

Both Jews and Moslems strongly debate issues in their respective religions, usually by trying to figure out the best interpretation of their written codes. On the other hand, we find Christianity is not a religion of law but a religious creed. Christians have always emphasized and focused on doctrine, which they believe, is a set of true beliefs that determine man's relationship with Almighty God.

It is also important to explain the difference between Christianity, Judaism and Islam, by stating that Jews and Moslems place their highest discipline on the law, whereas Christians place their highest emphasis on Christian theology. Just as John Locke wrote nearly 400 years ago, man is to apply his faculties to apply reason in understanding the nature and ways of God. We also find in Hinduism and Buddhism, there is no theology due to the fact their adherents are not called to investigate God's purpose using this approach.

Christian leaders are the ones throughout history who have continually asked the great questions of how did our world come into existence, what is the purpose of life, and how is God proven? St. Augustine, for instance, tackled a deep theological problem when he reasoned that before today there had to be yesterday. If there was a yesterday, then there had to be a yesterday before that, going back indefinitely into the past. Therefore, if that was the case, then the question became how could God create a universe that has always existed? Furthermore, if the universe had not always existed, then there had to be a beginning, which leads to the question: what had been going on before the universe was created? Augustine determined that when God created the universe He also created time itself. Think of an author writing a book. He stands outside the cast of characters, and is not inside the book itself, though He knows what will happen in future chapters. This makes God omnipotent, omniscient, and omnipresent.

The 4th century Christian analysis that time came into existence when the universe was created, has been fully accepted by modern day physicists and astronomers. Augustine's reasoning on the nature of time itself, was created solely from Christian theological reasoning, which has penetrated man's deepest thoughts ever since. This is just one of many examples of how Christian leaders like Augustine, and men like Thomas Aquinas, applied reason to explain man's relationship with God, and His very existence of being. This rational reasoning, which is the hallmark of Christian thinking, can be found in no other religion anywhere in the world. This form of Christian reasoning demonstrates that religion and science do not have to be incompatible as many scientists today believe. To be fair, however, there are many scientists who have come to embrace Christian principles of reasoning and thought, which are not incompatible with their scientific thinking.

The Oxford English Dictionary defines the scientific method as: "A method or procedure that has characterized natural science since the 17th century, consisting in systematic observation, measurement, and experimentation, and the formulation, testing and the modification of hypotheses." The chief characteristic is that this method allows reality to speak for itself. By continuing to build on previous knowledge, science helps us to better understand the world. There are a number of steps or principles involved: Formulation of a question; Hypothesis, Prediction, Testing, and Analysis. This model is in its simplest form, but underlies the scientific revolution that changed our world. Someone once stated somewhere between 33% and 50% of all scientific discoveries are estimated to have been stumbled upon, rather than actually being sought out. This helps to explain why Louis Pasteur, once said "Luck favors the prepared mind."

Although scientific experiments took place with pre-Socratic Greeks such as Thales, and later Aristotle, we later find in order for a true scientific method to develop, Aristotle could not be taken at face value due to errors he made in his works, *On the Heavens,* and *Physics,* which later had to be corrected. It was not until much later that the basis for a true scientific method would be provided by the Judeo-Christian perspective. We have since found the principles underlying the scientific method, which consists of testability, verification, and falsification, arose from a study of Judeo-Christian scriptures.

The experimental method was clearly nurtured by Christian doctrine, and it was early Christian leaders such as Basil of Caesarea (330 - 379), and Clement of Alexandria (150-215) who encouraged future generations to view the Greek wisdom as being "handmaidens of theology," and science was considered a means to a more accurate understanding of the Bible and of God. St. Augustine later promoted and advocated the study of science and was wary of any philosophies that disagreed with the Bible, such as astrology, and the overall Greek belief that the world had no beginning. This Christian accommodation with Greek science laid a foundation for the later widespread, intensive study of natural philosophy during the late Middle Ages.

Unfortunately, the split between Latin speaking Western Europeans, from the Greek speaking East, followed up by barbarian invasions, the bubonic Plague of Justinian (named after the Byzantine Emperor), and the Islamic invasion, caused Western Europe to lose access to Greek wisdom. We then find by the 8th century, Islam had overrun many of the Christian lands in North Africa and the Middle East, which still profess the Islamic faith to this day. This fast occupation by the Moslems resulted in a long lasting separation of Western Europe from many of the works of Aristotle, and other iconic Greek men of science.

With such a large body of valuable knowledge now under control of the Arabs, who were the enemies of Europe, and who viewed any language inferior to Arabic, the Arabs needed to acquire Christians and Jews to decipher these great works from Greek and Syriac languages into Arabic. The Arab world-view stuck closely to Aristotle, even though some questioned some of his works. This Arabic world-view, which included many folk religions where belief in astrology, and nature was alive and divine, made it difficult for Arabs to get beyond Aristotle. Arabs also restricted their scientific inquiries due to the belief that Allah is unlimited, in which case he is subject to change. It therefore follows that the unpredictability of nature is a direct result of his changeable will.

To get control of a universal scientific method for the ages, it became necessary to weigh and interpret the works of Aristotle and other ancient men of learning, in order to build upon their wisdom, while at the same time be willing to criticize mistakes when necessary. Men also had to be free from the idea that nature changes due to divine intervention, by also recognizing that it is governed by its own constant laws that can be discovered and become knowable. The Christian and Jewish communities embraced this thinking, and this began the impetus and discovery of the scientific method.

The scientific method that would create modern science came about through the exploits of the Fourth Crusade (1202 – 1204) when Western Christians on their way to free Jerusalem from the Muslims, ended up ransacking Constantinople, which was the Christian Byzantine Eastern Church. This allowed the West, for the first time, to gain access to the original Greek texts that eventually led to the beginning of the scientific method.

From that point forward there was no looking back, and soon other Christian men stood on the shoulders of other great Christian men to further the cause of science. Grosseteste (1175-1253), an English statesman, scientist, and Christian theologian was the principle figure in bringing about a more adequate method of scientific discovery. He in turn influenced Roger Bacon (1214-1294), considered by many as the father of the modern scientific method, and who claimed mathematics was integral to a correct understanding of natural philosophy. His later discoveries in the behavior of light, and correctly calculating the calendar, can be found in his seminal works, *Opus Majus* and *De Speculis Comburentibus*. Other Christian men of science such as men like Johannes Kepler (1571-1630), Blaise Pascal (1623-1662), and Isaac Newton (1642-1727), also come to mind as having made significant progress in furthering the knowledge of man.

CHRISTIAN SCIENTIFIC CONTRIBUTIONS:

Below is a short list of men who made significant contributions to science even though they were committed to Jesus Christ as the Son of God:

Isaac Newton (Calculus), Robert Boyle (Chemistry), Lord Calvin (Energetics), Louis Pasteur (Bacteriology), Michael Faraday (Electromagnetics), Gregor Mandel (Genetics), James Simpson (Gynecology), Matthew Maury (Oceanography), Robert Boyle (Gas Dynamics), George Stokes (Fluid Mechanics), William Herschel (Galatic Astronomy), William Ramsay (Isotopic Chemistry), Joseph Lister (Antiseptic Surgery), John Ambrose Fleming (Electronics), Blaise Pascal (Hydrostatics), John Ray (Natural History), Louis Agassiz (Glacial Geology), Georges Cuvier (Comparative Anatomy), Charles Babbage (Computer Science), Johannes Kepler (Celestial Mechanics), Henri Fabre (Entomology of Living Insects), Matthew Drury (Hydrography), and the list goes on… To make the claim creationists are not scientists is a little foolish when one considers all the facts.

Think for a moment about the many ways our lives today have been tremendously improved by the scientific revolution. Without Christ, and the legacy He left with His Christian followers, you would not enjoy anywhere near the benefits you have living in today's age of science. Think back to Chapter One where I mentioned the Pilgrims coming to our shores in 1620; they arrived on ships that were not much better built than those of ancient mariners. They toiled the land with ox and cart using farm tools that dated back eons. A lot of time elapsed before Christian principles were unshackled, allowing the faith to finally come into its own, and the rest as they say is history (His Story). The great Christian writer, Francis Schaeffer, stated many scholars have commented that Christianity gave birth to modern science. He writes:

"Both Alfred North Whitehead (1861 – 1947), and J. Robert Oppenheimer (1904 – 1967), have stressed that modern science was born out of the Christian world view even though neither man was a Christian. Whitehead was a highly respected mathematician and philosopher, and Oppenheimer, after he became director of the Institute for Advanced Studies at Princeton in 1947, wrote on a wide range of subjects related to science. Whitehead in his book, *Science and the Modern World*, commented Christianity is the mother of science because of the medieval insistence on the rationality of God."[7]

CHURCH INFLUENCE:

As the Christian church system grew larger over the centuries, it caused man to expand his charitable giving to the poor. The church created Christian hospitals, financed numerous missionary projects across the world, and resulted in civilizing millions of barbarian and primitive cultures, who otherwise may never have had the opportunity to learn about Jesus Christ and His teachings. Missionary work has also resulted in the codifying of many of the world's languages so Bibles could be read all over the world. We continue to live in the Church Age, and the church will continue to be used to exemplify God's glory here on earth.

As we approach the end of this chapter, I am confident in saying that the benefits to mankind that Jesus and His Christian followers have contributed to the good of man's society over the last 2,000 years, are inadequately mentioned here. A whole library of books could be devoted to the numerous accomplishments man has achieved based on the foundation of Christian principles taught to man by Jesus.

When we step back and pause to look at the "big picture," it is very difficult for someone like me to understand how European leaders, mentioned in chapter ten, have chosen to ignore numerous Christian contributions, which built the foundation transforming Europe into a powerhouse of scientific discoveries, and yet be willing to throw it all away in one hastily produced document. Other great societal contributions made by Christians include: art and music; the development of Christian ideals abolishing slavery; creating freedom for the common man; universal education for all; the creation of capitalism with opportunities to help man become fully self-actualized, and setting the standard by which the whole world sat back in awe.

We must not forget the exploits of European powers, backed by Christian missionaries, who have exported Christian values all over the world, especially during the last 350 years. Sadly, however, we are also witness to the steady regression against Christian values since the 1950's, causing me to wonder if Americans can learn from the European experience by strengthening their faith in God, or is America doomed to slip into the dark cave of secular humanism?

Christ is the only answer to the world's problems, yet when He was among us, He was a poor, wandering itinerant, who came from a humble family. He appeared, at least externally, like any other ordinary man, as presented in an excellent composition attributed to Phillips Brooks (1835 – 1893):

"He was born in an obscure village, the child of a peasant woman. He grew up in another village, where He worked in a carpenter's shop until He was 30. Then for three-years He was an itinerant preacher. He never wrote a book. He never held an office. He never had a family or owned a home. He didn't go to college. He never visited a big city. He never traveled 200 miles from the place where He was born. He did none of the things that usually accompany greatness. He had no credentials but Himself. He was only in His mid thirties when the tide of public opinion turned against Him. His friends ran away. One of them denied Him. He was turned over to His enemies and went through the mockery of a trial. He was nailed to a cross between two thieves. While He was dying, His executioners gambled for His garments, the only property He had on earth. When He was dead, He was laid in a borrowed grave through the pity of a friend. Nineteen centuries have come and gone, and today He is the central figure of the human race. All the armies that ever marched, all the navies that ever sailed, all the parliaments that ever sat, all the kings that ever reigned, put together, have not affected the life of man on this earth as much as that one solitary life."

I would like to add that Jesus did not come into this world to get married and have children; He did not come to pursue a career or start a Business. And He did not come here to live a long life and retire in comfort. He came into this world for one simple reason, which was to die. And by His death, His shed blood cleansed mankind's sins in order to allow eternal life with Him.

Jesus practiced ways of living that are counter intuitive to man's natural nature: love your enemies and pray for those who persecute you; if your enemy strikes you on the cheek, turn to him the other cheek; judge not less you also be judged. Concerning the woman who committed adultery, He advised her accusers to let him who is without sin cast the first stone; if someone wants to sue you and take your tunic, Jesus advised him to let him take your cloak as well. These, and many other teachings of Christ, have had a strong impact on man's treatment of other men since that time.

It is ironic, and the subject of a later chapter, that after many years of education and enlightenment about God's ways, we appear to be going full circle back to the days of ancient Rome and Greece, where life was cheap. In a country built on Judeo-Christian ethics we have, since 1973, when abortion became legal in the United States, killed nearly 60 million little Americans in their mother's wombs, many for their mother's convenience, so they can be free to pursue careers or fulfill their bucket list of needs. This staggering number is higher than the rate of infant killings during the Greek and Roman Empires, and it has all happened, notwithstanding all the knowledge man has learned during the last 2,000 years from Jesus Christ, who graciously died to cleanse mankind's sins. Worldwide figures on abortion are even more shocking. Jesus taught us the way, and His way is a good way, in fact the only way to live a clean, conscious free life-style where we can love our fellow man, forgive him when necessary, be non-judgmental when he fails, and above all love the one who gave His all for us. In the next chapter, with the help of God through Bible passages, we will take a peek into man's future. Unfortunately, it does not bode well for non-believers.

CHAPTER TWELVE

A GLIMPSE INTO THE FUTURE

In most of this book we have looked backwards by taking a panoramic view of man down through the ages, and his often tenuous relationship with God up to the present age. We have now accumulated almost 2,000 years of history since God walked among us, and showed us the proper way we should live. We have recorded the many mistakes made by man as he has pursued one religious or philosophical system after another in pursuit of meaning for his life, and we are now witness to the sorry current state of our world.

The evidence I have presented so far is overwhelming in favor of man needing a strong relationship with the monotheistic Christian God who created him; the God of Abraham, Isaac and Jacob; a God who is loving, righteous, and just; a God who is consistent in His application of spiritual laws, and can be depended upon to always do the right thing; a God who loves man so much He gave His only begotten Son as a sacrifice for man's sins, and He gave man the free will to choose Him or deny Him. He is also a God who has given man much opportunity to get his life right. Even as man continues to sin, God continues to forgive him through the redemptive nature of His relationship with those who love and believe in Him.

It is obvious by now that God loves us much more than we love Him.

God has also demonstrated tremendous patience over these many years with the iniquities committed by mankind, and all God has ever wanted is for man to love Him, obey Him, and accept His Son, Jesus Christ, as personal Lord and Savior. All man has to do is accept God's invitation to spend eternity with Him in heaven rather than spend eternity in hell. The process is easy, not complicated, except for man's free will getting in the way. A free will, I might add, that was given to man as a gift from a loving God who simply wanted reciprocal love. I sincerely thank God for not making me a puppet, and giving me free choice. It is that simple for me, yet that complex for some people.

Today the battle between light and darkness continues to rage on in the souls of men. Please keep in mind God is spirit. Satan is a spirit. Angels are spirits. A spirit cannot be destroyed. This explains why the Book of Revelation tells us in the end, the Anti-Christ and the False Prophet (explained later) will be thrown alive into the fiery lake of burning sulfur (Revelation 19:20), which is after the seven-year tribulation period, and then Satan will be chained in the abyss for 1,000 years (Revelation 20:2). The Bible does not talk about them dying. Man, however, is made of mortal flesh, blood and bone, with the spirit of God within him. When man's temporary earthly body eventually dies, his spirit does not, as it immediately goes either to heaven or to hell. In either place, man's spirit does not die, as spirits are eternal. If you are a believer in Jesus Christ as your Lord and Savior, then St. Paul clearly states: "I say I would prefer to be away from the body and at home with the Lord." (2 Corinthians 5:8). This a clear reference to heaven.

As I mentioned earlier, man grows physically and intellectually automatically, but the spirit within him does not. The spirit must be nurtured and developed or it stays dormant. The nourishment and protection of the soul must be developed through a relationship with God if man expects to live eternally with Him. Our life here on earth must be experienced backwards even though we have to live it forward. As the late Winston Churchill once said: "This is not the end. This is not even the beginning of the end, but perhaps it is the end of the beginning!" Yes, it is true that we make plenty of mistakes during our life, because we are matriculating students who don't receive our final test until we shed our earthly body and enter the spiritual realm. Then it will be too late to "crash" for the final examination.

I mentioned earlier how God has slowly revealed his divine law to mankind (Chapter Six), in at least seven major ways, causing man to have no excuse for not accepting God. I have also discussed three great chances man was given by God, in a very demonstrative way, which also went unheeded by many (Chapter Eight). We further reviewed how God, notwithstanding His many attempts to reconcile with man, even sent His Only begotten Son, Jesus Christ, to earth to walk among us, and show us very clearly what is expected of us during our short time on earth. This last chance still exists for you, if you wish to accept God's invitation. I recommend you read the first four books of the New Testament, Matthew, Mark, Luke and John, in order to gain a clear understanding of the teachings of Jesus; what He said, and what He did. Read Jesus' words for yourself;

don't allow others to read or interpret them for you. Many bibles indicate Jesus' words in red letters for easy identification.

Since Jesus walked among us, millions of people have taken up the cross of Christ and accepted Him as Lord and Savior. Unfortunately, the approximate two billion people on earth who claim Christ as their eternal savior, are trumped by the billions of other people who have either never heard of Christ, or have rejected Him for some other religious practice, which I have mentioned earlier in detail. Although man has been given many chances to get his life right with God, vast amounts of people today still don't understand what their life here on earth is all about. They fail to realize that this temporary life is in some ways a testing ground, a dress rehearsal if you will, that determines the eternal resting place for their souls.

In this chapter we will continue man's journey by looking forward. We will explore what God and the Bible have to say about future happenings. Many readers may not be aware there is an end to man's story here on earth, and I believe it informative for all of us to be aware of certain events God tells us will take place in the future.

Please note that this chapter and the next, although being provided as a simple over-view of upcoming prophetic events mentioned in the Bible, can be confusing to someone reading this type of material for the first time. My purpose, due to space limitations, is to provide you with a platform of upcoming events along with the appropriate Bible verses to support them. However, for those who wish to explore this subject in greater detail, there are many good books that can further enrich and amplify an understanding of this subject.

Why do we need to look into the future? Is it even possible? The answer is we need to know about the future in order to properly understand God's plan for mankind. We need to know the end of the story of man, and the only way for man to see the future is through the revealed words of God. God is all knowing, and He has all the answers. However, how much God reveals to man, and the timing of the answers, is entirely in the hands of God. In Deuteronomy 29:29 we find "The secret things belong to the Lord our God, but the things that are revealed belong to us and to our children forever." We also find in Isaiah 42:9 God saying "See, the former things have taken place, and new things I declare; before they spring into being, I announce them to you." With these two Bible verses in mind, let us now take a closer look at Bible prophecy in order to appreciate what God has provided man in the way of a roadmap towards the future.

WHY PROPHECY IS IMPORTANT:

A biblical principle known as "The Law of Proportion" mentioned earlier, means that we place importance on a subject based on the amount of attention that is focused upon it. If you consider nearly 25% of the Bible contains prophetic statements, this fact alone should make the study of Bible prophecy an important subject to pursue.

Consider the following points:

<u>Of all the written religious scriptures of major world religions, you will find the Bible is the only one that gives us detailed and specified, significant prophecies that have already been fulfilled.</u> Upon further research, you will not find any fulfilled prophecies made by Confucius, Buddha, the Hindu Vedas, or the Qur'an of the Muslims. According to John Walvoord,

past president of Dallas Theological Seminary, there are about 1,000 prophecies in the Bible, and about 500 have already been fulfilled. These facts alone separate Judaism and Christianity from all other faith systems, which fail to provide such future, specific, detailed predictions.

Bible scripture is authenticated by prophecy because all prophecies which have been fulfilled help validate the fact the Bible is the true word of God. This makes the Bible unique compared to all other world religious texts. In the Book of Daniel, we find him predicting the precise order of four great gentile (non-Jewish) empires that would arise hundreds of years before they became a reality (Daniel 2:36-45, and 7). In Jeremiah 25:11-12) he predicted the Babylonian captivity would last for 70 years, which it did. In Isaiah 44:28 and Ezra 1:1-3, we find the children of Israel would be sent home from Babylon by a man named, Cyrus, (a later king of Persia). Another example was when Jesus predicted the destruction of Jerusalem 40 years before it happened (Luke 21:6). Many more prophecies could be highlighted, but the point has been clearly made that the Bible is the most unique book in the whole history of the world. Why so many people don't read it is a mystery. Or in the words of Sir Winston Churchill, "It is a riddle, wrapped in a mystery, inside an enigma."

Jesus is clearly validated in the Bible where we find 333 prophecies concerning him alone, of which 109 were fulfilled by his First Coming, leaving 224 yet to be fulfilled in his Second Coming. Every part of the life of Jesus was prophesied including the place of his birth, Bethlehem, the nature of his birth (born of a virgin), the quality and purpose of his life; the agony of his death, and how He would die. In Psalm 22:16, it describes the

Messiah's hands and feet would be pierced. This prophecy was written by King David about 1,000 years before Jesus was born, and it was written at least 700 years before the Romans began using crucifixion as a means of executing people. How could that be? Consider the mathematical odds of so many proven prophecies coming true in the life of one person, and also consider the odds of the other unfilled prophecies not coming true. For instance, it has been proved that the probability of Jesus only fulfilling eight of the many prophecies would be 1 in 10^{17}. That's 1 in 100,000,000,000,000,000!

To put it another way, that would be like placing silver dollars to cover the entire State of Texas two feet deep, and then finding the one marked X. Now consider this. Upon further study, you will find the Bible has a 100% accuracy track record when it comes to predicting the future. That is something upon which you can depend!

Prophecy also provides man with insights of what God wants him to know about the future. Although God has not revealed everything about man's future, He does want man to know certain things in order to have hope for the future. St. Paul said, "Now we see but a poor reflection as in a mirror; then we shall see face to face." (I Corinthians 13:12). Through prophetic predictions we are able to know Lord Jesus is coming back, and He will resurrect us, and allow those who believe in Him to spend eternity with Him and the Father. We find in Deuteronomy 29:29, and Amos 3:7, what God wants us to understand about the future. Also, St. Paul states in 1 Corinthians 2:9, "However, as it is written: 'No eye has seen, no ear has heard, no mind has conceived what God has prepared for those who love Him'. . .but God has revealed it to us by His Spirit." (1Corinthians 2: 9-10).

A study of Bible prophecy can also help generate spiritual growth in Christians because it makes us more sensitive to our limited mortality, and the end of our life on this planet. Prophecy encourages patient waiting for the Lord (James 5:7-8), and provides hope for our future (Titus: 1:2-3). Peter also cautions us to prepare our minds for action; be self controlled; set your hope fully on the grace to be given you when Jesus Christ is revealed (1 Peter 1:13). We also find the Book of Revelation (1:3) provides a blessing to those who read it, and take it to heart, because all God's words are created to bless us spiritually (Psalm 119:114).

BIBLE PROPHECY UNFOLDING:

Numerous Christian theologians have studied eschatology (the study of end times), to gain insights into the future of man, and it is to be expected not everyone agrees on this subject 100% of the time. However, a large body of well respected men and women of God have agreed that certain action points take place in the future in a particular order to fulfill God's will for this earth and its inhabitants. It is this general consensus approach, of a dispensational pre-millennial viewpoint, I will be taking as we try to look into the future. Please also bear in mind good Christian men and women may differ in their understanding of these future events, but there are three non-negotiable events they all agree on: 1) The literal, physical and visible return of Jesus Christ to earth. 2) The bodily resurrection of the dead, and 3) the final judgment of all people.

For most of the past 2,000 years, Christians have been awaiting the Second Coming of the Messiah, Jesus Christ. However, no clear date could be established for the beginning of the end times as mentioned in the Bible (Matthew 24:36). Then, in 1948 a benchmark date was established with the re-creation of the Jewish State of Israel. Thus began the fulfillment of specific Bible prophecies regarding an international gathering of the Jews in unbelief, before the judgments to come, which will take place during the future Tribulation period. This re-gathering of the Jews had been predicted centuries ago, in fact even before the Jews were crushed and dispersed when Titus and his Roman legions destroyed the City of Jerusalem in 70 A.D. For almost 1900 years the Jews were without a country, making this 1948 event the first time in man's history where a nation destroyed came to life again after such a long interval, even to the point of rediscovering the old Hebrew language.

The prophet Ezekiel (36:10), who lived some 2600 years ago, speaking for God said: "I will multiply the number of people upon you, even the whole house of Israel, all of it. The towns will be inhabited and the ruins rebuilt." God also said, "I will bring them out from the nations and gather them from the countries, and I will bring them into their own land." (Ezekiel 34:13). In the vision of dry bones we find in Ezekiel 37, the Lord miraculously brings scattered bones back together into a skeleton, wraps the skeleton in muscles, tendons and flesh, and breathes life into the body. There is no question this chapter is speaking about Israel, for we read in verse 11 "these bones are the whole house of Israel." The larger point is that the Jews had to be re-gathered in Israel, which is a significant event from a prophetic standpoint. Even though Israel has been recreated, it should be mentioned that the Jews still live in unbelief. St. Paul states in Romans 11:25, "I do not want you to be ignorant of this mystery, brothers, so that you will not be conceited; Israel has experienced a hardening in part until the full number of the Gentiles has come in. And so all Israel will be saved." According to Joel 2:28-29, there will be a spiritual awakening in Israel, that will eventually occur in the future.

In the present age, known as the Church Age, or the Age of the Gentiles (non Jews), the Bible tells us we should prepare ourselves for the Second Coming of Christ. In fact all Christians should be looking forward to His return, which is unknown by everyone except God himself. However, we are told to look for certain signs of the times that will provide us with insight.

FUTURE SIGNS TO LOOK FOR:

In Jesus' Olivet Discourse (Matthew 24, Mark 13, and Luke 21) we read about wars, rumors of wars, famine, false impersonators of Christ, as just some of the signs we are to look for according to Matthew 24:4-8. We are also told in Mark 13:7, that when we hear of wars and rumors of wars, famines, earthquakes, nations rising against nations, we are not to be alarmed, for they are the beginning of birth pains, and the end is yet to come. We are further told in Matthew 24:29, and Luke 21:25, God's coming judgment will be preceded by eclipses, falling stars, earthquakes and other catastrophes, signaling God's final call to man to repent of his sins before it is too late. Most men will not. These terrible events, however, will be a reminder to all men that they cannot save themselves. Only Christ can save men from the evil in this world. In Mark 13:32 Jesus tells his disciples no one knows the date or the hour of

His return, but simply tells them to "Be on your guard!" (Mark 13:23). So that you do not become alarmed, it is best to focus on Jesus as the Blessed Hope, rather than worrying too much about signs. Watch for the signs, but don't get too carried away by them, for Jesus is our hope.

If you wish to gain insight into how God will judge mankind, you simply need to look at two parables, both found in Matthew 25:14-46. One talks about servants who have been left in charge of their master's money, and the other story concerns dividing people into sheep and goats.

Other signs of the times that we can be looking for are mentioned below:

An explosion of knowledge and travel	Daniel 12:4
People living as if God did not exist	Genesis 6:5, Luke 17:26-27
Deception and false Messiahs	Matthew 24:4, 5
Wars and rumors of wars	Matthew 24:6
Earthquakes and famine	Matthew 24:7
Worldwide acceptance of immoral behavior	Luke 17:26, II Peter 2:3
Increase in demonic activity	1 Timothy 4:1
Widespread abandonment of the Christian faith	1 Timothy 4:1-3, 2 Timothy 4:3-4
A diminishing of good world leadership	Psalms 2:1-3; Revelation 13:4-9
Evidence of family breakdown	2 Timothy 3:1-3
A common disrespect for the dignity of others	2 Timothy 3:2-4

An increase in selfishness and materialism	2 Timothy 3:1-5; James 3:14-16
Nation will rise against nation, kingdom against kingdom	Matthew 24:7
The ridiculing of God's word	2 Timothy 3:8, Jude 17-18
Big changes in political power and influence	Revelation 13:3-7
A human leader who declares himself God	2 Thessalonians 2:3-4; Revelation 13:14 - 15

TIME LINE OF FUTURE EVENTS:

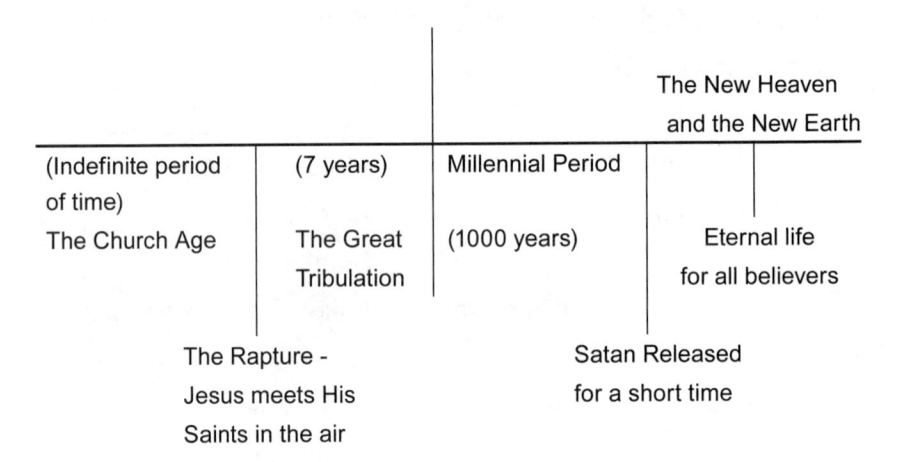

(Indefinite period of time) The Church Age	(7 years) The Great Tribulation	Millennial Period (1000 years)	Eternal life for all believers
	The Rapture - Jesus meets His Saints in the air (after "Jesus Returns")	Satan Released for a short time	The New Heaven and the New Earth

THE CHURCH AGE:

Jesus was crucified and resurrected. Fifty days later, at Pentecost (the birth date of the Church), the Holy Spirit was released into the world to combat the forces of Satan. We have all been living in the Church Age ever since. While in the

Church Age, believers are looking forward to the Rapture and the Coming of Jesus.

THE RAPTURE:

The Bible tells us there has already been six Raptures beginning with Enoch (Genesis 5:24; Hebrews 11:5), where it shows "Enoch walked with God; then he was no more, because God took him away." Elijah was "caught up" in heaven in a chariot of fire without dying (2 Kings 2:1, 11); Isaiah was briefly transported to heaven and came back to earth (Isaiah 6:1-3); Jesus bodily ascended to heaven (Acts 1:9 and Revelation 12:5); Paul was also "caught up" to paradise and then returned to earth (2 Corinthians 12:2-4). When Paul spoke about believers being "caught up" or Raptured in 1 Thessalonians 4:17, he knew of what he was speaking. Finally, in Revelation 4:1 we find John being ushered into heaven so God could tell him what would take place. Today, you will find more than half of all Americans believe in the coming rapture according to a Newsweek poll.

The next and final Rapture, which could happen at any time in the future, will cause all believers in Christ, both living and dead, to rise up and meet Jesus in the air where they will ascend bodily to heaven. Please note this is the first phase of Jesus' Second Coming. The second phase is when He comes to earth at the end of the Great Tribulation, which lasts for seven years. On its surface, the idea sounds implausible. The idea that millions of Christian believers will suddenly be ushered up to heaven to be with Jesus sounds impossible. Yet, a careful reading of God's Word in the Bible validates one day it will happen. We have to keep in mind what Jesus said: "With man this is impossible, but with God all things are possible."

(Matthew 19:26). Before we go further, let me provide a little perspective.

For illustrative purposes, let us suppose only five-percent of Americans are true believers in Jesus Christ as their Lord and Savior, and are subsequently Raptured to heaven. Five-percent of roughly 320 million Americans is about 16 million people who are suddenly out of the country permanently. Do you remember September 11, 2001 when some 3,000 people were killed in New York, and do you also remember the terrible effect on our economy that caused pandemic damage across our country? Then try imagining the effect of losing 16 million citizens in the blink of an eye: statesmen, military generals, captains of industry, and great civic and religious leaders. The event, I believe, would be catastrophic, and you can easily imagine the chaos caused if the number of Christians was much higher, which I believe to be true.

Some people state the word "Rapture" is not found in the Bible, which causes them to question the event, but neither is the word "trinity" or the word "Bible" for that matter. The actual word "Rapture" is from the Greek word "harpazo," which is in the Greek translation, meaning to be "caught up." The main Bible verses to support the idea of a rapture will take place before the seven year tribulation period, are to be found in John 14:1-4, 1 Corinthians 15:50-57, and I Thessalonians 4:13-18. Read the following words from 1 Corinthians 15:50-57 carefully:

"I declare to you, brothers, that flesh and blood cannot inherit the kingdom of God, nor does the perishable inherit the imperishable. Listen, I tell you a mystery: We will not all sleep, but we will all be changed - in a flash, in the twinkling of an eye, at the last trumpet. For the trumpet will sound. The dead will be raised imperishable, and we will be changed. For the perishable must clothe itself with the imperishable, and the mortal with immortality. When the perishable has been clothed with the imperishable, and the mortal with immortality, then the saying that is written will come true: 'Death has been swallowed up in victory.'" Please read the other two references on your own to see how the rapture is a future reality we must be aware of, and be looking forward to in our Christian walk. This is our "Blessed Hope!"

RESULTS OF THE RAPTURE:

Imagine millions of Christians around the world suddenly, in the twinkling of an eye, being ushered up to meet Christ in midair. Imagine the chaos it would cause just in America alone. Christian, government, business and military leaders, are suddenly no longer around to conduct their everyday affairs. In 2 Thessalonians 2:7-8 it states, "For the secret power of lawlessness is already at work; but the one who now holds it back will continue to do so till He is taken out of the way. And then the lawless one will be revealed." This verse indicates the lawless one (the Antichrist) cannot be revealed until the one who restrains is taken out of the way. Who is this restrainer?

The Popular Bible Prophecy Commentary claims the restrainer is the Holy Spirit. We also find God mentioning the Holy Spirit in Genesis 6:3, "My Spirit will not contend with man forever, for he is mortal; his days will be 120 years." Although this reference refers to a time-line God was giving man to renounce his iniquities, and live a righteous life before He flooded the earth, it nonetheless is most telling in that the Holy Spirit will not always be with man, and His restrainer, the Holy

Spirit, who lives in every believer, will one day be pulled from the earth. See also Galatians 5:16 for an explanation of how Spirit indwells in the life of all believers, but in the end times the Holy Spirit will depart. However, He will still work on earth as in Old Testament times to assist unbelievers, who were left behind, to come to faith in Jesus.

THE CHRISTIAN CHURCH:

The Christian Church, consisting of the universal body of believers in Christ, dating back to Pentecost right up to the present age, will all be caught up (Raptured) to be with Christ in the air.(I Corinthians 15:50-57 and Ephesians 2:6). With the church no longer here on earth, the Holy Spirit (the great restrainer), will also be removed. This creates an environment for entry of the Antichrist (explained in more detail later) who will attempt to run the world.

If you wish to become one of those people who are lifted into the air to be with Jesus, then now is the time to repent of your sins, and embrace the teachings of Jesus. In the words of Pastor John Hagee, "Look up, pray up, and pack up, because we're going up!" The evidence that Jesus was physically resurrected from the dead cannot be disputed (Matthew 28:1-15; Mark 16:1-11; Luke 24:1-12; John 20:1-18; Acts 1:3; 1 Corinthians 15:1-8; Colossians 1:18; Revelation 1:5,18). Furthermore, many witnesses came forward to verify it actually happened (Acts 2:32; 3:15; 10:39-40; 1 Corinthians 15:3-8). In John 11:25-26, Jesus says, "I am the resurrection and the life. He who believes in me will live, even though he dies; and whoever lives and believes in me will never die." Raising Lazarus from the dead is just one example of how Jesus proved His authority over the life and death of men.

THE BEMA JUDGMENT:

We are told in Scripture that Christ's judgment of believers will take place immediately after Christ meets them in the air (the rapture), and takes them back to heaven. There are no explicit verses in the Bible, but there are a number of factors that lead to this conclusion. Many biblical scholars believe the 24 elders in heaven mentioned in Revelation 4:4, 10, represent believers. They are portrayed as already having received their crowns in heaven at the very start of the Tribulation period (2 Timothy 4:8; James 1:12, 1 Peter 5:4, and Revelation 2:10). All this would lead reasonable minds to agree that the judgment of believers has already taken place sometime following the rapture.

At the judgment seat of Christ, also referred to as the Bema Judgment (named after the ancient Olympic Games where the judge sat at the bema seat to determine the winners of the race), we find that believers will be rewarded with crowns they will wear:

The Crown of Life is given to those who are steadfast and untiring under trial, especially to those who suffer to the point of death (James 1:12; Revelation 2:10).

The Crown of Glory is rewarded to those who faithfully and sacrificially minister God's word to the flock (1 Peter 5:4)

An Imperishable Crown is awarded to those who win the race of temperance and self-control (1 Corinthians 9:25)

The Crown of Rejoicing to believers who are Christ's glory and joy (1 Thessalonians 2:19-20)

Finally there is the Crown of Righteousness given for those who long for the Second Coming of Christ (2 Timothy 4:8).

When the bride of Christ (the church with the corporate body of Christians) return to earth with Christ at the Second Coming, the bride is adorned in "fine linen, bright and clean," indicating the "righteous acts of the saints" (Revelation 19:8). This has to demonstrate and lend credence to the idea that the judgment seat of Christ follows the rapture.

THE MARRIAGE OF THE LAMB:

After the Bema Judgment, the relationship between Christ and the church takes place in heaven. It is described as a marriage, with Christ being the bridegroom and the church as His bride (Matthew 9: 15; 22:2-14; Mark 2:19-20; Luke 5:34-35). We find the church is regarded as a virgin bride awaiting the coming of her heavenly bridegroom (2 Corinthians 11:2). See also Revelation 19:7-9. This will be discussed in further detail later.

INVASION OF ISRAEL:

Ezekiel, who lived some 700 years before Christ came to earth, prophesied that in the end times not only would the Jews be re-gathered from many nations to the land of Israel, but also there would be an invasion of Israel by a northern assault that includes Russia, and many Middle Eastern states, with ancient names that have been changed over the years. The Bible provides us with some possible answers.

Gog, for instance, is mentioned eleven times in Ezekiel 38 – 39, as the name title of the leader of the invasion. Gog probably refers to the ruler of the people who lived in Magog, and Magog was identified by Josephus (a Jewish historian), the lands of Russia, Kazakhstan, and part of Ukraine. Other allies names mentioned in Ezekiel 38:1-7 are: Meshech and Tubal (modern Turkey), Persia (Iran), Cush (northern Sudan), Put (Libya), Gomer (eastern Turkey and Ukraine), lateBeth Togarmah (part of Turkey near the Syrian border). See Ryrie Study Bible, page 1279 and footnotes.

The purpose of the attack on Israel will be to annihilate the Jews (see Ezekiel 38 and 39:1-24). Remember, 2600 years ago Islam was not even a religion, yet all the countries mentioned, with the exception of Russia, follow the teachings of Islam. They are all united in their quest today, with the current exception of Russia, to eliminate Israel from the map of the world. Note that all the nations geographically surrounding Israel today share the Islamic faith, and none of them show Israel on their maps. They refer to the area occupied by Israel as Palestine, even though Israel has been a sovereign state since 1948.

Obviously, we find several opinions existing regarding when this future great battle to crush Israel takes place, and the timing of the battle is the most debated. Therefore we should not be dogmatic about such issues. In general, however, it is believed that the battle will take place after the rapture, but before the seven year tribulation period begins. A careful reading of Ezekiel 38 tells us God will intervene by creating a great earthquake, the mountains will be overturned, and every man's sword will be against his brother. Ezekiel 39:9 goes on to say these armies will be completely destroyed, and the Jews will use the enemy's weapons for fuel and burn them for seven years. Please keep this thought in mind as we make further progress with the story. Meanwhile, the number of slain bodies will be so vast nothing but a deep valley – the Valley of Hamon-Gog – will be big enough to bury all the corpses, which will take seven months to complete the task (39:12). Following this seven month period the Jews will then cleanse all of the land by clearing all the bones of the dead (Numbers 19:11-22; Deuteronomy 21:1-9).

If Ezekiel 39:9 tells us the Jews will be burning their enemy's weapons for seven years, then a case can be made that perhaps the Tribulation takes place three and a half years after the rapture in order to allow the Jews time to burn all the weapons for seven years. This would allow the Jews to flee from Jerusalem in the middle of the tribulation period (the three and a half year point), as commanded by Jesus. In Matthew 24, we find Jesus urging the Jews to leave Jerusalem in order to take flight from the Antichrist, who will break the peace agreement, and set-up his headquarters there during the middle of the tribulation, where he will commit the abomination of desolation in the Jewish Temple (read Jesus' own words in Matthew 24:15, Mark 13:14, as He also refers to Daniel 11:31, and 12:11), a prediction that Daniel made hundreds of years before Christ came to earth.

So the question becomes one of figuring out how the Jews spend seven years clearing up and burning their enemies' weapons while simultaneously honoring Jesus by fleeing from Jerusalem at the three and one half year point of the tribulation, when the Antichrist breaks the peace covenant with Israel. This problem is avoided if the Ezekiel invasion of Israel takes place at least three and one half years prior to the beginning of the tribulation period, because then the burning of the weapons will have been completed by the midpoint of the tribulation, and therefore the Jews could obey Jesus' command to flee the city. We also have to bear in mind the beginning of the tribulation is not the Rapture, but rather the antichrist signing a covenant with Israel for peace (Daniel 9:26-27). Also remember that the rapture could happen at any time, meaning it could take place before or after the war mentioned in Ezekiel 38 – 39.

Some readers may have difficulty fully understanding the future events mentioned in this chapter, but I would advise them to keep moving forward with a reading of the next chapter, which will then give them a better overview of the "big picture" of what to expect in the future. It is also important to point out that no man knows all the details of what is to come, and learned men have several other versions as I mentioned earlier. So use the approach mentioned in this book as a template or foundation for further study and refinement, and allow God to point your way forward to the truth as you contemplate and pray about the words in Deuteronomy 29:29 and Isaiah 42:9, which clearly show that God is slowly revealing the future of man to those who earnestly seek the truth.

CHAPTER THIRTEEN

THE TRIBULATION AND BEYOND

THE SEVEN YEAR TRIBULATION PERIOD

The tribulation is a time period of seven years that takes place sometime after the Rapture when the forces of good and evil come to the forefront of man's existence. It will be a terrible time to be alive, as many of God's predictions mentioned in the Bible will come true.

Although I will be writing in a sequential manner, some of the actual events will take place simultaneously. Also, not to confuse you further, but some of the events during the tribulation take place in heaven, and others on earth. See chart below:

CHAPTER TOPICS OF THE BOOK OF REVELATION

Events	Church Age	Tribulation	Millennium	Judgment: Great White Throne	Eternal State
In Heaven	1	4-5	19-20	20	
					21-22
On Earth	2-3	6-19	20		

I previously mentioned that God intervened against a coalition of countries attacking Israel, and how they were all defeated. It is a common belief that this future event created a shift in the balance of power in the world. Russia and many of the Moslem countries are neutralized, and the Christians will have been Raptured to be with Jesus. These events pave the way for the Antichrist (see below) to gain power over the old Roman Empire countries of Europe. This allows the Antichrist to sign a peace covenant with Israel at the beginning of the seven year tribulation period, thus providing the Jews the opportunity to rebuild their temple and reinstate animal sacrifices. Unfortunately, the Antichrist breaks the peace covenant with Israel after three and one half years, (1260 days), which creates utter chaos throughout the remaining years of the tribulation period.

THE RISE OF THE BEAST (ANTICHRIST):

We were warned in 2 Thessalonians 2:3, 8-10 about a man of lawlessness, also referred to as Antichrist (see I John 2:18), who would ascend to great power during the tribulation period. This could only happen if the great restrainer (The Holy Spirit), who indwells in all Christians, pulls back His hold on the world. Remember, the Christian faithful of the Church at that point in time, have already been Raptured to heaven. However, the Holy Spirit will continue to work in individuals just as in Old Testament times.

In Revelation 13:1, it describes how the dragon (Satan) stood on the shore of the sea, and John saw a beast (Antichrist) coming out of the sea. He had ten horns and seven heads, with ten crowns on his horns, and on each head a blasphemous name. The ten horns represent ten kings that form a ten nation federation led by the Antichrist during the tribulation (Revelation 17:1).

However, in Daniel 7:24, it goes on to state that the Antichrist will subdue three of the ten, leaving seven. The seven heads, according to some Bible scholars, symbolize seven kings and seven hills, which could be a reference to Rome, which is known as the city on seven hills. Now the times are set for Antichrist to act. Scriptures reveal the Antichrist will be a genius in intellect (Daniel 8:23); commerce (Daniel 11:44; Revelation 13:16-17); making war (Revelation 6:2; 13:7); speech (Daniel 11:36), and politics (Revelation 17:11-13). He will perform many counterfeit signs and wonders, and deceive many people.

Revelation 13:16-18 demonstrates Antichrist will control the flow of all goods and services. He will force everyone, great and small, to receive a mark on their right hand or on their forehead, which is the name of the beast or the number of his name, 666, or six hundred and sixty six. This is referred to as the mark of the beast. Without this mark, a person will not be able to buy or sell anything. If anyone accepts the mark it will signal the beast's complete ownership. Consequently, they will be eternally doomed (Revelation 14:9-10). This mark will become mandatory during the tribulation. Do you see those trends today as we move further and further towards a cashless society?

Just as Jesus is the promised "offspring" of the woman (Genesis 3:15; Revelation 12:13-14), the Antichrist is the promised "offspring" of the serpent. Antichrist is an agent of Satan, and he will be opposed to everything Christ represents. Antichrist goes by at least 20 names in the Bible including: "King of Babylon" (Isaiah 14:4); "morning star, son of the dawn

(Lucifer)" (Isaiah 14:12); "little horn" (Daniel 7:8; 8:9); "Man of lawlessness" (2 Thessalonians 2:3-8; The "Antichrist" (1 John 2:18); "a beast coming out of the sea" (Revelation 13:1), to name a few.

Dr. Clarence Larkin, in his wonderful book, *Dispensational Truth,* used the King James version of the Bible to show a number of contrasts between Jesus Christ and the Antichrist:

Jesus came to us from above -(John 6:38)	Antichrist will arise from the pit -(Revelation 11:7)
Christ came in His Father's name -John 5:43	Antichrist will come in his own name -John 5:43
Christ was despised by men -Isaiah 53:3; Luke 23:18	Antichrist will be admired by men -Revelation 13:3-4
Christ came as humble man -Philippians 2:8	Antichrist will exalt himself -2 Thessalonians 2:4
Christ will be exalted -Philippians 2:9	Antichrist is sent directly to hell -Isaiah 14:14-15; Revelation 19:20
Christ came to do His Father's will -John 6:38	Antichrist will come to do his own will -Daniel 11:36
Christ came to save man -Luke 19:10	Antichrist came to destroy man -Daniel 8:24
Christ is the Good Shepherd -John 10:1-15	Antichrist is the evil shepherd -Zechariah 11:16-17
Christ is the true vine -John 15:1	Antichrist is the "vine of the earth." -Revelation 14:18-20
Christ is the "truth"	Antichrist is the "lie"

-John 14:6	-2 Thessalonians 2:11
Christ is the "holy one"	Antichrist is the "lawless one"
-Mark 1:24	-2 Thessalonians 2:8 (NIV)
Christ is the "man of sorrows"	Antichrist is the "man of sin"
-Isaiah 53:3	-2 Thessalonians 2:3
Christ is the "Son of God"	Antichrist proclaims to "be God"
-Luke 1:35	-2 Thessalonians 2:4
Christ is the "mystery of godliness": God manifest in the flesh	Antichrist will be the "mystery of iniquity": Satan manifest in the flesh
-1 Timothy 3:16	-2 Thessalonians 2:7

Antichrist will come on the scene, and assume power peacefully by diplomacy and intellect. He comes to power not by war but by deceiving other leaders of the world into the belief he can create peace (Revelation 6:2). This is further substantiated in Daniel 8:25. At the right moment he will destroy them all.

THE RISE OF THE SECOND BEAST (FALSE PROPHET):

In Revelation 13:11-15, the Apostle John saw another beast (the False Prophet) coming out of the earth. He had two horns like a lamb, but he spoke like a dragon. He will exercise all the authority of the first beast on his behalf, and made the earth and its inhabitants worship the first beast, whose fatal wound had been healed. *Whose fatal wound had been healed* refers back to Revelation13:3. This False Prophet performed great and miraculous signs, even causing fire to come down from heaven to earth in full view of men. He deceives the inhabitants of the earth, and he orders men to set up an image (which is the abomination that causes desolation – Daniel 12:11) in honor of the beast (Antichrist), who was wounded by the sword and yet lived. The False Prophet was given power to give breath to the image of the first beast, so that it could speak and cause all who refused to worship the image to be killed. See also Daniel 9:27; 11:31; 12:11; Matthew 24:15; Revelation 13:15. Thus the False Prophet completes the third part of the satanic trinity, which is explained later.

FIRST HALF OF THE TRIBULATION:

The Book of Revelation (chapter five) tells us where the Apostle John is shown a Seven Sealed Scroll, and in chapter six the seals are opened during the first half of the Tribulation period. The first four seals opened are referred to as the Four Horsemen of the Apocalypse:

THE SEVEN SEAL JUDGMENTS:

The First Seal opened releases a white horse ridden by a rider with a bow, but no arrow. Christian theologians differ as to who this rider is. Some claim him to be Christ, others antichrist, and yet others believe the rider is the spirit of conquest, which establishes a more natural sequence with the other three riders (bloodshed, famine and death).

The Second Seal opened is a red horse. "Its rider is given the power to take peace from this world, and to make men slay each other. To him was given a large sword." This horse is a symbol for war.

The Third Seal releases a black horse, a symbol for famine. The color black was used in the Bible before to depict famine as in Lamentations 4:8-9. Famine is typical at the end of war, as history verifies. The fact the horse is told "not to damage the oil and the wine," is reference to the rich not affected as badly as the common people.

The Fourth Seal allows the release of a rider on a pale horse, whose rider is named Death, and Hades was following close behind him. They were given authority and power over a fourth of the earth to kill by sword, famine and plague, and to use wild beasts to devour mankind.

The Fifth Seal allows the Apostle John to look under the altar at the souls of those who had been slain because of the word of God, and the testimony they had maintained. Crying out in a loud voice, they said: "How long, Sovereign Lord, holy and true, until you judge the inhabitants of the earth and avenge our blood?" Who are these people? Revelation 7 tells us at the beginning of the tribulation there will be a great soul harvesting that will take place throughout the world. The Fifth Seal teaches us that after the tribulation begins, there will be tribulation saints, who are individuals who had not accepted Jesus Christ prior to the time of the rapture, and therefore remained on earth. However, they later accepted Christ, many as a result of the 144,000 witnessing to them. For their faithfulness, many will be beheaded or die of famine by refusing to accept the mark of 666 (Revelation 20:4). Their later reward will be an imperishable body in communion with Jesus Christ. Those who have accepted Christ and manage to survive the tribulation, will enter the millennial period (mentioned later in this chapter) in their mortal bodies and repopulate the earth.

Upon the opening of the Sixth Seal, there is a great earthquake, the sun turned black, the moon turned blood red, and the stars in the sky fell to the earth. Men hid in caves, and among the rocks of the mountains. They call to the mountains and the rocks, "Fall on us and hide us from the face of him who sits on the throne and from the wrath of the Lamb!" (Revelation 6:16).

There is silence in heaven for about a half hour upon the opening of the Seventh Seal. John goes on to say, "And I saw the seven angels who stand before God, and to them were given seven trumpets." (Revelation 8:2). These seven trumpets are God's judgment on the earth. God clearly is sending these judgments to punish men for their iniquities. We will discuss these trumpet judgments further in this chapter.

THE FIVE EARTHS: [1]

In his book, *God's Plan for the Ages,* David Reagan discusses five earths, which are mentioned in the diagram below. You will notice in the time line paragraph mentioned earlier in this chapter, that the church age is an indefinite time period, in which we currently reside. At some point in the future the rapture will occur, and all believers in Jesus Christ will be air-lifted from earth to be with Him. This action is the forerunner of the tribulation period lasting seven-years. At that point, Jesus Christ returns to earth, and will reign over all the earth during the millennium (1000 years). The earth is restored after destruction caused during the tribulation, which creates the Fourth Earth as explained in the diagram below:

The Five Earths of the Bible

- **EARTH ONE** — Creation — Genesis 1-2
- **EARTH TWO** — Adam to Noah — Genesis 3-8
- **EARTH THREE** — Since Noah — Gen. 9 - Rev. 19
- **EARTH FOUR** — The millennium — Rev. 20 and Isaiah 65
- **EARTH FIVE (NEW EARTH)** — Eternity — Rev. 21 - 22

The First Earth was perfectly created at the beginning of earth's time as revealed in Genesis I, which allowed the first man, Adam, who was created in God's image, to live in it. However, when Adam sinned, he was cursed by God and banned from the perfect paradise, and the earth itself was also cursed. This changed the nature of God's original plan, and it caused nature to rise up against man, and the lion no longer lay down with the lamb; some plants became poisonous, and there was a change in climatic conditions. These events changed the earth.

The Second Earth was much different than the First Earth. Biblical evidence found in Genesis and Job indicates the possibility that this earth had a vapor canopy over it, which protected man from the harsh ultra-violet rays of the sun. This allowed man to live much longer, but he continued to sin, disobey God, and rebel against Him. This caused God once again to change the nature of the earth (Genesis 6:11-13), by creating a great flood, "and the floodgates of heaven were opened, and rain fell on the earth for forty days and forty nights." (Genesis 7:11). All the inhabitants of the earth were killed, except Noah, his family, and the animals that were aboard the arc. This cataclysmic change resulted in the creation of Earth Three.

Earth Three is a natural world affected by climatic changes, causing earthquakes, tornadoes, hurricanes, Tsunamis, and glacial warming. Man's lifespan is reduced by atmospheric conditions such as unprecedented ultra violet radiation, and a more polluted environment. This is the earth where we currently live.

Earth Four, will be much different again from our present earth. It will be referred to as the millennial earth, where believers reign with Jesus for one thousand years. We read in the Bible that the worst earthquakes in man's history happen during the seven year tribulation period leading up to the millennium, which changes the landscape of the whole earth. During the time of the millennium, life-spans will increase perhaps because the vapor canopy that existed during Earth Two (Job 38:8-11), which was taken away during Earth Three, will be restored (Isaiah 65:20-22).God's curse against man will be cancelled and Isaiah 11:6-8 tells us, "the wolf will live with the lamb, the leopard will lie down with the goat, the calf and the lion and the yearling together; and a little child will lead them."

Earth Five will come about as a result of Satan's last attempt to control the world when he is released one last time. His rebellion will result in the earth being polluted and devastated (Revelation 20:7-9). In 2 Peter 3:10-13, he describes how the polluted earth is laid bare, with the creation of a new heaven and a new earth. This results in the redeemed of the earth entering into the New Jerusalem. "Now the dwelling of God is with men, and he will live with them." (Revelation 21:1-4). Ecclesiastes 1:4, tells us the earth is eternal, "Generations come and generations go, but the earth remains forever." I point this out to simply say there will be five earths that man is to become aware of, but planet earth itself is not totally destroyed, but remade according to God's plan. "He who was seated on the throne said I am making everything new! Write this down, for these words are trustworthy and true." Jesus then said to John: "It is done. I am the Alpha and the Omega, the Beginning and the End." (Revelation 21:5-6)

THE BUILDING OF THE JEWISH TEMPLE:

Once the seven year peace covenant is signed between Antichrist and Israel, which will only last three and one half years, the Jews will be able to rebuild their ruined temple, and will reinstitute animal sacrifices as in ancient times. (Daniel 12:11).

The first temple was built by King Solomon because his father, King David, was basically disqualified by God from building it. The temple was eventually destroyed in 587 BC by the Babylonians. The second temple was not completed until 515 BC. This second temple had little of the former glory of the first temple, but it lasted about 500 years. Then, in 4 BC, King Herod started a very ambitious building program, and it was completed in 64 AD. This temple was destroyed by the Romans in 70 AD, as Jesus had predicted, and has remained that way ever since. Therefore, the rebuilding of the temple has been of paramount importance to the Jews.

144,000 WITNESSES:

In Revelation 7:4 the Apostle John states: "Then I heard the number of those who were sealed: 144,000 from all the tribes of Israel." This is a reference to 12,000 from each of the twelve tribes of Israel who will be living during the tribulation period, and preaching the Word of God. It is interesting to note, God chooses Jews to do His witnessing during this terrible time. It is not quite clear when their evangelism activity takes place other than during the tribulation period, but is generally believed to be during the first half. In Revelation 14:15b we find an angel shouting in a loud voice to him who was sitting on the cloud. He said: "Take your sickle and reap because the time to reap has come, for the harvest of the earth is ripe. So he who was seated on the cloud swung his sickle over the earth, and the earth was harvested."

TWO PROPHETIC WITNESSES:

Also during the tribulation, God will raise up two other mighty witnesses who wear sackcloth, and will testify on behalf of God with powerful voices heard around the world (when this prediction was made there was no television or technology capable of transmitting human voices or images around the Globe). Today we know better. (See Revelation 11:3).

In the Old Testament, two witnesses were required to confirm testimony, and it is generally believed the two witnesses fit the description of Elijah (1Kings 17; Malachi 4:5), and Moses

(Exodus 7:1,8-9). We do know their ministry on earth will last for 1260 days (three and one half years), and it is generally believed it takes place during the first half of the tribulation. This thinking is based on the fact they are both executed by the Antichrist, which would place the time at the midpoint of the tribulation when Antichrist also breaks his peace covenant with Israel, and madness and mayhem go unabated.

The two witnesses (who appear on earth during the sixth and seventh trumpets mentioned later in this chapter) will be supernaturally protected, have unlimited power, will be able to stop the rain from falling, and smite the earth with plagues. These two powerful witnesses for God will eventually be killed by Antichrist (Revelation 11:7). Their bodies will be left in the city for three and one half days while the people gaze at their bodies, gloat over them, and celebrate. In Revelation 11:11, however, we find God breathes life back into their bodies, and tells them "Come up here." Terror is struck in the hearts of the people as the two witnesses ascend to heaven. At the same time there is a mighty earthquake, and a tenth of the city collapses.

THE SEVEN TRUMPET JUDGMENTS:

The first trumpet judgment comes from the seventh seal. Revelation 8:6-13, tells us seven angels prepare to sound their trumpets. The first angel sounded his trumpet and there came hail and fire mixed with blood, and it was hurled down upon the earth. A third of the earth was burned, and a third of the trees were burned up. All of the green grass was burned up also.

Upon the second angel sounding his trumpet, we find something like a huge mountain, all ablaze, was thrown into the sea. A third of the sea turned blood, a third of the living creatures in the sea died, and a third of the ships were destroyed.

When the third angel sounded his trumpet, a great star, blazing like a torch, fell from the sky on a third of the rivers and the springs of water – the name of the star is Wormwood (a Middle Eastern bitter herb, known as hemlock in Hebrew). A third of the waters turned bitter, and many people died from the waters that had become bitter.

The fourth angel sounds his trumpet, and a third of the sun was struck, a third of the moon, and a third of the stars, so a third of them turned dark. A third of the day was without light, and also a third of the night.

John goes on to say when the fifth angel (Revelation 9:1) sounded his trumpet, "I saw a star that had fallen from the sky to the earth. The star was given the key to the shaft of the Abyss. When he opened the Abyss, smoke rose from it like the smoke from a gigantic furnace. The sun and sky were darkened by the smoke from the Abyss. And out of the smoke locusts came down upon the earth and were given power like that of scorpions of the earth. They were told not to harm the grass of the earth or any plant or tree, but only those people who did not have the seal of God on their foreheads. They were not given power to kill them, but only to torture them for five-months." (Revelation 9:4-5).

John continues in Revelation 9:13 - 15, "The sixth angel sounded his trumpet, and I heard a voice coming from the horns of the golden altar that is before God. It said to the sixth angel who had the trumpet, 'Release the four angels who are bound at the great river Euphrates.' And the four angels who had been kept ready for this very hour and day and month and year, were released to kill a third of mankind. The number of the mounted troops was two hundred million. I heard their number."

This chapter goes on to say a third of mankind is killed by the three plagues of fire, smoke and sulfur coming out of their mouths. Further, we find the rest of mankind, who were not killed by these plagues, still did not repent of the work of their hands, and did not stop worshipping demons, idols of gold, silver, bronze, stone and wood. Nor did they repent of their murders, their magic arts, their sexual immorality or their thefts.

When the seventh angel sounded his trumpet, there were loud voices in heaven, which said: "The kingdom of the world has become the kingdom of our Lord and of his Christ, and he will reign forever and ever."(Revelation 11:15).

THE MIDDLE OF THE TRIBULATION:

So far during the first half of the Tribulation, we have seen Israel enter into a peace covenant with the Antichrist for seven years (Daniel 9:27), and 144,000 Jewish witnesses for Christ are sent to evangelize the world. We have already seen the effects of the Rapture and the ushering away of believers to be with Jesus, which causes a power vacuum to come into being. This allows Russia and a number of Moslem countries to attack Israel (Ezekiel 38, 39), causing God to intervene, and save Israel by destroying her enemies. Meanwhile, Antichrist begins his quest for world power, and quickly consolidates his power through lies, deceit and trickery. He offers peace to the world, and Israel accepts his peace covenant, which allows them to rebuild their temple, and begin once again to practice their animal sacrifices in this new temple.

Unfortunately for Israel, we find the Antichrist breaking his peace covenant after three and one half years (Daniel 9:27), and he puts an end to animal sacrifices and offerings. On a wing of the temple he will set up an abomination of desolation until the end, as it is decreed (Daniel 11:31). This event is described by Jesus in Matthew 24. Jesus advises the Jews to flee Jerusalem and head for the mountains. Many believe the Jews will rush to the abandoned ancient City of Petra, in Jordan, that has many security benefits. In recent years I have visited Petra and found it to be full of deep caves representing a labyrinth able to protect millions of people in an emergency situation. There is only one narrow passage way through the mountain to enter the city, and it is easily defensible against superior forces, as the Romans found out when they fought the Nabataeans in the third century BC.

EVENTS DURING THE SECOND HALF OF THE TRIBULATION PERIOD:

The next major prophetic event is the pouring of the seven bowl judgments by seven angels. The time sequence of the seven bowl judgments is synonymous with this second half of the tribulation, also known as the great tribulation period, or the time of Jacob's troubles (Jacob was the son of Isaac, who was the son of Abraham, the founder of the Jewish people).

THE SEVEN BOWL JUDGMENT:

Revelation 16 provides details of the Seven Bowls of God's wrath upon the people of the earth, the non-believers, thus causing the completion of God's wrath:

An angel poured the first bowl, and ugly and painful sores broke out on the people who had the mark of the beast and worshipped his image.

The second bowl was poured out on to the sea causing it to turn into blood like that of a dead man, and every living thing in the sea died.

Afterwards came the third bowl poured by an angel onto the rivers and springs of water, and they became blood, which completed the second and third trumpet judgments.

We then find that the fourth angel poured out his bowl on the sun, and the sun was given power to scorch the people with fire. They were seared by the intense heat and they cursed the name of God.

Then an angel poured the fifth bowl onto the throne of the beast (Antichrist), and his kingdom was thrown into darkness.

We then have the sixth bowl being poured out onto the great river Euphrates, and it dried up to prepare the way for the kings of the East.

THE BATTLE OF ARMAGGEDON:

Armageddon is mentioned only one time in the Bible (Revelation 16 -16). The battle takes place in the Valley of Megiddo in modern day Israel. Revelation 16:14-16 refers to this battle as, "The Battle on the Great Day of God Almighty," which begins when the seventh angel pours his bowl into the air, and out of the temple came a loud voice from the throne, saying: "It is done!" This is followed by flashes of lightning, rumblings, peals of thunder, and an earthquake unlike any other experienced by man in the history of the world. Then the heavens stand open and Christ returns with His saints to strike down Antichrist.

Christ and His army, consisting of all believers, and His holy angels, totally destroy Antichrist and his army. Christ will consume His enemies with a sharp sword out of His mouth, (the Word of God), and their bodies will be eaten by the birds. Read also Ezekiel 39:17-20, and Revelation 19:17-18. We are also told in Revelation 19:20 that the beast (Antichrist) was captured, along with the False Prophet, who had performed the miraculous signs on his behalf. The two of them were thrown alive into the fiery lake of burning sulfur.

I had the privilege of traveling through the area where this last great battle of Armageddon will take place between the forces of light and darkness, located in central Israel in the Valley of Megiddo. When Napoleon Bonaparte traveled through this valley, he said with deep emotion, "This is the ideal battleground for all armies of the world." Megiddo is in the plains of Esdraelon. This is the place where most military contests were carried out in Palestine dating back to the days of Nebuchadnezzar, King of Assyria (2 Chronicles 36), up until the disastrous march of Napoleon Bonaparte from Egypt to Syria. Egyptians, Persians, Druses, Turks, Arabs, Saracens, Jews and Gentiles of many nations have been brought to death in this unique landscape. As my eyes viewed the panorama of this vast plain, it caused me to shudder not only at the tremendous bloodshed during many battles of the past, but also to imagine this last great battle on earth where millions will perish. It is an experience not soon to be forgotten.

THE MAGIC NUMBER SEVEN:

It is well worth including at this point the numerous times in the Bible the number seven is used. From the beginning of the first book in the Bible through to the very last one, you will find the number seven is repeated many, many times. Here is a short list where the number seven is used:

After creating the world, God rested on the seventh day	Genesis 2:2
In his dream, Pharaoh saw seven cattle coming from the Nile	Genesis 41.2
Samson's sacred Nazirite locks were braided in seven plaits	Judges 16:13
Seven devils left Mary Magdalene	Luke 8:2
In the seventh year the Hebrew slaves were to be freed	Exodus 21:2
Every seventh year was a sabbatical year	Lev. 25:4
Pentecost, the Feast of Weeks, is seven times seven days after Passover	Acts 2:1-31
Seventy times seven, the number of times that Peter should forgive a person	Matthew 18:22
Seven Churches of Asia	Revelation 1:4
Seven Spirits of God	Revelation 3:1
Seven Lamp stands (churches)	Revelation 1:12
Seven horns and seven eyes	Revelation 5:6
Seven Sealed Scroll	Revelation 5:1
Seven Seals	Revelation 5:1; 5:5
Seven Trumpets	Revelation 8:2, 6
Seven Bowls	Revelation 16:1
Seven angels	Revelation 8:2

Seven kings	Revelation 17:10
Seven Spirits	Revelation 1:4
Seven Stars	Revelation 1:16
Seven Thunders	Revelation 10:3
Seventy Sevens	Daniel 9:24

Is it just coincidental that the number seven, the number of completeness, is used more times in Revelation, the last book in the Bible, than any of the other books?

THE MILLENIAL RULE OF CHRIST:

Revelation 20:1-5 describes how an angel descends out of heaven with the keys to the Abyss, and is holding a great chain. He seizes the dragon, the ancient serpent, who is the devil or Satan, and binds him in the Abyss for one thousand years. The dragon will be released again for a short while. John then saw a throne on who were seated those who had been given authority to judge. "And I saw the souls of those who had been beheaded because of their testimony for Jesus, and because of the Word of God. They had not worshipped the beast or his image and had not received his mark on their foreheads or their hands. They came to life and reigned with Christ for a thousand years." This refers to the martyred tribulation saints; those who came to Christ after the Rapture.

The rest of the dead did not come to life until the thousand years were ended. This is the first resurrection. Jesus said, "Do not be amazed at this, for a time is coming when all who are in their graves will hear His voice and come out – those who have done good will rise to live, and those who have done evil will rise to be condemned." (John 5:28, 29). In Daniel 7:18, 27, in speaking for God, it says: "But the saints of the Most High will receive the kingdom and they will possess it forever – yes, forever and ever."

In Daniel 7:27 the Lord continues: "Then the sovereignty, power and greatness of all the kingdoms under the whole heaven will be handed over to the saints, the people of the Most High. His kingdom will be an everlasting kingdom, and all rulers will worship and obey him." We find a similar story in 1 Corinthians 6:2-3 when Paul is talking about believers resolving their disputes with one another rather than a lawsuit filed through ungodly courts. Paul goes on to say, "Do you not know that the saints will judge the world? And if you are to judge the world, are you not competent to judge trivial cases? Do you not know that we will judge angels?"

In the first book of the Bible, Genesis 1:27-28, we find God's original plan was to bring all things under the control of man, and to then submit all things to Himself through mankind. So without a literal Millennium ruled by His Son, Jesus, God would not be able to fulfill His purpose for this world. The Millennium will bring God's creation full circle as God is able to bring to pass with the second Adam, Jesus Christ, what the first Adam was unable to do (See 1 Corinthians 15:21-22).

SATAN RELEASED:

After a thousand years of the millennial reign of Christ, we find in Revelation 20:7 Satan is released from the abyss and is able to go out and deceive the nations one last time. He gathers followers from all four corners of the globe – Gog and Magog, and they attack the camp of God's people. But we find fire comes down from heaven and devours the enemies of

God, and Satan is thrown into the lake of burning sulfur, where the beast and false prophet have been thrown, where they will be tormented day and night forever and ever. Thus the satanic trinity will come to an end:

The Holy Trinity:	The Satanic Trinity:
God the Father	Satan the destroyer
Jesus Christ (the Son of God)	The Antichrist (total opposition to God)
The Holy Spirit	The False Prophet (unholy spirit)

THE GREAT WHITE THRONE JUDGMENT:

This is the final Day of Judgment for mankind. A reading from Revelation 20:11 states it best. The Apostle John goes on to say, "Then I saw a great white throne and him who was seated on it (Jesus Christ). Earth and sky fled from his presence, and there was no place for them. And I saw the dead, great and small, standing before the throne, and books were opened. Another book was opened, which is the Book of Life. The dead were judged according to what they had done as recorded in the books. The sea gave up the dead that were in it, and death and Hades gave up the dead that were in them, and each person was judged according to what he had done. Then death and Hades were thrown into the lake of fire. The lake of fire is the second death. If anyone's name was not found written in the book of life, he was thrown into the lake of fire." This is the ultimate judgment for all those who have lived and died here on earth who never accepted Jesus Christ as their Lord and Savior. But believers names will be in the book of life that provides eternal life for all who have accepted Jesus as their Lord and Savior.

THE NEW HEAVEN AND THE NEW EARTH:

The best part of the story is left for last, because it is the very best part for believers in Jesus Christ. Once the millennial period of a thousand years comes to an end, we will discover that Satan has been thrown into the lake of fire, to join the Antichrist and False Prophet, forever and ever. God, who had created our earth in the beginning, will now change it and create a new heaven and a new earth (Revelation 21:1-8). This event is also mentioned in other parts of the Bible including: Matthew 24:35; Isaiah 34:4; 51:6; Psalm 102:25-26, and 2 Peter 3:10.

In the Book of Revelation, chapters 21 and 22, we are introduced to the eternal future that is planned by God. It represents the final purpose that God has for the human race. Here we are told more details about the new heaven and the new earth than in any other part of the Bible. We are told about seven new creations that are revealed to us, each of which provides a glimpse into what we can expect to look forward to:

A new heaven (21:1)
A new earth (21:1)
A new city of Jerusalem (21:2)
New things (21:5)
A new paradise (22:1-5)
A new place for God's throne (22:3)
A new source of light (21:23; 22:5)

In the past, the earth was destroyed by God when He flooded the world and killed all mankind, with the exception of eight righteous people who were placed in an ark. In 2 Peter 3:10, we find in the future the earth being laid bare, but this time by fire, after which God will restore all things including a restored earth. "But the day of the Lord will come as a thief. The heavens will disappear with a roar; the elements will be destroyed by fire, and the earth and everything in it will be laid bare." Revelation 21:1 goes on to say, "Then I saw a new heaven and a new earth, for the first heaven and the first earth had passed away, and there was no longer any sea."

From time immemorial, Christians have pondered why God would also destroy heaven. The laying bare of earth can partially be understood due to the iniquities and rebellion of mankind. But heaven is another matter entirely. We first must realize there are three heavens. There is the atmospheric heaven around the earth; there is a stellar heaven, which contains all the great galaxies we are able to witness on a clear night. There is also the third heaven, or the throne of God (2 Corinthians 12:2; Revelation 4:1-5). There is no mention of God destroying the stellar heaven, or the third heaven, where He resides. The atmospheric heaven, however, is filled with evil. Ephesians 6:12 indicates Satan, who is "the power of this dark world," along with his cohorts are creating spiritual evil in heavenly places. So when God destroys the earth polluted with Satan's evil, He will also include the atmospheric heaven to ensure all evil has been eliminated.

The Apostle John describes in Rev. 21:2, "I saw the Holy City, the new Jerusalem, coming down out of heaven from God, prepared as a bride beautifully dressed for her husband."

This will be a city of righteousness, all prepared by God for the enjoyment of His people. 21:3 describes how God will dwell with men, and 21:4 states there will be no more death or mourning or pain or crying, and God will wipe away every tear.

God goes on to say He will make all things new (Rev. 21:5), and no longer will there be any curse. However, in 21:8 we find God saying: "But the cowardly, the unbelieving, the vile, the murderers, the sexually immoral, those who practice magic arts, the idolaters and all liars – their place will be in the fiery lake of burning sulfur. This is the second death."

The New Jerusalem is described as being 12,000 stadia in length, and as wide and as high as it is long (12,000 stadia is about 1400 miles or about 2200 kilometers). See Rev. 21:16. John continues by saying believers will be able to see God's face, and His name will be on their foreheads. There will be no more night, and they will reign forever and ever (Rev. 22:1-5).

This is the Good News, and the great hope for all who accept Jesus Christ as their eternal Lord and Savior. Nothing more needs to be said. "All Scripture is God breathed and is useful for teaching, rebuking, correcting and training in righteousness," (2 Timothy 3:16). "The fool hath said in his heart, 'there is no God'" (Psalm 14:1). Which one of these statements do you believe to be correct? The evidence is overwhelming in favor of the former.

TWO CHAPTER SUMMARY:

In the last two chapters we have covered some rather heavy material that is hard to digest in one reading, and therefore it is highly recommended for those who have a strong level of interest in knowing more about man's future, to seek other sources of help in illuminating and clarifying these very important concepts. Meanwhile, to summarize what we have discussed in the last chapter, and this one into a condensed narrative, the next big prophetic event in the future will be the Rapture, which will affect both believers and non-believers. The first part of Jesus' Second Coming will be realized when He will lift believers up into the air to be with Him in heaven, while non-believers are left behind. This event is preceded by the resurrection of all Christians who have died since the beginning of Christianity. They are not really dead since their souls and spirits have been: "absent from the body (at death) and are present with the Lord (2 Corinthians 5:8). This is what the Bible means to be "asleep in Jesus," a position in which deceased Christians remain until the return of the Lord. The reuniting of dead Christians with those who are alive to meet the Lord is a time of immense blessing, which is called "the blessed hope" (Titus 2:13). Also read Corinthians 15:50-58 that provides more detail about what happens when the Rapture occurs.

Those who remain on earth after the Rapture will experience the seven year tribulation period (Daniel 9:27), which is the heart of the Book of Revelation, and as mentioned earlier, it will be a terrible time for all who are living. Antichrist will be let loose on earth, and he will enter into a seven-year peace agreement with Israel, which he will break halfway through. Thus begins the great tribulation period (the second three and one half years of the seven year tribulation), when mankind will be forced to accept the sign of the beast on his forehead or right hand (666), in which case if he does, he will be forever damned by God. Each man can refuse the sign of the beast, and accept Jesus as his Lord and Savior, in which case he faces the possibility of starvation or beheading. Those converted Christians that survive, known as the tribulation saints, will keep their bodies when they enter into the 1,000 millennium period, when Jesus will rule the earth. The beginning of the millennium period takes place after the great Battle of Armageddon in which Jesus descends with all His angels and army of believers, to destroy the forces of Antichrist. The Antichrist and the False Prophet are then thrown into the lake of fire, along with Satan, but after the one thousand year millennium period, Satan is released one more time. Satan and his army attempt to overthrow Christ, but fail and all are cast into the lake of fire forever and ever.

The Great White Throne Judgment takes place at the end of the millennium period, and no one escapes the judgment of God. God opens the Book of Life, and anyone whose name is found in this book will enjoy the benefits of the new earth, but anyone whose name is not found in this book will be thrown into the lake of fire. Looking into the future to evaluate these events can be pretty scary for many people, but it is important to remember that the Book of Revelation is meant to prepare you, not to scare you! If you are part of the body of Jesus Christ, you should have no fear, for He will be with you always, even to the very end of the age (Matthew 28:20).

CHAPTER FOURTEEN

IS THE BIBLE TRUE AND AUTHENTIC?

Three score years and ten plus, may seem like a very long time for a young person to live on this planet, but for someone who has had the good fortune to stay the course, I must admit it seems like the twinkling of an eye. It reminds me of looking at the total face of a clock as representing the total time, according to scientists, that earth has been in existence, and then realizing that man has been on the face of the clock for less than one minute! Another quote in Job 8:9 goes on to say: "For we were born only yesterday and know nothing, and our days on earth are but a shadow." One moment I was young, and the next I was old, chronologically speaking that is. However, mentally I still feel young, which is the irony of getting older. However, getting old is one thing, but gaining in knowledge and wisdom is something else entirely. Gaining wisdom from God should be our life goal.

We are awash in information today, but can we discover the secrets of the ages, and get to the point where we fully understand our role as human beings, and the relationship we need to have with the one who manufactured us in the first place? That is the ultimate challenge for mankind. It is not just a question of existing in this world, and somehow trying to muddle our way through life. We have to reach a point of understanding what our lives are all about, which include knowing there is a life beyond this mortal existence. Are non-believers willing to throw away their only chance of living eternally with God by rejecting Him based on false evidence?

In this chapter, due to the long road we have traveled together, and the fact that hardened hearts may still need convincing that God is the answer to everything we can ever want, I have highlighted some additional evidence to support the truthfulness of the Bible, and in the next Chapter I will provide even more evidence to make the case that Jesus Christ truly is the Son of God almighty, and He represents the only way for us to live forever in His kingdom.

BELIEVE THE TRUTHFULNESS OF THE BIBLE:

A true Christian must believe in the inerrancy of the Bible, not only what it says about the past, but also about the future. As mentioned previously, you can search the whole world for a holy book that predicts the future, but you will find none but the Holy Bible. If we could find other holy scriptures that could provide verifiable predictions about the future, then there would be plenty of room for debate regarding which was the true religion for mankind. However, there is no debate on this issue. The holy Bible of the Judeo Christian faith based system, stands head and shoulders above all other scriptures, as some 500 prophecies out of approximately 1,000, have already been documented and verified as having been proven and realized. Any prophecies made by other holy scriptures are either highly skeptical or nonexistent. This alone makes the case that Christianity, of more than 4,000 plus world religions, is the only faith which has stood the test of time, despite being scrutinized, criticized and berated more than all other world sacred texts combined.

If you are still having a problem accepting proven Bible prophesies, then you need to do your own independent study to determine the truth for yourself. You are fortunate in that you live in a society where religious freedom is still tolerated, unlike many nations around the world where you can be persecuted for adopting a faith contrary to the government's position on religion. This freedom provides you with the privilege of seeking out the truth for yourself based on the numerous resources available in an open society.

As you delve into God's word you will be surprised at the number of great intellectuals who have come to know the Lord through their own investigations. Men like Isaac Newton, perhaps the best scientific mind in history; Louis Pasteur, the discoverer of pasteurization; Johann Kepler, the creator of modern astronomy; Robert Boyle, one of the greatest chemists of his age, and Lord Kelvin, the creator of thermodynamics. If these men, with their brilliant minds, all came to the same conclusion that Jesus Christ is the Son of God, the creator of the universe, then who are we to question their judgment based on their intense years of investigation? I am convinced that if any of us applied the same life time discipline to learn the truth, we would no doubt come to the same conclusions. The interesting irony, of course, is that man does not need a superior intellect to understand the Bible, as millions of poor, uneducated folks have learned for themselves. All it takes is a willing heart that surrenders to Jesus.

Some non-believers have a hard time accepting God's words in the Bible, because He is abstract and cannot be seen. Insurance is also abstract and cannot be seen, but it does not stop people from buying insurance to protect themselves against some future accident that may or may not happen. However, when it comes to their certain future death, and the protection of their soul, they refuse the insurance policy that comes with a zero premium, which will guarantee them eternal life with Jesus. How insane is that?

I am convinced many non-believers I have known do not accept the wisdom contained in the Bible, because they do not want to give up the sins they are committing, or believe they cannot stop sinning. Others I have known are so entwined in what is happening in this mortal existence they have given little thought about their eternal future, even though they often worry about their remaining future in this life. Other non-believers I have known have lost loved ones, and use this as a reason to disavow God by claiming He is unfair.

THE ACCURACY OF THE BIBLE:

Without even a proper reading of the Bible, many non-believers try to discredit it as fairy tales. Not that they have a better understanding of their lives; how they got here, and what happens when they die. They simply will not accept the fact, despite overwhelming evidence to the contrary, that the words of the Bible are inspired by God. Let me make my case by asking you to imagine any book other than the Bible, created in the way the Bible was. Bible Scriptures were given to man in a piece-meal fashion, at various times and places. Holy men of God spoke as they were moved by the Holy Spirit over a time period spanning more than 1500 years, from about 1492 B.C. to 100 A.D. You will also find the Bible actually contains 66 books within it, written by 40 different authors.

These authors were kings, like David and Solomon; statesmen such as Daniel and Nehemiah; a priest named Ezra; men that had been educated in Egypt like Moses; a man like Paul who was educated in Jewish law; by a herdsman, Amos; a tax collector, Matthew; great prophets like Isaiah, Ezekiel and Zechariah, and a physician, Luke.

The pages of the Bible were penned from locations all over the Holy Land and beyond, including the rugged desert and hills of Palestine, the Negev and the Sinai Peninsula; the courts in Jerusalem, and the Persian palace; the cities of Jericho, Babylon, and from a dungeon in Rome. John even wrote from the remote and isolated island of Patmos. Now, can you imagine any other book compiled in such a manner that could stand the test of time? Despite numerous authors and the time between the writing of the first book to the last, you will find the Bible is not a jumble of ancient history, legends, myths, speculation and superstition, as I have found in other writings. Upon closer examination you will find there is a progress of revelation and doctrine in it beginning with the first book, Genesis, all the way through to the last book, Revelation. Logically, you will notice the Judges knew more than the Patriarchs, the Prophets knew more than the Judges, the Apostles knew more than the Prophets, and Jesus is the central theme throughout.

Although Bible words are a revelation from God, it is not written in a superhuman celestial language, because man would not be able to understand it. The Bible's superhuman nature, however, can be seen in that it can be translated into any language and not lose any of its virility or spiritual life giving powers (this cannot be said for the Qur'an, which must be read in Arabic in order to maintain its clarity and beauty). Also, when it is translated into another language it manages to capture the language in its purest form. What other assortment of books written over many years by many different authors could accomplish what the Bible has achieved if it were not written in the words of God Almighty Himself? This wonderful, God inspired book, with thanks to the thousands of God believing Christian scholars who have studied it for hundreds of years, provides us today with greater understanding, and access to God's thinking, than at any other time in man's history. Yet the disbelief continues.

EVIDENCE FROM HISTORICAL DOCUMENTS:

Despite constant criticism from skeptics, scholars and the media, the Bible has proven its truth through the discovery of thousands of historical documents authenticating the words of the Bible. Evidence during the last century has revealed 41 kings of Israel and surrounding nations who have been confirmed by historical documents. It is also a historical fact that many biblical personalities such as: Nebuchadnezzar, Belshazzar, Darius, David and Cyrus, have now been reliably substantiated by these same records. Perhaps the foremost archeologist of the 20th century, Doctor Nelson Glueck, in his famous book, *Rivers in the Desert (1959),* has extensively searched the land of Israel for original records, and found not one biblical statement ever refuted by his archeological findings. He concluded after many years of research that the Bible is true and accurate in every area where he was able to examine the historical document evidence, as well as numerous physical sites to corroborate their existence.

I believe that 1947 is a seminal year in proving the authenticity of historical Bible documents. Prior to this date it was very difficult for Bible scholars to prove that the original Hebrew Scriptures from the Old Testament were without error throughout the last 2,000 years. For instance, the King James Version of the Bible (1611), was produced by translators who used Old Testament manuscripts that only dated back to 1100 A.D. In 1947, however, the long awaited truth came to the forefront when a young Bedouin discovered the Dead Sea Scrolls in Qumran near the Dead Sea. He searched several caves and discovered a treasure trove of more than 1,000 historical documents dating back before 68 A.D., when the Romans destroyed the Jewish village of Qumran during the war. Now biblical scholars were, for the first time in centuries, able to trace modern Bible translations back to the very beginning, and they all proved accurate. Therefore, the King James Version of the Bible, and all subsequent editions of the New International Version etc; are also true and accurate.

What a wonderful opportunity Bible scholars now have of reading all the books of the Old Testament, with the exception of Esther, in their original translations. Later, scholars were able to determine the most authoritative Hebrew text, the so called received text. This text was used by King James translators in 1611, and was identical with the historical documents found in the Dead Sea Scrolls. This one discovery eliminated once and for all any controversy that modern Bible translations had been changed and manipulated over time. This discovery should have put to rest, once and for all time, any further criticism of the authenticity of the Bible record, but it hasn't. Even proven hard evidence is disproved by some skeptics.

Today, the Bible has more than 5000 known Greek manuscripts, over 10,000 Latin Vulgate manuscripts, and as many as 9300 other early versions written in Slavic, Armenian, Arabic and Ethiopian languages. This means there are more than 24,000 manuscript copies of portions of the New Testament in existence today that prove that Jesus Christ did appear among men for a short period of time some 2,000 years ago.

Now when we compare these results against other ancient manuscripts, we find that Homer's Iliad has the second greatest number of manuscript copies of any work of antiquity with about 643 known copies, and the earliest copies are about 500 years removed from the original manuscript. Caesar's "Gallic Wars" has ten known manuscripts, and the earliest copies are some 1,000 years removed from the original. There are only seven ancient manuscripts of our famous Plato's "Tetralogies," and the earliest copies are more than one thousand years removed from the originals. It is quite clear that the New Testament manuscripts provide a much larger body of work for examination than other classical writers of the ancient world. Yet, historians are willing to accept other ancient documents as authentic with far less evidence to support their position. The Bible has been scrutinized by scholars far more than any other ancient documents, and the compelling evidence is strongly in favor that the textual accuracy of the Bible today is an accurate copy of the original.

EVIDENCE FROM ARCHEOLOGICAL DISCOVERIES:

During the latter part of the 19th century and throughout the 20th century, we have records of numerous brilliant scholars who have spent their entire careers in pursuit of the truth of the Bible record, digging into every archeological site in the Middle East. The result of this extensive body of research has confirmed the accuracy of the Bible in every area where biblical passages can be tested. This is a phenomenal statement to make, but it is true. The Bible claims to be the inspired word of God, so it is important to many people that Scriptural records be tested against all archeological discoveries uncovered at sites where many great events of the bible actually occurred. Their records show, as mentioned earlier, there is not one case where an archeological discovery disproves a statement made in the Scripture!

Perhaps the story of English scholar, Sir Mitchell Ramsay, will help reinforce my point further. More than a century ago, as a young man, Ramsay traveled throughout Asia Minor on a grant from Oxford University, for the sole purpose of trying to disprove the Bible's history as described by Luke in his Gospel, and in the Book of Acts, which Luke also authored. Ramsay and the other professors were convinced the New Testament record was not true; in fact they claimed it was totally inaccurate.

Digging through sites in Greece and Asia Minor searching for ancient names and boundary markers, Ramsay was convinced Luke had invented the history of Jesus and His church. To his amazement, and chagrin, Ramsay discovered all the statements made in the New Testament were accurate right down to the smallest detail. At the end of all his research he had developed a huge body of evidence to support the Bible was indeed true and accurate. Interestingly, as a result of his academic studies, and his numerous trips and archeological surveys and discoveries, Ramsay accepted Jesus Christ as his Lord and Savior. In later life he became both a Christian leader, and a biblical scholar of the first order. In his book, *The Bearing of Recent Discovery,* he ascertained all thirteen epistles written by Paul were not only accurate, but were indeed written by Paul, and not forgeries as some had surmised.

SCIENTIFIC EVIDENCE TO SUPPORT THE BIBLE:

As mentioned in chapter eight, there has been an epic war against God, particularly from the scientific community. Yet, upon closer inspection, we find there is a large body of evidence in the Bible mentioning advanced scientific knowledge. Although the Bible is not meant to be a scientific book, it nonetheless makes scientific statements that have proved to be accurate when investigated by scientists thousands of years later. Even King David wrote in one of his psalms: "By the word of the Lord were the heavens made, their starry host by the breadth of his mouth …For he spoke, and it came to be; he commanded, and it stood firm." (Psalm 33:6, 9).

Considering the billions of dollars scientists have spent on astronomy over the years, scientists have yet to come up with a credible theory to account for either the universe, or our own planet for that matter. A majority of these same scientists do not believe in God because he cannot be proven using the Scientific Method. So we have to ask ourselves the following questions: How can humans systematically observe God, measure facts, apply experimentation methods, create formulations through testing, and then modifying any identified hypotheses in order to prove God? We cannot. That is why faith in God beyond the limitations of our finite intelligence and limited facts, is critical to becoming a true servant of God.

When the Bible states God formed man of the dust of the ground, and breathed into his nostrils the breathe of life, and man became a living being (Genesis 2:7), we now see modern scientists agreeing with God since they have discovered clay and earth contain every single element found in the human body! Genesis also begins with the words, "God created the heavens and the earth." My readings tell me prior to 1950 most scientists believed in what is known as the "Steady State Theory," which implied the universe has always existed just as we observe it today. Of course, this position was in direct contradiction to God's statement that He created the universe at a certain point in time. Today, you will find the majority of scientists accept what is referred to as the "Big Bang Theory," which now suggests the whole universe came into being at a certain point in time, just like God had stated all along.

For hundreds of years, man in his ignorance, believed the world was flat, yet all he had to do was read Isaiah 40:22, which states, "He sits enthroned above the circle of the earth!" Also, in Job 26:10, it tells us God marks out the horizon on the face of the waters for a boundary between light and darkness, where evening and morning occur. The boundary is a circle since the earth is round. Even great men like Copernicus and Galileo were persecuted for stating the earth revolves around the sun, yet they were later proven correct. Yes, we have come a long way since the days when a man like Giordano Bruno was burned at the stake for saying the universe was infinite.

Science has made much progress over the last 150 years or so, but not at the expense of any Bible passages. Lord Kelvin, for instance, discovered the science of thermodynamics helping to describe the nature of our universe. His first law is known as the Law of Conservation of Energy, which states energy can neither be created nor destroyed. One scientist described it by saying energy can be transferred from one place to another or transferred from one form to another, but it can never be created or destroyed, which expands the definition further. This law says all the amount of energy that exists in our universe remains constant and can never be changed. This law has helped to describe the present state of the universe after its initial creation by our Almighty God.

Kelvin's second law of thermodynamics is the Law of Entropy. It states all systems and elements in our universe have a tendency to disintegrate to a lower order of available energy or organization. To put it another way, over a period of time all things, whether it be a human being, or things built by humans, will eventually disintegrate to rust and dust, which is a lower order of organization than the human being, or anything humans have originally built. We have been able to observe throughout our history, that matter decays from the moment of maximum order of organizational information at the beginning, through to the end when it ceases to function. At my age, I can certainly relate to this principle. Of course, if this law is true, and most scientists believe it is, then the whole idea of Darwin's Theory of Evolution cannot possibly be true. Why is this? Because evolutionists suggest all simple systems and elements become increasingly more organized and consequently more complicated by random chance. But the Law of Entropy under scientific examination, says just the opposite happens. This one law alone proves the whole Theory of Evolution makes no sense at all.

GOD'S LAWS FOR HYGIENE AND SANITATION:

During a trip to Egypt, I learned a great deal about their ancient medical practices. I found in the Ebers Papyrus in the Cairo Museum, for instance, one of the ancient Egyptian's most popular applications in their traditional medicines for allegedly curing patient illnesses, was to use manure, insects, animals, and even humans. You can imagine the results. Their ancient pharmacies provided prescriptions that included: excreta from both animals and humans, including donkeys, dogs, and cats, hippopotamus, and flies. They also used lizard blood, decayed meat, goose grease, and snake skin. Other prescriptions included ointments made up of the blood of worms mixed with the dung of a donkey. Despite their superior knowledge in the fields of engineering and astronomy, which made them the most advanced civilization in the world at the time, their knowledge of medicine was primitive to say the least. Consequently, thousands of Egyptians died each year due to medical malpractice and ignorance.

Yet the ancient Jews, contemporaries of the Egyptians, knew about good hygiene and sanitary laws thanks to Moses, who was raised Egyptian, but obviously did not get his medical knowledge from them. Yet Moses wrote all these laws down in the Torah (the first five books of the Old Testament). Of the 613 biblical commandments applied in Jewish law, some 213 were medical regulations used to ensure good health for the Jews. So where did Moses, a formerly well educated prince of Egypt, get such advance medical knowledge? It had to be divinely inspired from God, for Moses states in the Book of Exodus 15:26, where God says, "If you listen carefully to the voice of the Lord your God and do what is right in his eyes, if you pay attention to his commands and keep all his decrees, I will not bring on you any of the diseases I brought on the Egyptians, for I am the Lord, who heals you."

During the early 1400's the Black Plague destroyed the lives of about 60 million Europeans, about one third of the continent's entire population. The Jews were often blamed and persecuted for the plague mainly because they applied good sanitation, and general hygiene methods as laid down by God. Consequently, they were not dying at anywhere near the rate of the Gentile population. Eons ago, God had commanded the Jews to wash their hands in "running water" when working with people who had infectious diseases. For instance, in Leviticus 15:13, it says, "When a man is cleansed from his discharge, he is to count off seven days for his ceremonial cleaning; he must wash his clothes and bathe himself with fresh water, and he will be clean." Millions of lives could have been saved if European doctors had been conversant with Bible teachings.

There are other examples of man not heeding God's laws of hygiene and sanitation. Over the centuries, more battle hardened soldiers died from disease than were actually killed by enemies. Leviticus 13:46, lays down strict regulations for the treatment of infectious disease. I remember several years ago I saw a leper colony on the island of Molokai in Hawaii. Several leprosy patients still live there as a reminder that leprosy (Hansen's Disease), was not treated effectively until the 1950s! As late as the 19th century, lepers were burned to death in India!

Despite the wisdom contained in the historical Bible, as we delve into history we learn it was not until the 1840s that Europeans began to bathe regularly. For centuries prior to that, people would often go their whole lives without ever taking a bath! For instance, we are not aware that King James I of England ever bathed. He used talcum powder to reduce body odor. Many of the royal patrons in London and Paris used many forms of perfumes in court in order to reduce the stench that was obvious to all. When we think of how many millions of people have died unnecessarily over the centuries, for being ignorant of God's Word, it is enough to turn one's stomach.

The Bible, as I have mentioned many times in this book, is an absolute treasure trove of knowledge and wisdom that can help man lead a better, more productive and longer life, if he will only give the Bible a chance. It is fascinating to discover, for instance, that Moses made a remarkable statement in Leviticus 17:11, when he said: "For the life of a creature is in the blood." He said our blood is the essence of life. Today, all these many years later, we are able to determine there are more than 75,000 miles of blood vessels in our human bodies, and it provides nutrition to feed some sixty trillion cells. At the very center of all this rotating blood supply, flushing some half million gallons of blood through our bodies each year, is an organ weighing less than one pound – the human heart. Talk to anyone on kidney dialysis and you soon learn the importance of the need for rotating blood to cleanse our systems, to keep us healthy. Moses was right. Our blood is the essence of life, and years of scientific experiments have not changed our conclusions of what was said in the Bible some 3500 years ago.

In Arab countries, circumcision takes place by a boy's tenth birthday, with age seven being average. The Masai of Kenya and Tanzania circumcise boys at age 18. Have you wondered why Moses commanded the Jews to circumcise their baby boys on the eighth day after birth? Interestingly, the reason for Moses' commandment has been discovered by modern science. Medical scientists have been studying the biological processes leading to blood clotting. The findings demonstrate rapid healing of a wound begins with the clotting of blood. Scientists determined any wound that continued to bleed, especially in primitive times, would increase the possibility of infection. They further discovered two specific factors in our blood are related to helping our blood safely clot in order to prevent infections. Interestingly, Vitamin K and Prothrombin are at their highest level of a person's life (about 110% above normal), on the eighth day after birth! Vitamin K, it was further determined, is formed in the blood of a baby between five and seven days after birth. This led scientists to realize the eighth day of life is the very best day for circumcision due to the high level of Vitamin K and Prothrombin, which clots the blood and hastens wound healing. The important question to ask of course, is how did Moses, with no medical training, know this scientific information some 3500 hundred years ago, if it had not been commanded to him by God?

There are many biblical commands God gave to man so many years ago, but unfortunately man has not heeded them. God told Moses, for instance, it was all right to eat the ox, sheep, goats, deer, gazelle, roe deer, wild goats, ibex, antelope, and mountain sheep, because they were clean foods. God further stated that man can eat any animal with a split hoof divided in two which chews the cud, with the exception of the camel, rabbit and cone, because they chew the cud, but do not have a spit hoof making them ceremonially unclean. Pigs are also unclean, because although they have a split hoof, they do not chew the cud. Moses went on to say man can eat anything in the water that has fins and scales, but nothing else. Man can eat any bird, except an eagle, vulture, red kite, black kite, falcons, ravens, owls, gulls, hawks, osprey, cormorant, stork, heron, hoopee, and bat. Also, he said not to eat any flying insects that swarm. Never eat a dead animal, or a young goat in mother's milk (Deuteronomy 14). Later, under the New Covenant of Christ, we find Peter receiving a vision from God telling him to "Get up, kill and eat," and God continues, "Do not call anything impure that God has made clean." (Acts 10:13). This came about because Jesus had already laid the groundwork for setting aside the laws of clean and unclean food (Matthew 15:11).

I believe a strong and compelling case has been made that the words of the Bible are all true and authentic. Biblical words represent what God wishes to communicate to all His human subjects. The words of the Bible are meant to teach and instruct us in the right way to live our lives. In chapter three I spelled out a complete overview of the Bible and its history. In chapter twelve I demonstrated the Bible is the only book in the world that has made so many futuristic prophecies having already come true. Now in this chapter we have looked at the Bible through several other lenses to determine its authenticity. We have examined historical documents, and archeological evidence, both from a Christian viewpoint as well as a secular one, which has failed to make a case against the Bible. We have examined the Bible through the lens of the scientific community, only to find that all the Bible statements have been validated and corroborated by modern science, even though the Bible was not meant to be a science book. We have also examined ancient hygiene and sanitation laws laid down by God that are still valid today, and could only have been communicated to Moses by God Himself. These facts are verifiable, and your own investigation will prove them to be correct.

So here we are. The facts are the facts. The truth is the truth. As Winston Churchill once said, "The truth is incontrovertible. Malice may attack it, ignorance my deride it, but in the end there it is." So the only subject left for non-believers to scrutinize, to criticize, and in some cases even to condemn, is Jesus Christ himself, the only begotten Son of God, who is the subject of the last chapter.

CHAPTER FIFTEEN

THE CASE FOR CHRIST

Today, we find ourselves in a very interesting juxtaposition, where on the one hand we have access to greater resources of knowledge than any other generation before us, to prove the truth of Jesus as the Son of God, while at the same time we find more modern scholars disputing the historical accuracy of the Bible, and in particular Jesus Christ Himself. This onslaught of disbelief against Jesus has been going on now for more than 150 years, and the debate in intellectual circles still continues. This ongoing debate can be very confusing to casual observers who have not taken the time and trouble to evaluate the evidence for themselves. This causes many non-believers to accept the opinion of others, which is a rather lazy way to be playing around with their own destiny. In this chapter, I will provide the reader with more facts and evidence to support the truthfulness of Jesus Christ from learned men who are steeped in the details of Jesus' ministry, as well as naysayers who still need to be convinced.

Alan W. Hayden

COMMENTARY FOR AND AGAINST THE LIFE OF JESUS:

One example of Jesus' critics is the so called Jesus Seminar, where a group of 75 liberal New Testament scholars took the unusual position of examining Jesus' words, to see if they passed their approval. This is the height of man's arrogance, but nonetheless this is the position they took. One of its members famously declared, while rejecting most of the words of Jesus, that he thought Jesus was occasionally humorous! These scholars, many of whom are agnostic, have managed to spread their disbeliefs throughout the academic world, and the media.

Today, many biblical scholars see Jesus as a great moral teacher, but reject the claim of His deity, and that He died for our salvation on the cross. One of my favorite English Christian authors is C.S. Lewis. Here is what he had to say to those who reject the holiness of Jesus:

"Any person who did the miracles and spoke the messages ascribed to Jesus could not be a mere human teacher or an uninspired prophet, no matter how enlightened or exalted he might be. Anyone who performed the miracles ascribed to Jesus and made the statements Jesus made, about His nature and powers, must be the Son of God as He claimed, or a liar, or a lunatic. Anyone who claimed the things that Jesus said must be either insane, a demon from hell, or the true Son of God."

This three-part argument coupled to the overwhelming evidence produced in the New Testament, discussed previously, should demonstrate to all of us that Jesus was not a liar or a lunatic. Therefore, He is the Son of God!

For hundreds of years, numerous scholars have examined the evidence concerning the life of Jesus. When all bias is put to one side, and the evidence carefully examined on its merits, we find a huge body of accumulated evidence is truly loaded in favor of Jesus Christ being who He says He is.

THE TWELVE APOSTLES OF JESUS:

We know very little about the personal lives of the Old Testament Jewish patriarchs, prophets and priests, who were selected by God to set down in writing His revelations for mankind. In the New Testament, however, we find numerous historical evidences about the lives of the disciples, and apostles that are documented in the readings of the early church. Upon a close reading of the New Testament we find Jesus carefully chose his twelve apostles, who were ordinary men of no particular distinction: fishermen, a tax collector etc., Jesus' choice of men is noteworthy in that none of them were religious scholars or professional men. None of them were wealthy or natural leaders in their communities.

Jesus chose these men to fulfill and confirm, for all mankind, the words and deeds of Jesus during his short ministry here on earth. By their words, they confirmed the reality and the life, death, and resurrection of Jesus Christ. This was a totally new faith, and reliable eye-witnesses were required in order to later defend the faith against future cynics. Jesus asked these men to give up their present life, and follow Him into a destiny no other men had ever experienced. These men became so exalted, that even after 2,000 years we find mothers everywhere still naming their sons with apostle and biblically inspired names. As I write this chapter, I was informed by my dear friends that their son and his wife had just given birth to twin boys. Can you guess their names? James and Benjamin!

Later in the story we learn that for 30 pieces of silver, one of Jesus' apostles, Judas Iscariot, would have Jesus arrested, before Judas committed suicide. Another would totally deny Him. Others abandoned Him rather than be captured themselves. Yet, after His death and resurrection, He appeared to all the apostles and more than 500 of the brothers at the same time. (I Corinthians 15:6). Then the Holy Spirit was released in a powerful way at Pentecost. These disciples then went out into the world to spend the rest of their lives promoting the truthfulness of the words of Jesus as the true Son of God.

Based on Scriptures, early church writings and traditions, along with the writings of pagan writers of early times, we have good reason to believe each of these apostles were martyred for their beliefs with the exception of John. We have discovered Matthew was killed by sword in Ethiopia; Mark was dragged by horses through the streets of Alexandria, Egypt, until he died. The Greeks hanged Luke as a result of his preaching to non-believers. We find Peter the Rock, was crucified upside down on a cross in Rome; James the Just, who was the leader of the church in Jerusalem, was thrown from the top of the Temple after refusing to deny his faith in Jesus. There is also James the Greater, who was beheaded in Jerusalem for refusing to disavow his faith in Jesus; Bartholomew (Nathaniel), was flayed to death with a whip for preaching the gospel in Armenia; Andrew was crucified in Patras, Greece. Thomas was stabbed to death with a spear in India; Jude was killed by arrows when he refused to deny his faith, and Matthias, who replaced Judas Iscariot, was stoned and beheaded. We also find Barnabas, one of the 70 disciples, preached throughout Italy and Cyprus before being stoned to death in Salonika. Let us not forget the indefatigable Paul, who had formerly persecuted Christians before experiencing a dramatic conversion on the road to Damascus. He later wrote 13 of the New Testament epistles, before being tortured and beheaded by Emperor Nero in Rome. Finally, during a wave of persecution in Rome, we are also told that John was captured and boiled in oil, but he miraculously survived. He was then sent to work in the mines on the Island of Patmos where, after recording the last book of the New Testament, *The Book of the Revelation,* he died at a good old age, the only one of the twelve to do so. While not all of the details can be historically verified, we find these stories were recounted by the early church fathers, as well as the very first official in early church history, Eusebius in 325 A.D.

Now we have to ask ourselves an honest question. Why would the twelve apostles give up their families, wives and children, and follow Jesus, who was an itinerant preacher? By doing so, they risked everything for a belief in one man, when they could have stayed with their families and lived a far more peaceful and less traumatic life. Why would they later subject themselves to face relentless persecution, torture and finally face premature, violent deaths, without ever giving up their faith in Jesus Christ, if they did not think he really was the true Son of God Almighty? If there is nothing worth dying for, then there is nothing worth living for.

During their short lives, these men converted thousands of ordinary people to accept Jesus Christ as Lord and Savior. This happened, despite the tremendous fear, persecution, torture and death, decreed by Roman emperors, upon anyone who would not accept the emperor as god. People sacrificed their own lives as well as their families, in order to stay faithful to Jesus, fully knowing the horrors awaiting them. To the amusement of Romans, these early Christians were literally torn apart by lions and other savage beasts rather than renounce Jesus. They were greatly affected by Jesus' ministry, and these facts surely demonstrate there had to be more to this phenomenon than what the humanistic, secular world would have us believe. No one would ever sacrifice their family for a false prophet.

REPLACE YOUR FEARS WITH JESUS:

We all fear on one level or another, but non-believers fear far more than Christians, simply because non-believers don't understand the purpose for their life, as this book has demonstrated. Is there an antidote for fear? Yes, we need to trust God more, which allows us to fear less. It appears that fear is unwilling to share the heart with positive thoughts, happiness etc., Fear is defeatist, and never accomplishes anything. Fear (False Evidence Appearing Real), never put a man on the moon, or launched a new business. Courage and faith did that. Fear causes us to run for safety, and then safety becomes our god. When this happens, we find ourselves worshipping the safe-free life. At that point, can anyone achieve anything worthy for themselves, for others, or for God?

It is important to point out that Christians, just like non-believers, experience the loss of loved ones, experience serious illnesses, and face economic and other hardships. It's not the absence of fear that sets Christians apart. It is who Christians discover in the midst of their crisis – a bed rock of stability – Jesus Christ.

Fear corrodes our confidence. It makes us feel awful, and it can suck the life out of our soul. When fear arrives, many people try to insulate the fear by medicating themselves on drugs, alcohol, diet, or social withdrawal. Unfortunately, when they do this they exclude God from the solution, which makes the problem worse. Fear may fill our minds, but it does not have to fill our hearts. We can take positive steps to fear less tomorrow than we do today. We can do so by maximizing God in our lives, and minimizing ourselves. We need to make God larger, and ourselves smaller. We need to start living in the spirit rather than in the flesh. The promise we have from Jesus is, "Do not let your hearts be troubled. Trust in God; trust also in me."(John 14:1)

In the Gospels you will find more than 100 comments from Jesus that urge us "not to fear," "not to be afraid," "take heart," "be of good cheer," and "don't let your heart be troubled." Learn to start taking your problems to the feet of Jesus, and you will begin to experience more peace and contentment in your life, from this point forward.

COMPLETING THE JOURNEY:

Does God still consider us a blessed nation? Not too long ago, Judge Roy Moore, was removed from the Alabama Supreme Court for failing to execute a federal order to take down the Ten Commandments in front of the capitol building. The American Civil Liberties Union (ACLU) has filed hundreds of law-suits over the years attempting to take out any remaining vestiges of our Christian heritage from the public square. And, according to the Abortion Clock (www.abortionclock.org), nearly 60 million American babies have been slaughtered in their mother's wombs since 1973. And now in our contemporary times we are harvesting organs from these aborted babies, and selling them for profit. Are we still a blessed nation?

In the end, and there certainly is an end to everything in this world, we all have to resolve whether the Bible is true and accurate according to God's own words, and is Jesus Christ everything He claims to be? This book has supplied a preponderance of evidence in support of God, and all readers have the ability to verify this knowledge for themselves. Therefore, if there is still disbelief by some non-believers, then I ask them to analyze their own heart, and figure out what evidence they have to support an opposite point of view. God is real. Jesus Christ is real. Satan is real. In your lifetime you have made thousands of decisions – some small, and some that possibly included life and death. None, however, is more important than your decision to accept the Son of God, Jesus Christ, as your personal Lord and Savior for all eternity. Hesitate no more.

THE PROGRESS OF A CHRISTIAN:

Presently, a non-believer has the old sinful nature within him. He is a natural man, doing what he wants to do without conscience, or a conscience stunted or muted. He is living in the "flesh." Consequently, he is blinded by the sin he commits, and therefore continues to sin without remorse. Upon acceptance of Jesus Christ, a man, for the first time, begins to live in the "spirit." A new nature begins to form inside him, but the old nature does not go away. Therefore, it is still possible for a man to sin even though he has accepted Jesus as the new light in his life. Wouldn't it be ever so lovely if, once man accepted Jesus as his Lord and Savior, he stopped sinning completely, and the old nature disappeared from within him? But that is not the way it works, and man now has two natures that can often collide with each other. (See Romans 7:15-25).

BEING JUSTIFIED IN CHRIST:

The concept of Justification, however, allows Jesus Christ, the sinless one, to act as the perfect sacrifice, to die in our place for our sins, and thus accepting the punishment that we deserve.

In turn, sinners who believe in Christ as their Savior are justified by God the Father. This legal act means Christ's righteousness is credited to believers. Once justified in Christ, a process begins to take place whereby man wishes to maximize God in his life, and minimize himself.

THE PROCESS OF SANCTIFICATION:

The concept of Sanctification is the same as the Greek word "holiness," meaning once a man accepts Jesus Christ as his Lord and Savior, he is separated in a positional separation unto Christ as his salvation. What then takes place is a progressive holiness in man that continues throughout his life. This is where the power of Christ's nature within him helps him to fight the old nature, although it is still possible for him to commit sin.

OUR ULTIMATE GOAL – GLORIFICIATION:

Finally, there is the concept of Glorification, when we leave this mortal existence. We will find that God finally removes all sin from the life of saints (everyone who is saved) in the eternal state (Romans 8:18; 2 Corinthians 4:17). At Christ's coming, the glory of God, His honor, praise, majesty and holiness – will be realized in us. Instead of being mortals burdened with sin and nature, we will be changed into holy immortals with direct and unhindered access to God's presence. We will then enjoy Holy Communion with Him throughout eternity. In considering Glorification we need to focus on Christ, for He is every Christian's "blessed hope." We should consider Glorification as the culmination of Sanctification.

So now it is easier to see that becoming a Christian is a process of Justification, whereby we ask God to bring Jesus into our hearts so we can believe in Him as our Holy Savior, and enjoy eternal life with Him. We are then justified and saved in Christ. Justification is followed by Sanctification, whereby we are separated from secular man and his ways, and placed into a position of progressive holiness, which continues until Jesus returns. During this time we can still sin, but we are far more sensitive to sin, and quick to seek redemption through the shed blood of Christ. Although we are still physically in this world, we are no longer of it.

One of the reasons many young people today have little hope for their future, and often fear the future, is because they do not understand the redemptive nature of Christianity. They know they are steeped in sin, but see no outlet to cleanse it due to ignorance of Christian theology. If people are not raised in the Christian faith, do not go to church, and do not read and understand Bible teachings, they will find no matter how well educated they are about worldly ways, they are ignorant with reference to the spiritual side of their own natures. They are living a life with only half of an education. The other half of their unfinished education needs to be addressed so that they can enjoy wholeness in the eyes of God. You owe it to yourself to start learning about your spirit life right now, and I pray that this book will inspire you to do so.

GETTING INTO HEAVEN:

In Chapter Two I promised anyone reading this book, who currently is not a believer in the gospel of Jesus Christ, a step-by-step way to ensure a place in heaven after they leave this temporary existence. So let me share this with you now.

NON-BELIEVER STEPS IN BECOMING A MEMBER OF GOD'S FAMILY:

I sincerely hope and pray that this book has been of some interest to you in developing a greater understanding of what it means to be a Christian. I can assure you that there are numerous other Christian books available that can help shed further insights into God's ways, and I implore you to take advantage of them. Christian apologetics, for instance, is a special area of Christian theology that deals with the issues of proving God; why does evil exist in the world; free will versus predestination, and a whole host of other issues that have intrigued man from the beginning. As I mentioned earlier, Christianity is the most theological of all other religions. It is a thinking person's faith based system. There are no questions too difficult that Christianity cannot answer if you have a sincere desire to accept Jesus Christ as your Lord and Savior, and then diligently seek the answers through God's Word, and frequent prayer. In a free society such as ours, we are all without excuse not to make the attempt to seek out the answers. When you do find the answers, you will then know that there is a living, loving

God, who made us in His own image, and He will be proven innocent of all the charges ever rendered against Him.

If you are thinking seriously about how to become a member of God's family, then I implore you to seek help from a local Christian church, who can instruct you further. Meanwhile, here are the biblical steps you will need to take:

<u>STEP ONE – GOD LOVES YOU:</u> In 1 John 4:8, it states that "God is love." He loves you because He made you in His own image, and He is concerned about the way you live your life today (God is a loving God).

<u>STEP TWO – YOU HAVE SINNED:</u> The Bible also states all men have sinned. We find this in Romans 3:23, where it reads, "For all have sinned and fall short of the glory of God." In reading the books of the Old Testament it become evident that sin leads to trouble, and we are all pre-disposed to sin. Romans 6:23 goes on to say how bad this trouble will ultimately be: "For the wages of sin is death." Sin will always separate man from God, but there is hope. Read on.

<u>STEP THREE – GOD PAID THE PRICE:</u> Although Romans 6:23 says "the wages of sin is death," it also goes on to say "But the gift of God is eternal life in Christ Jesus our Lord." Knowing that sin leads to death, God loves man so much He gives him eternal life as a free gift.

<u>STEP FOUR – ASK GOD FOR HIS FORGIVENESS:</u> If you are willing to admit to yourself and God that you have sinned, and believe God gave His only begotten Son, Jesus, to die on the cross in your place, then God will forgive you and make you clean of all sin, and grant you eternal life. This is God's promise, and God never lies.

STEP FIVE – LIVE AS A CHILD OF GOD: It states in John 1:12, "Yet to all who received Him, to those who believed in His name, He gave the right to become children of God," and that means living with God for eternity.

It is a beautiful thing to become a Christian knowing why you are here, how you are to conduct your life, and to know where you will go after you die. This creates confidence and security to stand strong against the trials and travails we experience while living in this world. As we get older, and get closer to the death experience, we have greater confidence that everything is going to work out fine. Non- believers inwardly dread the future, but Christians have no fear of it. They know what is beyond the veil is far superior to this mortal existence, and just like my friend, who I mentioned earlier, you can experience calmness and joy when you come to the end of your life here on earth.

The alternative to the above road map to heaven is to not accept Jesus as your Lord and Savior in which case, according to the Book of Revelation your name will not be found in the Book of Life, and the Great White Throne Judgment of God will find you guilty. This is a sure one-way ticket to the lake of fire, where you will spend eternity in hell. Please don't take that chance.

WHAT HAPPENS TO CHRISTIANS WHEN THEY DIE?:

Non-believers may also be interested in knowing what happens to Christians when they die. So here are the biblical passages:

When Christians die, their spirit never loses consciousness (Philippians 1:21-23). Their spirits are then immediately ushered into the presence of Jesus. (2 Corinthians 5:8). We are then in a spiritual body with a conscious state until the Rapture comes.

At the time of the Rapture, Jesus reunites our spirit with our bodies, and then glorifies our bodies, perfecting them and rendering them immortal. (I Thessalonians 4:13-18). Also see I Corinthians 15:50-54).

We are raised to heaven imperishable and immortal, in our glorified bodies, to be with Jesus where we are judged for our works (Bema Judgment) to determine our rewards (2 Corinthians 5:10). Note that this is not the Great White Throne judgment, which comes at the end of the millennium, where the non-believers will be judged, and condemned.

When the judgment is completed we participate in a glorious wedding (the Marriage of the Lamb) to celebrate the union of Jesus and His bride, the church (Revelation 19:7-9). This takes place in heaven.

The marriage supper, following the wedding, takes place later on earth. "Blessed are those who are invited to the wedding feast of the Lamb." (Revelation 19:19). The guests will include the Old Testament and tribulation saints who are resurrected at the Second Coming of Christ (Matthew 22:1-14).

We witness His victory at Armageddon, we shout, "Hallelujah," as He is crowned King of Kings, Lord of Lords, and we revel in His glory as he begins to reign over all the earth from Mount Zion in Jerusalem (Zechariah 14:1-9, Revelation 19:16).

It is important to realize that even believers are judged by Jesus when they die. It is called the Bema Judgment, or the

Judgment Seat of Christ. This judgment is not to determine whether or not we have been saved, nor is it a judgment for any sins we have committed prior to accepting Jesus as our Lord and Savior. Rather, it is a judgment to determine our rewards for our faithful service after our salvation. Remember that believers are "saved by faith, and not that of yourselves; it is a gift of God, not of works, lest anyone should boast." (Ephesians 2:8-9). What are "good works"? Matthew 5:16 states, "In the same way, let your light shine before men, that they may see your good deeds and praise your Father in heaven." In other words, believers are an extension of Jesus' ministry. I Corinthians 32:13 tells us that some of these works will be gold, silver, precious stones, meaning that they will survive the fire (not to be confused with the lake of fire), and the believer will receive a reward. Other works, such as hay, wood and stubble, will not survive the fire, and those believers will suffer a loss of reward. They will be saved "so as by fire," or you might say, "by the skin of their teeth!" They will be saved, but their works will be lost.

When we are saved, it appears as though God sets up a heavenly bank account for each of us, and for the rest of our lives we can deposit into that account "treasures" or good works done in His name and for His glory. Then, when we die He opens up our bank account to see how much we have invested in His kingdom. He will then test our works by "fire" to see how genuine they are The Lord challenges us to "lay up for yourselves treasures in heaven, where neither moth nor rust destroys and where thieves do not break in and steal." (Matthew 6:20).

FIVE CROWNS OF REWARD

God will then present believers with the possibility of receiving one or more of five crowns, which are briefly explained below:

<u>The Crown of Righteousness (II Timothy 4:8)</u>
"There is laid up for me the crown of righteousness, which the Lord, the righteous judge, will give to me on that day, and not to me only but also to all who have loved His appearing."

<u>The Incorruptible Crown (I Corinthians 9:25-27)</u>
This is often referred to as the victors crown, as it is given to faithful servants who deny themselves personal desires in order to win the race in faithful service.

<u>The Crown of Life (James 1:2, Revelation 2:10)</u>
This is a special crown for persecuted Christians both here and around the world.

<u>The Crown of Rejoicing (I Thessalonians 2:19)</u>
This is a special soul winners crown for those who have led people to faith in Christ.

<u>The Crown of Glory (I Peter 5:1, 4</u>
This is the Elders Crown, given to those who share the Word of God. They can be ministers, Sunday school teachers, itinerant teachers, or anyone who teaches the Word of God faithfully to others. Perhaps this may be a good time to pause and reflect on which crown(s) you would like to have.

LOVE IS THE ANSWER:

We also need to remember that the great underpinning of Christian faith is very simple. There is nothing complex about loving God with all your mind, heart, soul and strength, and to love your neighbor like yourself. All other moral and ethical laws take second place to these two Godly commands, and anyone with a desire to love his fellow man, and wishes to know more about God, will always find an open door. Listen to what St. Paul has to say about love:

"If I speak in the tongues of men and of angels, but have not love, I am only a resounding gong or a clanging symbol. If I have the gift of prophecy and can fathom all mysteries and all knowledge, and if I have faith that can move mountains, but have not love, I am nothing. If I give all I possess to the poor and surrender my body to the flames, but have not love, I gain nothing. Love is patient, love is kind. It does not envy, it does not boast, it is not proud. It is not rude, it is not self-seeking, it is not easily angered, it keeps no record of wrongs. Love does not delight in evil but rejoices with the truth. It always protects, always trusts, always hopes, always perseveres. Love never fails. But where there are prophecies, they will cease; where there are tongues, they will be stilled; Where there is knowledge, it will pass away. For we know in part and we prophecy in part, but when perfection comes, the imperfect disappears. When I was a child, I talked like a child, I thought like a child, I reasoned like a child. When I became a man, I put childish ways behind me. Now we see but a poor reflection as in a mirror; then we shall see face to face. Now I know in part; then I shall know fully, even as I am fully known. And now these three remain: faith, hope and love. But the greatest of these is love." - St. Paul – I Corinthians 13:1-13

FINISH THE GOOD FIGHT

So now we come to the end, of the book that is. Your earthly life, just like this book, will also come to an end one day, and I hope that when it does happen, you will be fully prepared to face your maker: He is the potter, you are the clay.

You have read about my tortuous struggle with ignorance and darkness, and how, through the grace of God, I was able to reach a point of being able to bask in the light of Christ, because that is what my soul yearned for, and God heeded my need. My sins have been forgiven, my slate is made clean, and I enjoy peace and contentment beyond all human understanding. I am not afraid of death, because I have a promise from God that I will enter a much better place than this veil of tears here on earth. That is worth more to me than any treasures I leave behind.

Intertwined throughout this book I have shared with you my personal spiritual journey, which in many ways parallels the stories of millions of men and women who have gone through similar experiences. These people, just like myself, are part of the larger struggle that mankind has experienced in overcoming the power of darkness, and discovering the royal road to a contented heart. Jesus said, "Ask and it will be given to you; seek and you will find; knock and the door will be opened to you. For everyone who asks receives; he who seeks finds; and to him who knocks, the door will be opened." (Matthew 7:7). Sacrificing some things in this world to obtain greater rewards in the next is like giving up something you love, for something you love more. We have all been given the opportunity to get a free, one-way ticket to heaven. I implore you to use it by turning your life over to Jesus. Each day you wait you are that much closer to death. There is no escaping it.

As we come to the end of the book, I believe it fair to state that none of us will ever gain all the answers to life's mystery this side of the veil. Obviously, if we had all the answers the decision would be easy, but then there would be no need for faith, and it is by faith alone that we enter into a relationship with God. We cannot get into heaven on our own merit, and all the good works in the world are not good enough. We need help from God that only comes through our faith in Him, which causes Him to give us mercy through His divine grace. Mercy is God giving man what he does not deserve (salvation), whereas grace is God not giving man what he does deserve (condemnation).

God bless you, and I thank you for reading the whole book. Christianity is the most theological of all the major religions, and most people don't like the idea of twisting their brain into a pretzel to master its content. Although I have covered some of the tougher theological issues, I have only done so to provide you with an overview of Christianity in order to encourage you to do further study, and to also demonstrate that man cannot go it alone without God. The blood bath of the 20th century, with its alternate godless ways of Fascism, Communism, and Nazism, resulting in some 170 million casualties, should have laid that issue to rest long ago. Some statesman once said that the Bible was killed in the 18th century; God was killed in the 19th century, and man was killed in the 20th century. Let us pray that in the 21st century we can learn the great lessons of our past history, but more importantly apply them in our everyday lives in order to make a better life for ourselves, our families, and our world.

I have presented the material to you, not from a seminary trained individual viewpoint, but rather from the viewpoint of someone who has "walked the walk," and understands what it is like to be lost and frustrated with a life that has no meaning. At one time my life had no meaning. I was living in ignorance and darkness, but today I am experiencing what it is like to bask in the light of He who created me. For me to think God sacrificed His only begotten Son to cleanse me of my personal sins, and thus allowing me a final eternal place beside Him in heaven, is the greatest sacrifice anyone has ever made for me, or ever will. I know I do not deserve it, but I believe in, and have faith in, His solemn promise.

So, to all my non-believing friends, I pray you now have a way out of your circumstance, and you embrace God with all your heart, mind, soul and strength, so the rest of your life will be rich in the light of Him who created you. There is no other way. As mentioned earlier by C.S. Lewis, "All that is not eternal, is eternally useless!! Keep these words in mind as you progress forward.

My final prayer is that you will review the contents of this book more deeply, pray to God for direction, and then let the Holy Spirit invade your soul so that you can enjoy an eternal life beyond this one. Check in with headquarters (heaven) every day for your marching instructions. We call it prayer! We know that Jesus paid it forward. We can do no less.

Today is God's gift to me. What I do with today is my gift to God!

THE END

BIBLIOGRAPHY – END NOTES

INTRODUCTION
(1) Department of Justice
   The National WW II Museum – New Orleans
(2) "A Mass Murderer Repents: The Case of Rudolf Hoss, Commandant of Auschwitz
   - John Jay Hughes (1998)

CHAPTER ONE
(1) World Population Clock
(2) www.universetoday.com
   www.skyandtelescope.com
(3) How many Cells in Your Body? – Carl Zimmerman: Phenomena – Nationalgeographic.com
(4) Arizona Republic Article – April 7, 2013

CHAPTER TWO
No sources cited

CHAPTER THREE
(1) How We Got Our Bible – Dr. William H. Griffith Thomas (1861 – 1924)

CHAPTER FOUR
No sources cited

CHAPTER FIVE
(1) The God Squad – Rabbi Marc Gellman, Monsignor Tom Hartmann, Apr 24, 2007
(2) Tao – A Source Book in Chinese Philosophy – Wing Tsit Chan – Princeton University Press (1963)

CHAPTER SIX
(1) Israel Government Decision 7/20/1958
(2) Israeli Supreme Court Decision (1960)
(3) www.jinfo.org/nobel_prizes.html

CHAPTER SEVEN
(1) Thomas Carlyle – 1840 Lecture on "The Hero and the Prophet."
(2) The Meaning of the Glorious Qur'an – Marmaduke William Picthfall (1930)
(3) Temporary Marriages – Light of Islam – Sayyid Mujtaba Busavi Lavi
Htpp:/homeswipnet.se/islam/English.htm
(4) Holy Terror – Inside the World of Islamic Terrorism – Amir Tahiri (1988)
(5) The Spirit of Allah: Khomeini and Islamic Revolution - Amir Tahiri (1986)
(6) Associated Press Article – February 20th, 1989
(7) The Closed Circle - David Pryce Jones – (1989)
(8) Ibid
(9) www.religionofpeace.com

(10) World Health Organization – "Female Genitalia Mutilation and other Harmful Practices" www.wgo.int/reproductivehealth/topics/fgm/prevalence/en/index/html
(11) Consag.net
(12) The Closed Circle - David Pryce Jones (1989)
(13) Communicating Christ in Animistic Contexts – Gailyn Van Rheemen (1991)
(14) Ibid

CHAPTER EIGHT

(1) Death By Government – R.J. Rummel
(2) The Captain of Industry – Our Darwin Legacy - Ralph Ancil
(3) www.pbs.org/wgbh/amex/carnegie/peopleevents/pande03/htm
(4) "Darwin and the Darwinian Revolution" – Gertrude Himmelfarb (1959)
(5) Department of Justice
(6) Telegram from Minister of the Interior, Talaat – quoted from "Boyaakiam – 1972
This telegram was included in the preface of the book, *La Passion dela' cilicie* (1919 – 1922), by the governor of Adana, Paul de Veou
(7) NationalWW2Museum.org
(8) White and Jacoby (1946)
(9) Hitler, a Study in Tyranny – Alan Bullock (1962)
(10) The Harvest of Sorrow – Robert Conquest (1988)
(11) The Gulag Archipelago – Aleksandr Solzhenitsyn (1953)
(12) Mao's Great Famine – The History of China's most Devastating Catastrophe (1958 – 1962) – Frank Dikotter

CHAPTER NINE

(1) The End of Free Will – Ashlee Vance – Bloomberg Business Week – Apr 16, 2012
(2) Seventeen Magazine Article – May, 2000 – Dr. Judith Reisman
(3) 1998 Study: Sexual Abuse of Boys – William C. Holmes M.D., Gail B. Slap M.D.
(4) Malcolm Moore Article, Beijing Reporter for UK Telegraph, March 15, 2013
ww.telegraph.co.uk
(5) Abortionist Whistleblowers Tell All – Whistleblower – Jan 2003
(6) ibid
(7) Catholic Business Journal – Barbara McGuigan – Feb 2011
(8) Wikipedia 2015
(9) A Proclamation to create a National Day of Humiliation, Fasting and Prayer - President Abraham Lincoln – March 30th, 1863

CHAPTER TEN

(1) The Demons of Europe – Commentary – January, 2004
(2) Men Have Forgotten God – The Templeton Address – Aleksandr Solzhenitsyn
(3) www.religioustolerance.org/const.eu.htm
(4) Christianity and World Religions-Disputed Questions in the Theology of Religions Gavin D'Costa (2009)
(5) Eurostats – Statistics Explained 2011
(6) Warning Bell for Developed Countries Declining Birth Rates –Lee Kuan Yew
Forbes Magazine – October 16th, 2012

(7) www.pewglobalorg/2011/1/17. The American Western European valuesgap
(8) Religious Beliefs in Europe. Factors of Accelerated Decline – Dagan, \Mattei (2003)
(9) Gallup.com/poll/13117/religious-europe-trust-falling-pew.aspx
(10) ec.europa.eu/public-opinions/archives/eh/eb66-higlights-en.pdf
(11) Money.cnn/interactive/pf/costofchildren
(12) Pew Research 7.2.2013
(13) Free Inquiry (1982)

CHAPTER ELEVEN
(1) Pagans and Christians – Robin Lane Fox (1988)
(2) www.heritage.org – September 14, 2014
(3) www.NPTrust.org (National Philanthropic Trust)
(4) The Roots of Capitalism" – John Chamberlin – D. Van Nostrand 1959/65
(5) Christianfinancialconcepts.com
(6) Religion and the Rise of Capitalism – R.H. Tawney – Holland Memorial Lectures 1922
(7) A Thumbnail Sketch for the Battle of Truth in the Mind of Man – Francis Schaeffer

CHAPTER TWELVE
No sources cited

CHAPTER THIRTEEN
(1) God's Plan for the Ages – Dr. David Reagan (2005)

CHAPTER FOURTEEN
No sources cited

CHAPTER FIFTEEN
No sources cited